THE AMERICAN INDIAN MIND
IN A LINEAR WORLD

THE AMERICAN INDIAN MIND IN A LINEAR WORLD

American Indian Studies and Traditional Knowledge

Donald L. Fixico

Routledge
Taylor & Francis Group
New York   London

Published in 2003 by
Routledge
Taylor & Francis Group
711 Third Avenue
New York, NY 10017

Published in Great Britain by
Routledge
Taylor & Francis Group
2 Park Square, Milton Park
Abingdon, Oxon OX14 4RN

Library of Congress Cataloging-in-Publication Data
Fixico, Donald Lee, 1951-
   The American Indian mind in a linear world : American Indian studies and traditional knowledge / Donald L. Fixico.
      p. cm.
   Includes bibliographical references and index.
   ISBN 0-415-94456-2 — ISBN 0-415-94457-0 (pbk.)
   1. Indian philosophy—North America. 2. Indians of North America—Psychology. 3 Indians of North America—Education. I. Title: American Indian studies and traditional knowledge. II. Title.

E98.P5F59 2003
191'.089'97—dc21   2002037051

An earlier version of Chapter 6 appeared in the *Journal of the West*, Vol. 39, No. 1. Copyright ©2000 by Journal of the West, Inc. Reprinted with permission of *Journal of the West*, 1531 Yuma, Manhattan, KS 66502 USA.

To
My grandmother,
Lena Spencer Fixico
"Whose beliefs and traditions are my strengths"

TABLE OF CONTENTS

LIST OF ILLUSTRATIONS

PREFACE

As a child raised in the Seminole and Muscogee Creek traditions, I used to watch our elderly men at our campground talk as they spoke the native language and sat under an arbor. Our ground is Gar Creek, near Seminole in Oklahoma. The men sat close to the Earth, and with sticks they drew on the ground to illustrate points they were talking about. This was the way things were done, talking about all that was concerned and related. This is the way of my people, and I am a part of it and so are my relatives, especially my grandmother, who I remember so well even though she passed away many years ago. My grandmother was the matriarch of our camp, and her way of doing things and her logic was in the Seminole–Creek tradition. Her ways of doing things were taught to me as I learned from my relatives and elders, as they saw the world and the universe in a special way. This native ethos has remained much a part of me, and it is the same for all American Indians who are close to their tribal traditions. In our world, relationships are important and sustaining them is valued.

Many years ago as a child in grade school, I often wondered why I thought in a different way than my classmates, and why I did things differently from a mental point of view. My fourth-grade teacher at Star Elementary School in Oklahoma City, Oklahoma, where we lived, was teaching our class how to do math—fractions. Fractions have sometimes been the bane of frustration for fourth-graders, especially for those who do not do well in math. But I usually did well in the subject. It is just that I thought about solving math problems in a different way. Most of the time, I was convinced that I was wrong, but I came up with the answer to the question that the teacher had asked. What was confusing, besides this point, was how the teacher had arrived at the same answer. I often wondered if I was the only one thinking the way that I did, and usually I was the only American Indian in school, except for my brother, who was two years younger. I may not have used the logical way of solving a problem as taught by my teacher, but my way was logical to me from my point of view. Later, I wondered if other Indian people thought the same way that I did, and I found that Indians raised in traditional ways did think in a distinctive way. I began to understand that one perspective is just as valid as another in solving problems and responding to questions, although the American mainstream does not typically hear or pretend to begin to understand different points of view for fear of their authority being challenged.

Thinking Indian or Indian thinking is the native logic of American Indians, based on their tribal cultures and how they see the world and the universe. Traditionalists view the world according to relationships with the natural environment and a circular philosophy based on cycles of seasons, migrations of animals, and the rotations of the Earth and the stars.

Given the scope of Indians and education, this book spans a length of relations from the polarized positions of the traditional mind of the tribal full blood to the Western mind of empirical evidence. As a policy historian and ethnohistorian, I approached this study as an ethnohistorical examination of the Indian point of view involving indigenous thought. Cultural analysis is also involved. In between, the traditional Indian mind and the white linear mind is the majority of the Indian population, which is mixed blooded and educated in the mainstream school system, especially during the twentieth century. Hence, this study strives to explain the complexity of the American Indian mind in its traditional cultural and natural environment. This indigenous ethos is the focus while demonstrating how this perspective has evolved toward the linear world and how modern Indians have adapted their thinking to adjust to the American mainstream.

Indian thinking is argued in this book to be visual and circular in philosophy. Imbedded in an Indian traditional reality, this ethos is a combination of the physical reality and metaphysical reality. Listening and observing the natural environment is essential to the Indian mindset. Decision making is responsive in nature due to considering all of the physical and metaphysical factors affecting one's life. Coming to a consensus is coming to a balance of all factors so that the right decision is the best decision for all concerned. Although this logic may not be direct, it includes human and nonhuman entities. This type of thought is the basis of an indigenous ethos that is defined by tribal cultures within the natural environment of the people, the basis of chapter 1.

Chapter 2 addresses the importance of "story" about truths and its multiple purposes and how they can teach people to learn. The power of story through the oral tradition is also explained and how all of this transcends time, thus making time less relevant to the power of oral narrative told effectively. Story is the basis of traditional knowledge, and such knowledge is explained as well.

In chapter 3, the significance of the circle is the central governing subject of Indian traditions and ethos. The premise here is that the circle includes all things. All things are within it and it contains spiritual energy that becomes power. Furthermore, it is argued that traditional Indians have observed migration patterns and cycles of seasons such that they have influenced native thought where plants and animals are brothers to human beings in the whole natural order of life. This discussion helps to complete the argument for the indigenous mind, leading to chapter 4, which demonstrates the distinction of the linear mind set and how this mind set has led to a Western mentality.

Chapter 4 on the Indian genius and native intellectual addresses the point that Indian intellectualism has been grossly neglected by mainstream academia, and how the American public does not consider Indian people to be intellectuals. It has been an uphill battle for sufficient recognition of Indian intellectuals in comparison to other minorities and mainstream scholars. The final point is that Indian genius and the American Indian mind is all about understanding "relationships." Seeing all relations within the totality is the source of traditional knowledge, thereby manifesting a traditional ethos from various tribal perspectives. These points set up the scene for the continual conflict of the traditional mind set of early boarding-school Indians struggling with white teachers in linear-taught schools.

Chapter 5 covers personal narratives about boarding-school learning, loss of language as basis of resistance of assimilation of the Indian mind, colonized assimilation while destroying Indian thinking, resilience of native intellect, seeing dual perspectives, and federal programs negating native ethos. The survival of ideas, perspective, and Indian thinking is amazing after all these attempts to change the Indian mind.

Chapter 6 focuses on origin, definition, history of struggle of American Indian studies, the need for it, and how it is striving to become an academic discipline. American Indian studies as another form of traditional knowledge is the final message in this chapter. An earlier version of this chapter appeared in the *Journal of the West*, Vol. 39, No. 1

(2000). It is included here with changes with permission from Editor Robin Higham of the *Journal of the West*.

Chapter 7 focuses on the increase of Indian scholars culture ownership or cultural patrimony, respecting Indian artifacts, and developing research protocol in Indian communities. The mainstream exercise of academic freedom has exploited tribal artifacts, burial remains, and sacred sites, while suppressing the academic freedom of native scholarship.

Chapter 8 addresses the Native American fear of institutions, native acceptance of institutions, Indians in control-building institutions, institutions as new places of keeping traditional knowledge, and the tandem of Indian–white institutional practices. Yet, it is ironic that American Indian educators and tribal leaders have established tribal colleges and tribal museums to form their own institutions.

Finally, chapter 9 summarizes the importance of the Circle of Life and discusses the center of the Circle of Life and its meaning to American Indian ethos as a special way of indigenous thought. The center is about balance of well-being and beauty in life, and it is not the human being, but how the human being feels.

In completing this book, I am appreciative of the various audiences who listened to my presentations over the years. Due to invited presentations at various universities, the basis of those presentations became the chapters of this book. Sometimes I found that I had used some material in more than one presentation, so the chapters have been reconstructed to build on original points while additional analysis has been added to provide depth and expansion of ideas and relevant points of conference and invited papers that I delivered.

In particular, I am grateful for the invitations by certain friends, colleagues, and associates who enabled me to try my ideas at certain conferences and in invited lectures. Thank you, Professor Maureen Smith, Chuck Marecic, Victoria Kane, and the administration at the University of Maine for the invitation to give a keynote presentation at the conference, "Initiating the Dialogue: Academic Research Ethics in Indian Country," sponsored by the Native American Studies Program and the University of Maine in April 2001. I am grateful to Professors Dee McBride, Sterling Evans and the other faculty and staff at Humboldt State University for the invitation to deliver "American Indian Minds in Public Schools," an invited keynote presentation, for the California Content Standards and American Indian Civics and Government Symposium, Humboldt State University and DQ University, April 5–6, 2001. Some years earlier, I delivered another paper, and I am grateful to my friend Anne Medicine for the invitation to present some ideas in a paper, "Traditional Knowledge and American Indian Intellectualism in History," given at Stanford University in 1990. I am indebted to Professors Carol Lujan, Bo Colbert, James Riding In, and the staff of American Indian Studies, for the opportunity to give a keynote address, "Relationships/Partnerships Between American Indian/Indigenous Studies Programs and Native and Non-Native Faculty Across Disciplines," at the American Indian Studies Directors' Conference, held at Arizona State University in February 2001. Three years earlier, I spoke at ASU, and delivered a paper, "The Emerging Voice of American Indian Studies," an invited paper presented at Arizona State University, Tempe, on September 25, 1998. I am grateful for the invitation from James Riding In, and enjoyed visiting his family, as well visiting with Peter and Kaaren Iverson while I was there.

I am also grateful for the invitation to deliver another keynote address on the "Institutionalization of American Indian Intellectualism and Traditional Knowledge" at the Annual Canadian Indigenous/Native Studies Association Conference held in May 2001 at the Saskatchewan Indian Federal College in Saskatoon, Canada. I am thankful to Professors Rob Innis, Lenora Stiffarm, and the many others at SIFC who made me feel so welcomed. In the end, this address at Saskatoon became the basis of another chapter of this book.

I am also thankful to those individuals, including friends and relatives, who have been an inspiration much more than they would believe. Their subtle encouragement, direct advice, and kind words helped me in various times of my life as a scholar to step forward and try to be more original in my work. They helped me to learn to think in the linear way, but also influenced me to go on with my work.

In the Center for Indigenous Nations Studies at the University of Kansas, I am grateful for the help of the following individuals who assisted in the final stages of this book. I am grateful to research assistants Melissa Fisher Isaacs, David Querner, Stephanie Al Molholt, Viv Ibbett, and Elyse Towey. In the daily operation of the CINS office, I am grateful for the assistance of Denise Lajetta, Dianne Yeahquo Reyner, Antonie Dvorakova, Gil Hood and Regina Toshavik who I depend on so that I could complete this writing project. I appreciate the support of my work from Chancellor Robert Hemenway, Provost David Shulenburger, Interim Dean Kathleen Fawcett-McCluskey, Dean Kim Wilcox, and Associate Dean Carl Strikwerda at the University of Kansas. I am very grateful to Jean Bowlus and the rest of the Bowlus family. The late Thomas Bowlus sponsors my Distinguished Professorship, enabling me to have the funding for the research of this book project.

In the final stage of this book, I am grateful to Professors April Summitt and especially Margaret Connell Szasz, who spent precious time reading and making this manuscript a much better book. I am also appreciative of Bill Welge, Chester Cowen, and Lillie Kerr at the Oklahoma Historical Society for helping me with photographs, John Lovett of the Western History Collections at the University of Oklahoma, Barbara Sorensen at the *Winds of Change,* Sarah Hartwell, Joshua Shaw, Dr. Jane Westburg, Victoria Smith at Dartmouth College, Rob Spindler and Elizabeth Bentley of the Archives and Manuscripts, University Libraries at Arizona State University, and Dr. Beverly Singer at the Alfonso Ortiz Research Cultural Center at the University of New Mexico. At Routledge, I am very grateful for the assistance of Karen Wolny, Publishing Director; Nicole Ellis, Production Editor; Jaclyn Bergeron, Editorial Assistant; and Sara Folks, Assistant Editor for producing this book that I have thought about for many years. Completing this book has taken me away from my family, Sharon O'Brien Fixico and Keytha Fixico. I am indebted to them and my parents, John and Virginia Fixico.

Finally, this book is written for the full bloods and those who live the Indian way of traditionalism, and for Indian people who think in the Indian way, meaning in a circular philosophy based on close relations with the natural environment. Furthermore, there are people who are not Native American, but see things in a similar manner. For Indian people brought up in the traditional way of our people, we think differently, and it is very natural to us. To us, the linear world thinks differently than we do. Some Indians will likely disagree with parts of this book, saying that they do not think this way. They may more than they realize, and many of them are assimilated at various degrees into the mainstream and are comfortable with their lives. This book is about the traditional Indian mind that the linear mainstream overlooks and tries to suppress. For whatever criticism that might rise, I accept responsibility for the following words. Simultaneously, the book is intended for explaining the position of the traditional elder and/or full bloods like my Muscogee Creek grandmother, Lena Spencer Fixico, who spoke broken English and who knew her language. These wise elders have been ignored, subordinated, and criticized by mainstream academia of the linear world. Yet, their wisdom and knowledge have sustained their communities for each new generation.

Donald L. Fixico
University of Kansas

1

"INDIAN THINKING" AND A LINEAR WORLD

"Long, long ago the Muscogee Creek people lived in a dark misty fog and they were cold. They felt along the walls of something damp and realized they were moving upwards. Slowly they emerged from the Earth and the fog blinded them. Unable to see and stricken with fear, the people and even the animals cried out until the wind blew away the fog so that they could see. Perceiving animals and people to be equal, the Creeks named groups of people after animals and called them clans.[1] In all four cardinal directions, the forces of fire confronted the people, and they had to make a decision. From the south, a yellow fire faced the people, a black fire burned in the west, a white fire was aflame in the east, but the people chose the red and fire from the north.[2] The fire of the north warmed the people and provided light over the world and enabled the plants to grow, so that the Muscogee Creeks learned to respect all of the elements for life and they celebrated the harvest of the green corn (busk) in ceremonials. Should the people fail in their respect for nature and forget the busk ceremonies, the people would disappear from the land and it would fall beneath the waters of the ocean. The Muscogee Creeks stressed the importance of community and generations of ceremonials reinforced it. As the ceremonies became ritualized, the Muscogees developed ceremonial laws to maximize the community's confirmations of successful ceremonies, and thus the way of life of the Creeks was the correct way."[3]

Muscogee Creek myth, 1922

* * *

"Indian Thinking" is "seeing" things from a perspective emphasizing that circles and cycles are central to the world and that all things are related within the universe. For Indian people who are close to their tribal traditions and native values, they think within a native reality consisting

1

of a physical and metaphysical world. Full bloods and people raised in the traditional ways of their peoples see things in this combined manner.

Seeing things in this special way is thinking like an Indian who has been raised in a tribal community operating according to tribal beliefs. This point of view is a different perspective from that of the American mainstream, based on the Western mind believing in empirical evidence. "Seeing" is visualizing the connection between two or more entities or beings, and trying to understand the relationship between them within the full context of things identified within a culturally based system. It is like seeing the molecule first instead of seeing the atom and all of the atoms that make up the molecule. This holistic perception is the indigenous ethos of American Indians and how they understand their environment, the world, and the universe.

Perception is nature's way in which humans and animals see things. Although we all see things differently from various perspectives based on different cultures and different personal experiences even within our own families, it is suggested that Native Americans, who are knowledgeable of their cultures, see things in more than a human-to-human context. It is a perspective that involves human beings, animals, plants, the natural environment, and the metaphysical world of visions and dreams. This broader context of perception involves more accountability and responsibility on the part of native people for taking care of and respecting their relationships with all things. Like the creation story of the Muscogee, the people established their relationships with each kind of animal and plant with the help of *He-sa-ke-tv-me-se,* the Giver of Breath or Life. This system of relations set the kinship of community for all beings, and with other peoples or tribes.

This inclusive kinship conflicts with the mainstream linear way of seeing things in the world where everything is based on a human-to-human relationship. The late Muscogee elder Jean Hill Chaudhuri and her husband, Joyotpaul Chaudhuri, observed the Muscogee tradition of thinking and how it differed from the linear way of thought. "For instance, mainstream Christian thinking conceives of a bracketed, reified, individual self and soul. Fundamental Creek thought also eschews the existence of atomistic permanent souls, selves, and entities. The Creek entities—'all my relations'—male, female, human and non-human, known and unknown, are all part of a continuum of energy that is at the heart of the universe. The continuum of energy and spirit, *boea fikcha/puyvfekcv,* and the ever-present principles of transformation and synergy illuminate the meaning of all-important entities in the Creek world."[4] Due to the spiritual energy within all things, all things should be respected for their potential. In this way of understanding, the totality that the Muscogee Creeks call *Ibofanga*, is the existence of all things and energy within all things. In this belief, all things are capable of possessing spiritual energy.

"Seeing" in the traditional perspective is understanding the totality of one's universe. But, such an understanding does not occur immediately with realizations. Patience is a part of the "seeing" or the way in which Indian people think about such things. The point of knowledge or an idea may not be apparent at the moment of its introduction, but, with patience, the message becomes clear. Sometimes, this realization takes several minutes, days, or even years. Its importance or relevance derives from the realization or with the help of a wiser person or special person who is gifted to interpret insightful experiences such as dreams and visions. Among the Muscogee Creeks, a *Kerrata* (key-tha) is a gifted person like an interpreter with special insight to help people understand a vision, dream, or an unusual experience. Many tribes have such a person whose role is that of a metaphysical interpreter or translator. A well-known example is Black Elk, the holy man of the Oglalas. Black Elk described his personal vision as a young boy, saying, "It was the pictures I remembered and the words that went with them; for nothing I have ever seen with my eyes was so clear and bright as what my vision showed me; and no words that I have ever heard with my ears were like the words I heard. I did not have to remember these things; they have remembered themselves all these years. . . That evening of the day when I came back, Whirlwind Chaser, who had got a great name and a good horse for curing me, came over to our teepee. He sat down and looked at me a long time in a strange way, and then he said to my father: 'Your boy there is sitting in a sacred manner. I do not know what it is, but there is something special for him to do, for just as I came in I could see a power like a light all through his body.'"[5] Like a *Kerrata* among the Muscogee Creeks, Whirlwind Chaser of the Oglalas could tell that Black Elk could "see" into the future as a prophet, and that he was sensitive to all things in his understanding of the universe. His role in life became that of a cultural interloper or interpreter. His gifted powers to see things connected with the metaphysical world made him valuable to his people as a mediator between the two realities of the physical and metaphysical.

"Seeing" involves mentally experiencing the relationships between tangible and nontangible things in the world and in the universe. It is like living one's dream that seems so real while you are sleeping. It is acceptance of fact that a relationship exists between a tangible item like a mountain and a dream. In his visionary experience, Black Elk spoke of "seeing." As he stood on a high mountain [Harney Peak], he recalled, "Then I was standing on the highest mountain of them all, and round about beneath me was the whole hoop of the world. And while I stood there I saw more than I can tell and I understood more than I saw; for I was seeing in a sacred manner the shapes of all things in the spirit, and the shape of all shapes as they must live together like one being. And I saw that the sacred hoop of my people was one of many hoops that made one circle, wide as daylight and as starlight, and in the center grew one mighty flowering tree to shelter all the children of one mother and one father. And I saw that it was holy."[6]

Many Indian people have had such experiences as Black Elk in an actual vision or a dream or both. They seldom talk about it for fear of others not believing them, or perhaps they do not take their dreams very seriously as signs and messages connecting them with the metaphysical world. Such fear and the thought of being ridiculed by one's peers causes a suppression of such metaphysical opportunities to learn more about things beyond the limitation of the physical world. The interface between the physical and the metaphysical (the conscious and subconscious mind) is of the traditional American Indian mind.

"Indian Thinking" is "seeing" and "listening." Listening for sounds of what is most relevant about the interaction between two things is a part of the realization of relationships and learning their importance about life. Listening does not necessarily involve only hearing sounds. Actually, listening involves hearing and realizing as a receiver while understanding the objective of seeing. It is the counterpart to Indian "seeing." Perhaps, it bears repeating that "seeing" in this way involves trying to understand the significance of relationships. Without listening, seeing only provides images to the mind with limited information and hearing sounds adds substance or more pertinent knowledge to the visual experience. In this light, it is imperative for traditionalist and linear thinkers to look around themselves while trying to understand the natural and man-made environments.

All of the interrelationships is a system called the Natural Order of Life for the American Indian who knows his or her traditional beliefs. Their perception is defined and determined by their natural environment in a type of Natural Democracy, for they treat all things with respect. This democracy is based on respect. In this belief, all things are equally important. Where a native person grows up is relevant to how one understands all things around him or her. One's natural environment is pertinent to how things are perceived, and this set of surroundings become fixed in the mind like reference points for later in life, especially as one travels to distant places away from one's home space or homeland.

Understanding relationships has developed from the Indian thinker "seeing" connections by becoming familiar with his or her natural environment which might be called a homeland. In fact, this situation typifies the American Indian mind in the traditional sense. One's natural surroundings aid the Indian thinker, as thoughts are based on understanding relationships within the environment called the homeland. It is being familiar with the Earth while possessing local knowledge about the streams, creeks, rivers, valleys, deserts, meadows, woods, hills, mountains, and knowing all of the names of plants and animals that are also a part of one's homeland. It is knowing the smells and aromas like the Earth when rain falls lightly, the smell of a meadow of grass or bountiful flowers, and realizing the beauty of life like seeing a newborn kitten.

Listening as a part of oral tradition is essential for understanding relationships and their multiple meanings. Elders tell stories in the oral tradition of tribes, where it was equally important to listen to the story as well as tell the story. Both storyteller and listener engage in reviving an experience of the past that becomes alive again, thereby transcending time from the past to the present. Both tenses of time blur, becoming one and the same. More of this discussion is covered in the next chapter, but the salient point here is that listening is a part of "seeing" the world in the mind of the American Indian.

A part of patience to the path of knowledge is silence and learning to accept the significance of quiet in our lives. Silence is imperative in listening for reflection and self-examination as information is related to the seer. At the beginning of this chapter, the Muscogee creation story related a difficult situation, for the people had to listen and tried to understand the strange new sounds that bewildered them as they later saw the various species of animals that became the clans in their society. Originally, Creek elders said that there were twelve clans of animals and plants in the Muscogee world view, although more clans developed to accommodate the expanding Creek universe as all things are a part of the Natural Order of things.

Silence is the test for patience. In silence, two people are still engaged in the same experience of concentrating on the same item or piece of knowledge. In this way, learning to deal and function with silence is a means for securing one's thoughts and confirming one's beliefs. In this way silence is an opportunity, not a negative. Such silence is uncomfortable to the mainstream person whose world is filled with many man-made noises. This opportunity is for self-reflection and introspection in the process of understanding one's own mind, and finding balance within oneself. Personality is shaped, changed, and refined. Character is built.

For what all of us see, we must relate carefully to how it is related to other things or how it is related to us. For Indian people who are close to their traditional way of life, "thinking" is seeing visions and dreams in a visual reality, unlike seeing things in a linear manner. Seeing and understanding things in a visual context is the basis of receiving information or the processing of information. As a result, a story can be told, thereby providing information as a means of sharing via the oral tradition of the community or tribe. The process is re-creating a vision of the experience via a story in the minds of the listeners.

Seeing involves observing for signs to learn about life with an open mind, so that a full context of information can be absorbed. As a result, one must be an acute observer and be receiving of all things without doubt that might provide relevant information to one's concerns. Native people acutely observe nature and watch for the instincts of plants and animals in action. Developed over centuries, plants and animals act in concert with the Earth via circular rotations, migrations, and seasonal changes. By observing a single act or unusual act of nature, we can tell what is not right about a course of events that is supposed to ensue, according to regularity. These clues are the signs of nature, such as the coat of a horse will develop thicker for a hard winter that is coming. Other animals will respond in the same manner as nature has helped to prepare them with instincts in this way for survival.

Native elder Ed McGaa observed that "each animal has its own power or gift to convey because they were so endowed by *Wakan Tanka*. Does not a mountain lion tell us that we can become independent and walk those lonely chasms of change undauntedly? Doesn't a portrait of the owl, the eagle of the night, tell us not to fear the dark or mysterious places? Surely the beaver conveys a serene security and peace brought forth by a steady endeavor if we can be so fortunate to find our own bliss. And yes, we all need endless scenes of the freedom of hawks, eagles, wolves and the great orcas of the seas to forever implant a resolve that we must never lose our connection with the vast soothing solitude of Nature. Each winged, four-legged and finned [animal] has a meaning to convey that can be beneficial to our intricate two legged lives. Yes, even a common field mouse or a disciplined, dedicated badland ant has a message to convey if we will stoop to study and look for it."[7] All animals have special talents and certain roles in the living world. The way of the traditionalist is to understand these special talents and roles of his or her brethren. Generations of survival among animals have instilled in them keen instincts and certain qualities have evolved in them that have been helpful as ways of knowledge to the American Indian.

Indian thinking is inquiry into relationships and community, and it bears reminding us that community extends beyond human relationships. How all of us as individuals place ourselves within a system of relationships is very important for understanding our own thinking about achieving balance within oneself and within the community. Seeking balance between one's aggressive and peaceful emotions, between one's evil and good thoughts, and between one's negative and positive relationships with others is a continual struggle that has been deemed by the Creator of All Things so that a balance is sought within one's self and within one's community consisting of the family or extended family, clan or society, community, and/or tribe. It is understanding one's relationships that is paramount to living a life in the beauty of balance and harmony.

Seeing, *hecvs* (in the Muscogee Creek language), is cultural awareness of all relations to the seer. To see properly, one must be aware of all surrounding things, including those that might not be in a physical sense, but choose to exist in the metaphysical sense. This type of perception calls for an open-mindedness and sensitivity. Many native people see visions, ghosts, and spirits, but this is not unlike biblical characters who saw angels and Jesus. Angels mostly appeared in the Old Testament of the Bible; one source of the Church doctrine claimed the number of angels on Earth was fixed at the time of creation at 301,655,722, according to fourteenth-century cabalists, and this is a modest estimate.[8] In the linear world of Catholicism or Judaism, or any other mainstream religion of the Western world, such spiritual aberrations enlightened hungry souls desiring to know more about the afterlife.

Religious believers who are willing to risk the limitations of western beliefs defined by scientific empiricism become increasingly likely to see like traditional American Indians. By following the religious tenets for believing, the linear mind and the American Indian mind decrease the vast gap that polarizes them. This compromise of the linear mind enables non-Indians to have a better chance to experience the metaphysical. The biases of the linear mind become obstacles unto the linear person who wishes to think like the American Indian.

Can non-Indians "see" in an Indian way like a traditionalist? This perplexing question of the 1980s and 1990s has continued into the twenty-first century as indigenous knowledge and the academic writings of indigenous scholars have received increasing respect from the mainstream academy. The answer is affirmative, if the non-Indian learns the traditional ways of an Indian community and accepts the values and beliefs of the indigenous culture. Seeing and learning is accepting that you will be enlightened by listening and witnessing the signs. Non-Indians can "see" in this manner, if they believe in the same ethos of the native community or tribe.

For the present, the indigenous way of seeing things like traditional Indians is becoming increasingly incongruent with the linear world. The linear mind looks for cause and effect, and the Indian mind seeks to comprehend relationships. Hence, mental perception is relevant to both the Indian mind and linear mind seeing the world in their own ways.[9] But how are the Indian mind and linear mind different, and why are they different?

Too often, studies about American Indians have been produced from the non-Indian point of view. In the history of Indian–white relations, understanding the native perspective or comprehending the Indian point of view can be referred to as the three dimensions of constructing new American Indian history (which are basically the First Dimension of general narrative description "about" Indian history, The Second Dimension of historical analysis of the dynamics of Indian–white relations, and the Third Dimension consisting of historical analysis of the Indian point of view). The First Dimension is like a door or window, and it is basically the linear mainstream's interpretation or perspective "about" American Indian history. Written from an external point of view, these works can only best describe American Indians.

The Second Dimension is the two-way door like a mirror effect, which allows a common subject like treaties or war between Indians and whites to be viewed by both sides. Contact literature including both the perspectives of the colonizer and colonized is a part of this Second Dimension, in which the scholarly studies involve speeches and quotes from native leaders to help balance the perspectives on a particular battle, treaty, or issue that involved both Indians and whites. Theoretically this type of historical analysis renders equal partnership to the role of Indians in the history of Indian–white relations.

The Third Dimension is actually the native perspective about an issue, a battle, an event, or about an entire history. From the true Indian point of view, this Third Door is actually the First Dimension to the indigenous person. Respectively, from right to life, it is the Third Dimension in the proposed equation of Indian–white relations. Specifically, this view of the traditional American Indian mind originates from the other side of the bridge or from the Indian side of the Indian–white equation. In the course of scholarly investigation and literature on the subject, most of the literature is on the first approach. In the 1990s, scholars have been working on the second approach, in the application of ethnohistory, and only a few have been able to adequately produce studies on the third approach. This Indian–white equation of the three dimensions, especially the Third Door addresses the Indian point of view in relationship to traditional knowledge and developing an Indian intellectualism.

Due to cultural differences, everyone perceives everything differently. It may even be said that individuals of the same culture perceived everything differently, according to their personal point of view as dictated by their personality. However, it is maintained here that persons of the same culture will likely perceive an idea, point of discussion, or solution to a problem in a similar general way. These categorical perceptions are governed by their cultural influences and changes with the development or regression of the basic culture.

From this premise, we can assume that persons of a tribal culture of American Indians perceive subjects differently from those of a non-tribal culture like the American mainstream. Hence, there is a fundamental difference of perception between Indians and white Americans. They understand things differently and accept truth and facts differently. Whereas the Indian mind is more accepting of the truth and facts, the Western linear mind must pursue empirical evidence to prove something is true so that it can become factual in the scientific sense.

But what about the extraordinary—the unexplainable? A gifted mind in mainstream America might be called a genius. If a person scores above ninety-eight percent of the general population on a recognized standard IQ test, then this person would qualify to be a member of Mensa, (Latin for "table"), an organization for extraintelligent people. Founded in 1945 by Roland Berrill and Dr. L.L. Ware in London, Mensa expanded to several other countries with American Mensa established in 1961. With 70,000 members world wide, about 48,000 people classified as being in the top two percent of intelligent people, belong to more than 120 chapters of American Mensa.[10]

In observing American Indians researching at the National Archives, a mainstream scholar disclosed that "when the American Indian scholars come to the National Archives and read the histories from those sources, their interpretation of the action of the Bureau of Indian Affairs, for instance, is quite different from mine. Sometimes the interpretation is parallel, but sometimes it is exactly opposite from mine."[11]

This observation would seem logical along the premise that has been established, but it also notes two polarized perceptions. Why they are of opposites is clear, but how they came about invites suppositions about their origins. Because they are opposing points of view and both are products of their cultures, then they would have to be exemplary of their cultures. It can be assumed the situation of one person as a member of an Indian tribal culture and the other person as a member of the American mainstream hold opposite views, or different views on a point or subject of discussion. Theoretically they are different, but realistically they are not equal in their degrees of retention of cultural backgrounds. If we assume that a person who is also a member of the same tribal cultural background, but is less traditional than a traditionalist, then the second person is more likely to have a similar perception of the mainstream individual. In other words, the diminishing of a culture from traditionalism in the direction of less traditionalism would have a decreasing traditional point of view of that tribal background. Evidence of this occurrence is the changed point of view of the traditional full blood of a tribe who has become educated in the white man's school, and this person may have a different view of his perception. Or a mixed blood who is both from a tribal background and a mainstream background may have a combination of both polarized perceptions.[12] This decrease in traditionalism is discussed in chapter 8.

How humans perceive is through sight performed by the eyes. Unfortunately, we depend too heavily on this physical gift, and do not pay as much attention to the feedbacks of our other senses, both physical and innate senses, so that physical sight is the immediate detector for perception, which influences our perspective. It is maintained here that perception is not perspective but helps to determine it.

Sight also reveals to all of us color, shape, quality, and unusualness of a subject to our mind. Because human minds are also products of culture, we quickly categorize the "seen" subject into our memory banks of knowledge, and all too often form immediate opinions. In ethnocentric cultures, judgments are quickly formed, as linear thinkers naturally learn by comparisons. Relatively, the Western mind compares other things to what it has experienced, and other people to itself, and other cultures to Western culture.[13] The result is Amerocentricism.

Cultural influences act as governors of the way all people think and how the mind responds to what is seen and heard. The retention of culture involving beliefs, philosophy, and values dictates thoughts and therefore forms opinions and determines points of view for both the American Indian mind and the linear mind. These cultural influences are fundamental, but they interact with the present state of mind, which may be involved in emotional stress, anger, happiness, or some other emotion.

There are fundamental foci that perception engages: time, mass, space, and sound. In the Muscogee Creek way of thinking, this type of "seeing" is understanding and accepting the totality of *Ibofanga*—that all things have a spiritual energy. These elemental qualities make up the whole order of the universe. How people perceive them through their cultural lens reflects linear or Indian perspectives and possibly other human perspectives. Normally, a person overly depends on sight, and is not aware of the other senses that are possessed, that is, smell, taste, hearing, and touch. A wiser individual takes into account all of his or her human senses in order to understand what he or she has seen. Indian people have learned to do this, especially by observing and understanding how animals see the world around them. In the linear mainstream, a good hunter would practice the same way of seeing things. To be a good hunter is to hunt like an animal such as a wolf who relies upon all senses for its survival.

In this vast world of diversity, we are of many types of humans, animals, and plants. Former Navajo Tribal Chairman Peter MacDonald observed the Navajo way in his words. "We Navajo call ourselves the Diné, which means 'the only human beings in the world.' That sounds arrogant to those who do not understand our culture and history, and it has caused us to experience great hatred and violence. Yet the concept developed from our efforts to understand our place in the world at large and was our way of determining how we differ from the birds, the animals, and the other creatures with whom we share the earth."[14] The Navajos look at the world in a special way of kinship. This communal sense is common to Native Americans who believe that traditionally the community includes animals and plants. We forget the fact that historically animals and plants were much more a part of our natural environment in colonial America and in Indian Country.

The late Tewa anthropologist Alfonso Ortiz observed the same sense of totality as he noted, "but what would be some of the constituent parts or categories of a world view? Space and time are, of course, the obvious initial candidates, if only for the reason that phenomenologists—including anthropologists, philosophers, and historians of religion—have compiled an impressive record of evidence that space and time do provide man with his primary level of orientation to reality." Ortiz also held that, "this is true enough if we but add the cavil that none of the pueblos, to the best of my knowledge, has abstract terms for space and time; space is only meaningful as the distance between two points, and time cannot be understood apart from the forces and changes in nature which give it relevance and meaning. It is precisely when time becomes cut up into arbitrarily abstract units (weeks, hours, minutes, seconds) that tribal peoples lose all similarity in their time-reckoning customs with those of Western peoples. And these smaller units of time-reckoning are precisely the ones which concern Western minds the most."[15]

Such deep observations have sustained the chasm between the traditional American Indian mind and the mind of the linear world. Cultural stereotypes negatively portraying other cultures hinders the process of learning and education. Academia allows the participation of minds from various cultures and backgrounds. But, a comparison of the performance of minority groups with the mainstream has produced some interesting results. Minority scholars—African Americans, Hispanic Americans, and Asian Americans—have been surveyed for their academic performances. Concerning young minority intellectuals, Sanford M. Dornbusch, professor of sociology at Stanford, while surveying 7,000 high school students in the six schools in San Francisco, discovered that Asian Americans consistently earned better grades than any other group of students, regardless of their parents' level of education or their families' social and economic status, the ususal predictors of success. In fact, in Asian American homes where English is spoken often, or whose families lived longer in the United States, the students did slightly less well.[16] The Asian American students have evaluated their academic situations and opportunities with the help in many cases of their parents, and they have applied the effort of working hard with an attitude of determination. Hard work and determination are not solely Asian American cultural habits, but they are becoming typical to those Asian American students who succeed, and the mainstream has mistakenly presumed that Asian American students being brilliant is a cultural trait. This is not traditional knowledge, as it actually derives from culture over time.

The basis of traditional knowledge derives from identification of identity and culture. Through centuries, generations of people practiced ways of doing things and emphasize the importance of certain items that are concrete and abstract. Much of this traditional knowledge originated from the practicalities of life on a daily basis in relationship to an environment and its climate. As people have made these adjustments, cultural identities have developed and evolved from the peoples' actions within a group that is generally called a nation.

Simultaneously, much of traditional knowledge comes from mundane daily living, thereby establishing cultural norms that may be called an order to life. Tribal elders have taught this observation for generations. By maintaining order in life, a balance occurs and decreases the chance for confusion and chaos. Hence, it is the role of the elders to maintain peace and order, to supply advice, teach, and to advise, and it is the role of the younger to hunt, to fight in war, and to protect the people. They are also to listen to the elders for advice on how to regain the balance between peace and war, between good and evil. This respect for elders is valued by many tribal cultures around the world.

It can be assumed that in life people are "doers" and "reactors"—people who act and people who react or respond. For example, to acquire knowledge, Creek and Seminole traditionalists learn by first waiting and listening and watching for signs. For instance, much can be learned from the larger order of life—the universe. Humans can learn more from the Natural Order of things than from the order that man has established.

The traditional educational system is to learn by two methods. The first is to listen, observe, be patient for a sign (which has caused others to call traditional Indians passive), and lessons are learned by receiving or taking in this information. An important point may be that it may not be most effective to try to deliberately obtain knowledge, as only information would be gained (not knowledge) and frustration usually happens in this acquisitive process.

After receiving knowledge, which may not always be understood at first, then a person reacts by imitating the elder who might be a teacher, or reacting to the instruction learned from nature, and knowledge is learned in this way like the mainstream by doing—the practical experience and this knowledge of doing one's job, taking an exam, hunting, and so forth is application of knowledge received by using this knowledge.[17]

Philosophical differences between American Indian intellectualism and mainstream intellectualism are actually based on the differences among the various tribal cultures. Hence, the difference is not accurately between "Indian intellectualism and mainstream intellectualism" but between mainstream intellectualism and the different tribes' intellectualism. This may seem obvious, but stereotypes negate the multiple differences between the various tribal nations and their cultures and promote a generic "Indianness," which is categorically convenient for discussing American Indians as a group.

The abstract of nativism versus the concreteness of mainstream academics is an ongoing incongruence. It is a noticeable characteristic of tribal elders (traditionalists) who frequently have a tendency to generalize rather than supplying a direct answer or specific detail. This indirectness means that they communicate in a more abstract way so as not to decrease the opportunity for further information that might cause confrontation or rejection of what they said, for example, suggestions or advice. This makes it difficult to understand elders sometimes, as they expect the younger ones to understand, so other examples are often given to help illustrate what they mean.

In addition, by being general, with the responsibility placed on the listener to learn, the possible ill reaction is not necessarily placed on the speaker, who might use the pronoun "we," or the "tribe." It has always been important to promote harmony in the tribal community. Because the mainstream is more detail oriented, it must have concrete details to work with for understanding.

The abstract also involves another reality of life—the afterlife. Life on Earth is only a segment of time and life here is obviously a struggle. Hence, the tribal individual entertains thoughts about the reality of the afterlife, and strives to communicate with that world, especially through holy men, priests, or prophets. A story of the oral tradition provides clues about the spiritual world around us and helps to comfort the living. Hence, effective communication is very important.

Language has not always been the expression of traditional knowledge. In some languages like one of my peoples, the Muscogee Creeks, it is simpler than English as it has a smaller vocabulary. It is simple to prevent misunderstanding, but takes longer to speak. When elders speak, they converse for hours, and often they sit outside on a porch to visit, and may use the ground to draw to convey their meanings and explain points of interest. One example is the word or explanation of "treaty." In the Muscogee Creek language, it is described as *patvkva*, meaning blanket or top covering of the Earth. Words were described to be placed on the blanket, and to be moved around like putting words down on paper. This was the explanation of the concept of "treaty" among the Muscogees and Seminoles.

It has been theorized that American Indians biologically function from the right hemispheric side of their brain. Although some scholars say that this has been debated and it has been proven that there is not a hemispheric difference, it is apparent that some people are more musically and visually inclined than their opposite colleagues, who are more mathematical and uncompromising in a scientific way of wanting empirical evidence.

This contrasts with members of the American mainstream, who operate from the left hemispheric side. Whether this hypothesis is true or not, it offers some intriguing ideas as to why Indians may approach scholastic endeavors differently from that of the mainstream, which is responsible for course curriculum and instruction. It should be noted here that some readers will say that this hemispheric theory had been disproved, whereas others will continue to ask why there remains such a dissimilarity between Indian/artist thinking and linear thinking. Supposedly, people (and some mainstream individuals function in thought from the right side) of the right hemisphere are said to be oriented toward philosophy and art. People of the left side are inclined toward science and mathematics. What is most important to realize is that native people have a wider perspective due to a holistic approach in seeing the world and accepting truth instead of trying to prove it on every occasion when there is doubt.

Due to this difference in perspective, class instructors (who are mostly from the mainstream, thus from the left hemisphere), should, nevertheless, respect the perspective of the American Indian student. To discriminate against a differing point of view, especially from the instructor, or even harboring prejudice against another viewpoint, is biased and disallows academic freedom. Furthermore, it is a negation of the cultural existence of the Indian intellectual.[18]

America has been criticized by global communities for its ethnocentrism, and it is important to hear different cultural perspectives for the sake of academic freedom. By continuing to hear only the same school of thought from one culture, then the opportunity to learn progressively is obstructed. This is regression in the American mainstream, especially for a society consisting of various ethnic peoples of diverse cultures.

The wars fought between Indians and whites were more than just over land—they were wars of the minds. The American mainstream thinks in a linear fashion, which is very different from the circular fashion of traditionalists. These two are at odds when both are not realized, as by one not knowing the other one. This neglect presumes that there is only one correct way of thought—the linear way.

Basically, linear thought is rationalizing how something originates at point A, is affected by some force or influence and transforms into point B, to point C, and so forth. Intuitiveness is less relevant to the linear mind of problem solving and philosophy. The problem for the linear mind is dealing with the abstract.

The circular method is a circular philosophy focusing on a single point and using familiar examples to illustrate or explain the point of discussion. The circular approach assures that everyone understands, and that all is considered, thereby increasing the chance for harmony and balance in the community and with everything else. As each person or being relates to the focal point, and if lines were drawn to indicate this relatedness, then the results would be the spokes of a wheel, and all the participants are encircled by the unity of this experience. This might be called an "Internal Model."

The community is a product of the culture, which consists of several important elements that can be theorized as the "Internal Model." The internal consists of the person, families, societies like clans, or councils, and all these units are related by kinship and interrelated. This network or system makes up the tribal village or towns, or possibly a band, and these units make up the tribal nation. Hence, identity of the tribal nation derives from the community of internalness, the keeper of traditional knowledge. The identification of tribal nation is more identified with the modern era of American Indian history, especially in the twentieth century, whereas before 1900, tribes more likely viewed themselves as communities in their tribal languages.

The Internal Model frequently comes into conflict with external forces deriving from another community, nation, culture or civilization. The obvious example is the confrontation of the tribal communities or nations like the Muscogee Creeks and the white American mainstream. There are three experiences that occur in this arrangement: (1) the existence or evolution of the tribal community, (2) the existence or evolution of the other (external) community, and (3) the interchange or dynamics of exchange between the two spheres of cultures.

In modern society, American Indians of traditional thought are functioning outside of their cultural worlds for a large percentage of their life. Furthermore, they are products of two educational means and two cultures. Initially, this is difficult as the traditional person strives to learn in the non-Indian educational system. But, once this is achieved, then this individual can draw upon the traditional knowledge and mainstream knowledge to put forth a modern Indian intellectualism.

The importance of Indian intellectualism is contributing answers to difficult questions today. It is very possible that many answers can come from tribal cultures and be applied to mainstream problems. How would this happen? If order exists in a traditional perspective, how can traditional knowledge of a tribal culture be applied to a problematic condition of the mainstream?

Hypothetically, the problem has to exist in an order of things or systems. The first task is to learn all the factors involved, to research for all the items influencing possible cause of the problem. This would involve studying and determining which items are directly or internally involved, and which are indirectly or externally influential. Beyond observing and studying, the next step is finding out how all the internal and external factors are involved, as it may be that the problem is caused by another problem. Hence, the problem has to be understood before it can be permanently solved (thus avoiding temporary solutions and quick results that permit the problem to occur again). It may also be determined that the problem is unsolvable and this is a part of accepting the Natural Order of things.[19]

Next, what are the possible sources to use to solve the problem? The best of all worlds would be to apply something that is familiar, but this may not be possible. It has to be determined what the possible resources are for the solution. In fact, this situation may present a problem. If the resources are not accessible for a proposed solution, then one must be patient for indicators, probably while studying the situation, for ideas, and perhaps a vision of the whole matter, which would likely put everything—the problem, solution, and human relationships—into the context of the vision, which may be called a mental image.

An Indian way of "seeing" exists, according to a native perspective about all things. It is a cooperative effort between the subconscious and conscious mind and influenced by one's tribal culture and personal experiences. As a result, dreams, daydreaming, imagining, and visions are pertinent to "Indian thinking" and this realization becomes a part of the logic and decision-making process of thought. In every dream and vision are clues of knowledge and/or revelations about what all people seek to understand. Although the conscious mind is the rational part of thinking, native people have learned to consider carefully what the subconscious part of the brain has to offer. "Seeing" in the Indian way is how traditionalists of indigenous cultures understand life, and it is the basis of their indigenous logic. Although many Native Americans have been educated in mainstream public schools, American Indians who are close to their traditions still "see" things from an indigenous perspective. This logic derives from their natural ethos as a people whose communities still believe in the old ways of life, and they remain viable in the twenty-first century.

NOTES

1. Angie Debo, *The Road to Disappearance: A History of the Creek Indians* (Norman: University of Oklahoma Press, 1941), 15.

2. For the origin of the Muscogee Creeks, see John R. Swanton, *Early History of the Creek Indians and Their Neighbors*, Bureau of American Ethnology Bulletin 73 (Washington: Government Printing Office, 1922) and John R. Swanton, "The Social History and Usages of the Creek Confederacy," *Forty-Second Annual Report of the Bureau of American Ethnology* (Washington: United States Government Printing Office, 1928), 1–900.

3. For discussion of Muscogee Creek traditions and other members of the Five Civilized Tribes in the late nineteenth century, see Theda Perdue, *Nations Remembered, An Oral History of the Five Civilized Tribes, 1865–1907* (Westport, CT: Greenwood Press, 1980), 87–115. For history and cultural information about the Creeks, see Angie Debo, *The Road to Disappearance*, 3–399; Michael Green, *The Politics of Indian Removal: Creek Government and Society* (Lincoln: University of Nebraska Press, 1982), 1–237; J. Leitch Wright, Jr., *Creeks and Seminoles, The Destruction and Regeneration of the Muscogulgee People* (Lincoln: University of Nebraska Press, 1986), 1–382. For cultural information on the Seminoles of Oklahoma, refer to James H. Howard in collaboration with Willie Lena, *Oklahoma Seminoles, Medicine, Magic and Religion* (Norman: University of Oklahoma Press, 1990), 1–279.

4. Jean Chaudhuri and Joyotpaul Chaudhuri, *A Sacred Path: The Way of the Muscogee Creeks* (Los Angeles: UCLA American Indian Studies Center, 2001), 2.

5. John Neihardt, ed., *Black Elk Speaks: Being the Life Story of a Holy Man of the Oglala Sioux* (New York: Pocket Books, 1973), seventh printing, 41.

6. Neihardt, *Black Elk Speaks*, 36.

7. Ed McGaa, *Native Wisdom: Perceptions of the Natural Way* (Minneapolis: Four Directions Publishing, 1995), 36–37.

8. Gustav Davidson, *A Dictionary of Angels: Including the Fallen Angels* (New York: The Free Press, 1967), xviii.

9. Jamake Highwater's *The Primal Mind* (New York: Harper and Row, 1981) is a philosophical study of the American Indian, and the author demonstrates how Indians differ in their thinking from the dominant society.

10. Marvin Grosswirth, Abbie F. Salny, Alan Stillson, and members of the American Mensa, Ltd., *Match Wits with Mensa* (Cambridge, MA: Perseus Books, 1981), xiii–xiv.

11. Floyd O'Neil, "Commentary" on "Perspectives on The Writing of Indian History from the Indian Point of View," *Breaking Barriers*, edited by David L. Beaulieu, "Occasional Paper Series," No. 1, December 1974, 38.

12. Studies that point out the different perspective of Indians from the mainstream include Robert C. Breuing, "Hopi Perspectives on Formal Education" (Ph.D. dissertation, University of Kansas, 1973) and Laura M. Lowry, "Differences in Visual Perception and Auditory Discrimination Between American Indian and White Kindergarten Children," *Journal of Learning Disabilities*, Vol. 3, No. 4, July 1970, 359–363.

13. Some years ago, Judith Kleinfield, an anthropologist, observed that children of the Tlingit Indian village of Angoon frequently crowded the local cinema and could recall minute details of the films they had watched. This extraordinary visual ability is applied as a learning technique among American Indian groups. See Estelle Fuchs and Robert Havighurst, *To Live on This Earth: American Indian Education* (Garden City, NY: Anchor Press, 1973), 122.

14. Peter MacDonald with Ted Schwarz, *The Last Warrior: Peter MacDonald and the Navajo Nation* (New York: Orion Books, 1993), 4.

15. Alfonso Ortiz, "Ritual Drama and the Pueblo World View," in Alfonso Ortiz, ed., *New Perspectives on the Pueblos* (Albuquerque: University of New Mexico Press, 1972), 137.

16. Fox Butterfield, "Why They Excel," *Parade* magazine, *South Bend Tribune*, January 21, 1990, 1.

17. Some insight into traditional Indian learning methods is in J.A. Fitzgerald and W.W. Ludeman, "The Intelligence of Indian Children," *Journal of Comparative Psychology*, Vol. 6, No. 4, August 1926, 319–328.

18. See Robert Berkhofer, *The White Man's Indian: Images of the American Indians from Columbus to the Present* (New York: Alfred A. Knopf, 1978), 1–261.

19. See Benjamin Lee Whorf, "An American Indian Model of the Universe," in Dennis and Barbara Tedlock, *Teaching From the American Earth; Indian Religion and Philosophy* (New York: Liveright, 1975), 121–129.

2
ORAL TRADITION AND
TRADITIONAL KNOWLEDGE

"My father found an eagle starving to death in a coyote trap. Its leg was badly mangled. He took a blanket out of the car to capture it with the least harm and received a lifelong scar on his forearm from the eagle's claws. We attempted to nurse the eagle back to health in the chicken coop. We had a big orange-colored rooster that was so mean that he would even chase us kids. This rooster never lost a fight and was not even afraid of dogs. The eagle sulked in the chicken coop looking out at us through an iron gate that covered the opening. A smaller hole was beneath the gate that we used to place jackrabbits through. Chickens could pass through this opening, which we kept covered although they stayed away from the chicken coop because of the eagle. My father was worried about the eagle losing its strength. Then one day the big rooster went through the opening. I guess he must have thought that he could whip the eagle. Some people, even some countries have been like that, making some ill-advised decisions to go off and fight a force much larger than themselves. All of a sudden, there was nothing but orange feathers in that chicken coop. The eagle ate the rooster and from then on devoured our rabbit offerings. He became so healthy and strong that the Hill City zoo offered one hundred dollars to my father. This was a large sum of money in those days. Most people would have taken the offer, but not my father. We were poor, but he took the eagle back to the badlands and released it. The eagle circled high above my father before it flew to some distant buttes. At times, my Dad would go back to that place and hold up his big cowboy hat, waving it at the buttes. Often the eagle would come and circle over my Dad. He was proud of his scar and the fact that money could not buy the eagle."[1]

Ed McGaa, Oglala Lakota, 1995

* * *

"Story" is the basis of American Indian oral tradition. Story is the vehicle for sharing traditional knowledge and passing it from one generation to the next. Its purposes include sharing information, providing

21

lessons in morality, confirming identity, and telling experiences of people. Stories sometimes tell us about the future. Powerful and vivid, each account is an entity of power. When the story is told effectively, it transcends time, as traditional knowledge lives on with each new listener becoming a part of them and a part of the next generation.

Native Americans, who are close to their traditional beliefs, and people of mainstream America have a different understanding of history, especially when their history involves their relationship with each other. The linear mind primarily depends on archival documents to write history and the other relies on oral tradition to account for the past. Even their definitions of "history" demonstrate their cultural differences. Native Americans stress a sociocultural kinship of relationships, whereas mainstream Americans rely on a factual interpretation of historical events and human deeds recorded in written documents. What is real? And, to whom? The linear thinker is convinced that history is a measurement of the past and that each new event becomes a part of the collective past in chronological order.

To the American Indian, history is better explained as the importance of "experience." People recall an experience in greater detail because of the emotions involved, vivid colors, familiar sounds described, and the people and/or beings involved. When retold, the experience comes alive again recreating the experience by evoking the emotions of the listeners, transcending past-present-future. Time does not imprison the story. The vehicle for transmitting this same reality of past and present is the oral tradition, which differs from oral history. Oral tradition is the process; oral history is an event told orally. Orality is the way of the American Indian mind.

The debate of written history versus oral history is a continuous one. It focuses on the assertion that oral history is not as reliable as history documented by written evidence.[2] In the linear world of academia, only things written down in the past are taken seriously. Mainstream academia calls them facts, although they are subjective observations of biased minds filled with many influences. The printed document is accredited with more relevance than a verbal account retold.

Oral history and oral historians of the academic mainstream have argued for the validity and recognition of oral history. As a result, general works written by mainstream oral historians have set standards for obtaining and using oral history.[3] Having been established as a field, and becoming increasingly recognized by historians and other academics, oral history has gained increasing respect since the 1970s as the interviews of America's heroes and politicians seemed to be important for collecting before these great men died. For example, Studs Terkel's oral history, *The Good War: An Oral History of World War Two*, won the Pulitzer Prize.[4] Another decade or so elapsed before women began to be seriously given the same recognition that their male politicians and heros received. Unfortunately, a scant number of studies of women in oral history have received recognition in mainstream academia at this date. One might think that this is not true, but a quick computer survey or look in book stores reveals a limited number of women's oral histories.

Narrative and oral tradition are essential tools for building a bridge between these two interpretations of history.[5] In practice, oral history has certain attributes and it can be used very effectively. In actuality, American Indian history is tribal history told individually via the oral tradition, and not all of the 562 federally recognized tribes at this date have a written history.[6] An estimated 20 tribes have no written history at this date.[7] In other words, mainstream scholars should include Indian oral tradition when writing about American Indians, but this is not usually the case.

A definition of "history" for Native American groups depends on each community's world view and the elements which define and shape their knowledge of the world. For instance, among the Muscogee Creeks and Seminoles of Oklahoma, perception, reality, and causality interacted for their understanding of history. These two peoples traditionally relied on oral tradition, like many tribes, for telling about historical events and recording occurrences in forms of myths, legends, stories, and songs.[8] These venues are also ways for helping the people remember the oral history and placing their lives in a context of collective history about their people as a community.

Storytelling is an intuitive tradition. Within a family or a gathering of relatives and friends, stories are told, becoming the fabric for holding groups together, even momentarily. Sometimes storytellers embellished the stories for entertainment, and at other times they told the same stories in a mild way to convey the importance of the story as a message or lesson in human behavior or to share some ethical or cultural action as a lesson for the youth.

Oral tradition represents the forms just mentioned, and oral history is the spoken record of events. Furthermore, the oral tradition among tribes does not function with the sole purpose of becoming oral history, although mainstream academics typically classify it that way. As mentioned, the oral tradition becomes a socio-cultural history of the community and it may contain some biographies, hero accounts, women's studies, environmental knowledge, and metaphysical experiences.

Essentially, oral tradition conveys what is important to the community. Configured more on a daily basis, the oral tradition consists of stories, like the eagle and its caretaker, that are about people and what happened to them, and perhaps about "what they did," but not necessarily about "what they accomplished." What is important in the story is the difference between the American Indian mind and the Western mind. This kind of oral tradition weaves together the community, telling us about the human beings, animal beings, and other beings. As certain stories are repeated, and others are not, then sorting out what is important becomes a part of the process of determining what is germane to the community. Relevant values and what is important, according to the people are reinforced by the retold stories. Oral tradition is the basis of American Indian history from a native perspective (although as more Indian minds are educated in mainstream ways, this point is diminished).

Typically, American Indian history, produced by linear scholars, is written from a "window" perspective "about" Native Americans. This characteristic is changing. Within this generation of scholarship since the 1980s, historians and insightful scholars are addressing the dynamics of cross-cultural experiences between Indians and whites. But what is needed is a new bridge of innovative theory and methodology to understand Native American history from an Indian and/or tribal perspective. Michael J. Hill (Blackfeet), Associate Dean for Students at Northwest Indian College, Bellingham, Washington, observed that "western science looks down on aboriginal people. Our stories, our oral traditions are just myths to them . . . all of our oral traditions are invalidated."[9] In this age of scientific America, linear scholars place little credibility in Indian myths for explaining history.

The following theory of the Third Dimension mentioned in chapter 1 involves constructing such a bridge from the Third Dimension to the other two portrayals of history for an Indian or native perspective based on insights with the tools of narrative and oral tradition within the indigenous cultural context. In order to understand this viewpoint better, the story about the rooster and the eagle becomes significant at this point. Stories in the oral tradition of native people have purposes and lessons for teaching about morality or the future. They are lessons in life about vanity, pride, showmanship, hidden danger, and how life can be lost—all as a part of the natural laws of the universe.

Stories are a large part of Indian life, a type of oral literature.[10] As a child in rural Oklahoma during the 1950s, I grew up with stories, told by relatives, usually elders. They talked mainly about "what happened" to someone that everyone knew. And they usually told who these people were related to and discussed why it happened. Stories perpetuated life. Contrary to the historic stereotype of the "silent Indian" or "stoic

Indian," Indian people, at least my people, the Seminoles and Creeks, talk a lot. They use narrative in developing an oral tradition that consists of stories, myths, and legends. The late Jean Hill Chaudhuri described the importance of stories in the following way: "the full-blood storytellers, using Creek language through the late [nineteen] forties and early fifties, were the intellectual guardians of a major watershed in Creek history. They were connected with the Trail of Tears themselves or in their immediate family circle."[11]

Telling stories shared information, passed time, communicated positive feelings, and reassured listeners, especially children, that things were all right, making them feel safe and secure. Storytelling is enriched by the person telling the story. A good storyteller is known for providing a brief history of kinship of the person(s) involved, presenting the plot of "what happened," and usually speculating "why" it happened. Sometimes the stories are serious, describing danger or bad things happening, sometimes they make us laugh. Such humor breaks tension and brings people together, solidifying them into one group. Narrative is powerful and it remains evocative among the Seminoles, Creeks, and many other tribes. Converse to the stoic stereotype, Indians laugh a lot. They are masters at teasing and superb joke tellers.

"Story" among American Indians consists of at least five parts: time, place, character(s), event, and purpose. Together, they are the sum of an "experience." Each part connects the other parts for the storyteller to weave his or her story in the art of storytelling that is poetry and fine entertainment and knowledge sharing in Indian communities.

Time as a part of the story of when it happened becomes less relevant as the story continues to be told. Time becomes less important as the characters come to life and relive the experience. The storyteller breathes life into the story by describing the characters involved and vividly describing the event. The past becomes the present and when common patterns are a part of the experience told about, they are lessons for the future. "When" something happened is not so important as "why" and "how" something happened.

Place plays a prominent role in the story to give it texture, so that the listeners can relate to the origin of the story. Place becomes a reference point that is needed in life so that we know where we come from and who our relatives are. Reference points of experiences become landmarks and even sacred places or special sites where they remind travelers of certain paths, rivers, trees, valleys, and mountains that have become touchstones for memory. In this way, every place has a story relating to human experience.

The characters in a story are one or more, human and/or an animal or both such as a trickster, and the characters represent heros, cultural heros, tricksters, ghosts, spirits, or even the Creator. The characters carry the story, thus allowing the listeners to relate to them and to form opinions of whether they like them or not, respect or disrespect them, and admire or fear them. For many tribes, "Coyote" is the clever trickster. Other groups say their trickster is the "Great Hare," while others have tricksters who also might be called culture heros.

The event or incident of the story is the "experience" shared by the storyteller with the listeners. The "experience" is the heart of the oral tradition for native peoples. Native people recall the past via remembering experiences, which are told via stories. The participation of "listening" is equally important to the role of the storyteller. Listening and interpretation is imperative for understanding properly the information and knowledge that were transmitted via the story.[12]

At the beginning, the purpose of the story is not always clear to the listener(s), but there is/are objective(s) for sharing it. The purpose may be teaching youth about life. As mentioned, the story can pass along information, or share knowledge. Or the story's purpose can also be for mere entertainment. But when the story is told effectively, it becomes powerful, and it empowers its listeners by touching their emotions and increasing their awareness about life.

The power of a story is vastly underestimated for its influence on society in general. Local history, sharing news, spreading gossip, and understanding the structure of a community are all involved in the power of story and storytelling. Although scholars of American Indian Studies might argue that this emphasis is folklore and involves twisting the truth, American Indian oral tradition and power of a story is much more than the story and the storyteller. It is an Indian reality.

It bears repeating the important point of the totality of *Ibofanga*. All things contain spiritual energy, and the release of such power unmeasurable. For example, the rooster badly underestimated the growing energy and power of the hurt eagle. Stories of the Indian oral tradition have the powerful nature to transcend linear time, which is governed by the power in the story itself and the power of the storyteller. The power of a story contained energy waiting to be released at the appropriate time of story telling via the oral tradition. From a traditional perspective, one might say that the story, like the rooster and eagle, is spirituality in the form of released power or energy with its effects on listeners of the audience. The quality and depth of the story convey the strength of the power of the story, and thereby such power is waiting to be acted upon by the storyteller and the audience or listener. No doubt, you are thinking about the rooster and the eagle right now. The power of the story has the potential to influence you to visualize the rooster fighting the eagle. In your mind, they are struggling now.

The spirituality of any entity is timeless, such that a story is reawakened and moved through linear time. In the full release of its power and its effects on the audience, the story is enlivened such that the past becomes a part of the present, and the past and present is projected into the future. All three parts of linear time—past, present, and future—are a part of the American Indian circular understanding of a time continuum. Told again and again, the story's power becomes known and acknowledged such as a person of known reputation, for example, as good or bad story, interesting or dull, short or long, and so forth.

The storyteller is powerful, much like a lightning rod conducting the electrical power of visual energy. Storytellers vary in style and success to electrify an audience, the spirit or power of the story remains encapsulated. Talent, experience, and timing are important variables in this dimension of the oral tradition. For example, a talented storyteller with limited experience can encounter a difficult time in telling a story with the results being a bored audience, or a "so-what" feeling. However, perfect timing with a talented storyteller and listeners prepared to listen can convey the full power of the story's spirituality, thus awakening time, place, character(s), and events of the story. You can actually see the characters in your mind.

An audience is reactionary power waiting to be acted upon. The audience is essential for the story to live on as a part of the circular time continuum. In the sequence of a story, the storyteller, then the listener, like a chain reaction, the audience is also an integral part of the American Indian oral tradition of oral history. Hence, "listening" is pertinent to the success of the story. The linear world needs to properly understand the words of Indian people. President Karen Gayton Swisher of Haskell Indian Nations University (Standing Rock Sioux), noted that "the words 'voices,' 'stories,' and 'perspectives' are prevalent in recent reports of research and typify the intent of educational researchers to present more accurate interpretations of the qualitative research experience. Among the current methods being used to attempt to capture authenticity is: listening to the voices of the people and making sure they are heard through the writing; telling the stories of the people as metaphors and examples of schooling experiences; and presenting the perspectives of others in an attempt to encourage readers to see through a different lens."[13] The voices are channels of energy in action, transmitting ideas, feelings, and knowledge impacting the listeners whose emotions and intellects have been affected by such oral energy.

Stories possess a special power, a kind of emotional energy that can produce tears of laughter or sadness, depending on what the story is about. Among the Seminoles and Creeks, including many Indian groups, stories are usually about ordinary people. They are not normally about someone's great deeds of personal victory or a battle, or the signing of a treaty. Most stories are simply about people and their experiences. But they evoke something that we feel in common and something that we can relate to such as people we know and are familiar experiences that we have had.

The emotional energy can be felt in a story by the listeners as they relate to the characters involved. The more vivid the storyteller makes the story—the momentum increases, falls, then rises again, then falls. It draws the energy from each listener, pulling them into the story as an experiential happening. Simultaneously, the storyteller labors to bring realism and importance to the story, expelling energy in the process. Energies are exchanged, engaging each other. The rooster and eagle are fighting. You believe that rooster will win. I think the eagle might win. In the end, both storyteller and listener feel the emotional drain, or increased anxiety permeates their personal beings.

Certain stories are special. These accounts are about extraordinary people, beings or places. Spirits and Indian people are a part of each other, and the former are among us when they want to be. They remind us that we are not as powerful as we think that we are, and that we can make mistakes that will make us the folly like the rooster in the story with the eagle. It causes us to think about our relationships and to think about how they are important to our place in community.

The ability to think about things is based on memory. The role of memory in oral history is an integral part of the oral historical process and transmitting traditional knowledge.[14] Memory also makes oral history vulnerable due to the limitation of recall and getting facts correct, thus an outdated argument of historians criticizing oral history and American Indian oral history.

In the Western world, the printed word carries much weight and supersedes a verbal agreement and a confirmed handshake. People would rather have a contract in writing than believe what a person has said, such as a promise to do something. It has been said that the printed word is more reliable than the spoken word.[15]

For American Indians, oral tradition is imperative to holding communities together. A story unites us with a common understanding of kinship, giving us a common experience, and creates a group ethos. This is how native people think. Community is central to indigenous societies and holds more importance than individual status in the community. Community is the most important social unit among Native Americans.

Narrative and oral tradition produce a kind of social history, telling you also about the culture of the people. Stories are clues of what they are like, what they like, and what they think are important in their lives. It is also a kind of community history of oral tradition, and these stories actually bond the community members together. The stories, as they are told, weave a fabric of continuity, holding the community together. They give a sense of place, time, people, feeling, and identity. Indian people enjoy good stories, good humor, but we are also affected by the bad stories, by bad things that have happened to people. All of these expressions are about human nature and story is a means of bonding people.

Narrative and oral tradition help to build an oral history for accounting for the past of a community. They tell us about the social, everyday life of people. Instead of writing about Indian people from the window of a library or archives using historical documents, oral tradition and listening to stories allows people to "feel" and become a part of the past and sharing a sense of time and place with the people.

The presence of community begins with origin and where native people come from. Hence, creation stories are significant to the identity of native communities. Native peoples have stories passed down through generations about the origin of their peoples.[16] Such stories render group identity and tell us who we are and where we came from.

According to Navajo leader Peter MacDonald, "for the Navajo, the most important deity was Changing Woman, also known as the Turquoise Goddess or Estsánatlehi. During the time of darkness, Mother Earth rose up to meet Father Sky. A great mist appeared on the sacred mountain, and when the mist rose, a child was heard crying. This was Changing Woman, who went from infancy to adolescence to adulthood to old age in just four days. Later she would be thought of in relation to the seasons, as an infant in the spring, a teenager in the summer, an adult in the fall, and an old woman in the winter. . . . Changing Woman was responsible for all creation on earth. First she had intercourse with the sun and gave birth to two monster-slayers, the deities Nayenezgáni (Warrior God) and Tobadsistsini (Child of Water). Then came the Diné, all of whom first lived in the Fourth World, a land populated by monsters, which made the Warrior Gods important protectors . . . As it evolved, our religion became more complex in order to explain everything there was to know about life. Changing Woman was created after First Man and First Woman, but she is the most important deity on earth. It can be said that she is the child of the mountain, her father being the sky. With such a history, you can understand why certain mountains and other places were considered sacred to the Navajo. Such mountains defined territory that was never to be abandoned, even at the expense of one's own life."[17]

Stories involve place, usually homelands with deep human attachments. Homelands, especially in our minds, can never be taken away as long as the Indian mind wants to recall such places. Activist Russell Means reminds us that "one must understand that to an Indian, ownership of land is a foreign concept. The earth is our Grandmother, who provides us with everything we need to survive. How can you *own* your grandmother? How can you *sell* her? How does a piece of paper that you probably can't read prove ownership of something that can't be owned? Even if you're white, and think you *really* own some land, try skipping property-tax payments for a few years."[18]

Means told a story about his grandfather telling about his special relationship with *his* grandfather. He stated that "the best part of my Greenwood summers was when Grandpa John took my hand and walked with me for hours along the river or across the prairie. Afterwards, we would go down to the store. Together, we sat on the front steps while I drank an icy strawberry soda and munched a bag of salty potato chips. Those were among the most wonderful moments of my life . . . What Grandpa John taught me on those walks was the most important part of my childhood. As we ambled through the trees and fields, he carefully pointed out the tracks of various animals and birds, showing me how to distinguish one from another. The tracks of a dog, he said, are usually steady, because the dog is familiar with its territory and knows where it's going. A coyote or a wolf is more wary, stopping frequently to check things out. Domesticated dogs are much like domesticated humans in that their toes are close together, explained Grandpa, but wolves or coyotes are free, so their toes are open. When we were free Indians, he said, *our* toes were spread apart."[19] For Indian people, hundreds and thousands of sacred places exist throughout Indian Country.

Such experiences and places that Means talks about are important to Indians in life. Places become significant in personal ways, and there are places with power such as sacred sites. Natural sacred places to native people that are special to understanding and learning about life and the universe include the Black Hills, Blue Lake of the Taos, Mackinac Island, Mount Rainier, Mount Taylor, and Bear Butte.[20] Other sacred places to indigenous peoples include Uinta in Utah, Tucumcari in New Mexico, the Black Hills in South Dakota, and the Four Corners area of the Southwest that held special meaning for the Hopi, the Diné (Navajo), and early Spanish peoples.[21] There are hundreds of such places, even thousands.

Such places of power contain knowledge. By understanding the relationship of them within the natural environment, important information can be accessed, even by personal experiences with sacred places. Hearing the wind whisper through the pine trees in the Black Hills, listening to the waves lapping against the shore at Taos Blue Lake, and concentrating at other sacred places enable the channel of communication to be open between the American Indian mind and nature.

Identifying documentary evidence left by Native Americans is important to both the Indian people and the linear world. This suggestion means entertaining more than one methodology, but the other forms of historical evidence need to be identified. Over time, Native Americans have supplied some written evidence of their natural world and events. Early written evidence includes petroglyphs, rock writing or rock art, and hide paintings. In more recent time, during the early nineteenth century, the invention of Sequoyah's syllabary of eighty-six distinctive characters enabled the writing of Cherokee documents. Additional written evidence has been left in the forms of picture writing and Navajo sandpaintings. These forms often are derived from the memory of an individual, but can also include the subconscious dream, for example, or a historical event.

Written native evidence is also in the form of winter counts. Plains Indian groups, in particular, recorded an accounting of the past of important events. These counts were often drawn, according to the seasons of the year, and related "what" happened during these periods. They described battles, supernatural phenomena, and other special events as deemed important by the person recording the winter count.[22]

For the last ten years, a resurgence of oral history publications of various forms has been occurring. In a rough estimation of the following categories by the year 2000, at least fifteen publications exist on general Indian oral history or Indian oral history collections. By the 1990s, a rough estimate includes six autobiographies and/or published volumes of recollections, nine publications using oral history and nonwritten sources, five publications on oratory and speeches, and thirty published articles and books on myths, stories, and legends. This is about fifty total published works using the oral tradition. In the 1990s, at least eighteen Indian oral histories' works were published, eight were published in the 1980s, 18 works were published in the 1970s, eight works in the 1960s, and three works were published in the 1950s. According to percentages, about 75 percent of the published oral history works have been published since 1975.

How stories are told and the kinds of stories or oral accounts have produced various categories of oral histories. General works in comprehensive collections include all types or oral accounts. Richard Erodes and Alfonso Ortiz compiled a wide range of tribal myths and legends in *American Indian Myths and Legends* (1984). Another insightful compilation is Jay Miller, *Earthmaker, Tribal Stories From Native North America* (1992). A similar compilation with geographic representation is Terri Hardin, ed., *Legends & Lore of the American Indians* (1993).

Indian oratory and commentary consisting of speeches on a variety of subjects are in W. C. Vanderwerth, ed., *Indian Oratory: Famous Speeches by Noted Indian Chieftains* (1971); Colin G. Calloway, ed., *The World Turned Upside Down: Indian Voices from Early America* (1994); Steven Mintz, *Native American Voices: A History and Anthology* (1995); Arlene Hirschfelder, ed., *Native Heritage: Personal Accounts by American Indians, 1790 to the Present* (1995); and in Peter Nabokov, ed., *Native American Testimony: A Chronicle of Indian-White Relations From Prophecy to the Present, 1492–1992* (1995). Although Calloway's and Mintz's editions stress Indian accounts during the colonial era, Hirschfelder collected more or less contemporary personal accounts about basic areas of life. Nabokov gives the fullest range of individual Indian perspectives from historical leaders to contemporary spokespersons.

Related to oral tradition are works focusing on the generic Indian trickster and world view. These insightful works are Frank B. Lindera, ed., *Old Man Coyote: The Authorized Edition* (1931); Paul Radin, ed., *The Trickster, A Study in American Indian Mythology* (1956); Berard Haile, *Navajo Coyote Tales: The Curly to Aheedliinii Version* (1984); Ekkehart Malotki and Michael Lomatuway'ma, eds., *Hopi Coyote Tales: Istutuwutsi* (1984); Heister Dean Guie, ed., *Mourning Dove Coyote Stories* (1990); and Deward E. Walker Jr. in collaboration with Daniel N. Matthews, eds., *Nez Perce Coyote Tales* (1998). Howard L. Harrod, *Renewing the World: Plains Indian Religion and Morality* (1987) and

Michael Kearney, *World View* (1984) focus on the world at large. The latter focuses on a model and theories about the world views of native communities in general around the world. A work often referred to is A. Irving Hallowell, "Ojibway Ontology, Behavior, and World View," in Stanley Diamond, ed., *Primitive Views of the World: Essays From Culture in History* (1964). To understand how legends and traditions help to explain tribal origin, Harold Courlander, *The Fourth World of the Hopis: The Epic Story of the Hopi Indians as Preserved in their Legends and Traditions* (1971) remains a reliable narrative description and has valuable insight into Hopi life and their world.

As the oral tradition is practiced, over time the stories add to the Third Dimension of the Indian point of view. Actually the stories become a sociocultural history about the community in general, conveying values, ideas, beliefs, and providing much insight about the people. As a result, cultural information or ethnographic data is a product of the oral tradition.

Stories told by men and women differ in the methods of telling them and in subject areas. Temperament reveals the tone of the story and which details are stressed. On a daily basis, Indian women account for daily experiences that are more family oriented and tell stories about events that occurred to the people. As a result, Indian men tell stories differently from Indian women.[23]

For example, women among the Muscogee Creeks and Seminoles in Oklahoma experienced a different reality than their male counterparts.[24] Their perception and recollection of events presented a different view and a different reality in conjunction to the reality of their menfolk. Because even a lesser amount of historical documents accurately conveys how native women view things, trying to research this perspective on reality is even more challenging for fully understanding the importance of oral tradition among Native Americans as a part of their histories.

Indian men tell stories of travels and experiences that happened to them while hunting and in war. Their accounts include stories about feats and deeds of great warriors and about the supernatural that they may have encountered while hunting or traveling.

By learning about the oral tradition of a community, then scholars can begin to understand the Third Dimension. However, this is actually an introduction into the reality of the native community, and why it functions as it does. Listening carefully is imperative to understanding. The oral tradition is like a metaphorical key for opening a door to the other side of understanding a community and how its people think, conceptualize in their logic, and draw conclusions based on their prior knowledge. In a way, this is a cultural reorientation, and the reality in which the people and their community exist.

A part of passing through the door to the other side includes understanding the thought process of the indigenous people. In retrospect, the Muscogee Creeks came from the dark, misty spiritual fog into life upon Earth. So, the other side of the spiritual and abstract are always near by. For Native American groups, who are closer to their historic traditions, their sense of logic is related to a circular thinking process. Unlike the linear process of western society, the circular process addresses items as to their relationships within a system or base of knowledge. Basic elementary functions of perception, causality, and reality work in a circular fashion that does not differentiate time and historical events, so that the conscious knowledge becomes a part of the subconscious knowledge.

This kind of circular thought and logic thereby influence the logic of Indian people and how they "see" and "understand" the world. For them, reality combines the opposites of conscious and subconscious in one mind set. For them, the mind combines the physical and the metaphysical to achieve a balance that influences native logic or acting and reacting to stimuli. The real world and the surreal world are one, due to the metaphysical forces that have power over human life.

Reality for Indian people and their communities is very different from the reality of non-Indians. This combined reality of the physical environment and metaphysical environment reflect the people's belief in a combined reality. Stories convey this reality of spiritual beings interacting with people on a regular basis. That nature and its phenomena of metaphysics interact with people in a nonconcrete fashion that Western society usually dismisses. This metaphysical and physical combined reality is natural to Indian people, and it is much a part of their lives and the realm that their community functions within. This is the "other side" of the equation of the history of Indian–white relations.

Oral history has been a conduit for Native American communities. Oral history contains the oral tradition of native groups in the forms of oratory, myths, legends, songs, parables, and prophecy that would help to present the reality of the native community in question. Oral history is the non-Indian interpretation and understanding of native oral tradition.

The oral tradition of story remains one of the essential elements bonding the various entities of Indian communities. Due to the lack of a written language and the power of the spoken word, the oral tradition was the essential means for communication. Although current oral tradition seems less unimportant, what is said today in the form of the story becomes increasingly important as knowledge with the passing of linear time.

Thus, oral tradition is the conduit for sharing traditional knowledge within the community. In modern American Indian history since the turn of the twentieth century, an increasing amount of the oral accounts have appeared in print. In his book, *Land of the Spotted Eagle*, published first in 1933, Luther Standing Bear described how his people learned the traditional ways of the Lakota and he described how his people passed this information to the next generation. He wrote, "In Lakota society it was the duty of every parent to give the knowledge they possessed to their children. Each and every parent was a teacher and, as a matter of fact, all elders were instructors of those younger than themselves. And the instruction they gave was mostly through their actions—that is, they interpreted to us through actions what we should try to do. We learned by watching and imitating examples placed before us. Slowly and naturally the faculties of observation and memory became highly trained and the Lakota child became educated in the manners, lore, and customs of his people without a strained and conscious effort. I have known children to become very apt in learning the songs they heard. One singing would sometimes suffice and the child would have the words and tune so well in mind that he could never forget it . . . This process of learning went on all the time."[25]

Other types of events such as Indian–Indian accounts have also been passed along to succeeding generations. In a historic confrontation between the Lakota and the Crow in the nineteenth century, the white Crow Indian Thomas Leforge described the dire situation for the Crow warriors who were fewer in number that day against their arch enemy. He described, "Our Crow warriors were doing their medicine, each according to his own way of imitating the vocal noises and the actions of his own special animal-friend which he believed protected him in time of danger. There was a tumultuous mingling of whoofing like a bear, talking like a magpie, howling like a wolf, screaming like a curlew, hooting like an owl, mimickings of the sounds and movements of a crane, a badger, an eagle, and elk, of many varieties of lower animal life. I was wearing dangling from my long black hair my red plume that had been given to me by a medicine-man. Yes, I believed in it as a helpful charm."[26] That day in battle was lucky for the Crow. After some sparing of Lakota and Crow riding the line in front of the enemy and drawing their fire of arrows and bullets, the Lakota decided to retreat at the end of the day.

After many generations of observing animals, Plains Indian people imitated them for their strengths and characteristics to draw upon the powers of the animals, if their requests for such assistance were granted. Using traditional knowledge in a meaningful way was wisdom. Frank Rowland, Cheyenne scholar, noted that "for the Cheyenne, wisdom was learning how to use profound knowledge to help the community. If knowledge was gained but was not used to help the community, it was meaningless."[27]

The use of oral history has been a means for tribal prophets to report their visions and messages from the other side, the afterworld. Oral history was the Indian counterpart to the "white man's" written history of Indian–white relations. Practice of oral tradition accounts for the same historical events as do written documents, and although the memories of individuals are depended on, the events are relived. This quality gives oral history greater dimension than written history. The Indians' own accounts of history were based primarily on oral traditions. Memories today of past events include the emotions and intensity exhibited during treaty making, battles, and the telling of stories that described vividly native leaders and their peoples. Elders shared their knowledge via the oral tradition, passing down historical accounts of the people from one generation to the next. Whether myth, legend, tale, or song, the oral tradition was a means of sharing knowledge, and it served several purposes. Oral accounts contained parables and lessons, and the young people learned from them; morals of stories told by their elders enlightened them on virtues, values, and the importance of respecting taboos. Stories and tales served in other ways as well. Although they were entertaining, frightening stories were used to discipline the young when they misbehaved. At the philosophical level, the oral tradition explained the origins of the people and the creation of the universe, and it prophesied the future.[28]

In conclusion, the "story" holds an important place in native cultures, and it has multiple purposes for learning and sharing traditional knowledge. A story possesses power and life of its own and it transcends time as an experience comes alive again in the minds and ears of listeners when the storyteller touches the emotions of them. It permeates the mind and soul. Story is the heart of the oral tradition between Indian people and they enjoy a good story. Yet, it is much more than hearing a fine entertaining account. The story has power and energy, and it brings the past into the present. Oral tradition is not oral history, rather it is the process of oral expression via speech, oratory, argument, and story. It is much more than oral history, and it invites criticism from linear scholars, especially historians depending on the printed word, and they devalue the oral tradition of American Indians. For American Indians, stories live on, and they will live longer than all of us.

NOTES

1. Ed McGaa, *Native Wisdom: Perceptions of the Natural Way* (Minneapolis: Four Directions Publishing, 1995), 34–35.
2. See Ruth Finnegan, "A Note on Oral Tradition and Historical Evidence," *History and Theory* Vol. 9, 1970, 195–201; Ruth Finnegan, "How oral is oral literature?" *Bulletin of the School of Oriental and African Studies,* Vol. 37, 1974, 52–64; David William Cohen, "The Undefining of Oral Tradition," *Ethnohistory* Vol. 36, No. 1, 1989, 9–18; and David P. Henige, *Oral Historiography* (London: Longman, 1982); Patrick H. Hutton, "The Problem of Oral Tradition in Vico's Historical Scholarship," *Journal of the History of Ideas,* Vol. 53, No. 1, 1992, 3–23; and Mabel L. Lang, "Herodotus: Oral History with a Difference," *Proceedings of the American Philosophical Society,* No. 128, 1984, 93–103.
3. See Paul Thompson, *The Voice of the Past: Oral History,* (London: Oxford University Press, 1978).
4. Studs Terkel, *"The Good War": An Oral History of World War Two* (New York: Ballantine Books, 1984).
5. See Jan Vansina's two works, *Oral Tradition* (Chicago: Aldine, 1965) and *Oral Tradition as History* (Madison: University of Wisconsin Press, 1985); refer also to Francis West, "Oral Tradition," *History and Theory,* Vol. 5, 1966, 348–352.
6. For helpful information on tribal history, see Duane Kendall Hale, *Researching and Writing Tribal Histories* (Grand Rapids: Michigan Indian Press and Grand Rapids Tribal Council, 1991).
7. See Perry K. Blatz, "Craftsmanship and Flexibility in Oral History: a Pluralistic Approach to Methodology and Theory," *Public Historian,* Vol. 12, Fall 1990, 7–22; Elizabeth Tonkin, "Implications of Oracy: An Anthropological View," *Oral History,* Vol. 3, No. 1, 1975, 41–49; Elizabeth Tonkin, "The Boundaries of History in Oral Performance," *History in Africa,* Vol. 9, 1982, 273–284; Elizabeth Tonkin, *Narrating Our Pasts: The Social Construction of Oral History* (Cambridge: Cambridge University Press, 1992); Ronald J. Grele, ed. *Envelopes of Sound: Six Practitioners Discuss the Method, Theory and Practice of Oral History and Oral Testimony* (Chicago: Precedent Pub., 1975); Sarah C. Gudschinsky, *How to Learn an Unwritten Language* (New York: Holt, Rinehart and Winston, 1967); Haim Seligman, "Is Oral History a Valid Research Instrument?" *International Journal of Oral History,* Vol. 10, No. 3, 1989, 175–182; Allen Smith, ed., *Directory of Oral History Collections* (Phoenix: Oryx Press, 1988); Robert Harms, "Oral tradition and Ethnicity," *Journal of Interdisciplinary History,* Vol. 10, No. 1, 1979, 61–85; Beatrix Heintze, "Oral Tradition: Primary Source Only for the Collector?" *History in Africa,* Vol. 3, 1976, 47–56; and Philip D. Curtin, "Field Techniques for Collecting and Processing Oral Data," *Journal of African History,* Vol. 9, 1968, 367–386; David King Dunaway, "The Oral Biography," *Biography,* Vol. 14, 1991, 256–266; David E. Faris, "Narrative Form and Oral History: Some Problems and Possibilities," *International Journal of Oral History,* Vol. 1, 1980, 159–180.
8. Indian nations accounting for their own histories begin with the oral tradition, thus providing an oral history of legends and myths, which accounted for creations and metaphorical stories for morals and values among the people. Jan Vansina's *Oral Tradition as History* (1985) and Donald A. Ritchie's recent *Doing Oral History* (1995) provide instruction on how to interview people in collecting oral history and its im-

portance. The difficulties of collecting Indian oral history is told by a frustrated Fred McTaggart in his insightful experience, *Wolf That I Am: In Search of the Red Earth People* (Boston, MA: Houghton Mifflin, 1976).

9. Michael J. Hill, "Science Should Serve the Community." *Tribal College Journal*, Vol. 7, No. 4, Spring 1996, 12.

10. A. Lavonne Brown Ruoff, "American Indian Oral Literature," *American Quarterly*, Vol. 33, 1981, 309–326.

11. Jean Chaudhuri and Joyotpaul Chaudhuri, *A Sacred Path: The Way of the Muscogee Creeks* (Los Angeles: UCLA American Indian Studies Center, 2001), 4.

12. In regard to the role of the listener and interpretation of oral history, see Jack Campisi and Laurence M. Hauptman, "Talking back: The Oneida Language and Folklore Project, 1938–1941," *Proceedings of the American Philosophical Society*, Vol. 125, No. 6, 1981, 441–448; Ruth Finnegan, *Oral Traditions and the Verbal Arts: A Guide to Research Practices* (New York: Routledge, 1991); Jane H. Hill and Judith T. Irvine, eds., *Responsibility and Evidence in Oral Discourse* (New York: Cambridge University Press, 1993); Trevor Lummis, *Listening to History: The Authenticity of Oral Evidence* (New York: Barnes and Noble, 1988); and P. M. Mercer, "Oral Tradition in the Pacific: Problems of Interpretation," *Journal of Pacific History*, Vol. 14, 1979, 130–153.

13. Karen Gayton Swisher, "Why Indian People Should Be The Ones To Write About Indian Education," *American Indian Quarterly*, Vol. 20, No. 1, Winter 1996, 83–90.

14. J. Bradshaw, "Oral Transmission and Human Memory," *Expository Times*, Vol. 92, 1981, 303–307; Karl Figlio, "Oral History and the Unconscious," *History Workshop Journal*, No. 26, 1988, 120–132; David P. Henige, "Oral Tradition and Chronology," *Journal of Africa History*, Vol. 12, 1971, 371–389; Charles Kemnitz, "The Hand of Memory: Forging Personal Narrative," *Genre*, Vol. 16, 1983, 175–189; Lance J. Rips and Margaret E. Stubbs, "Genealogy and Memory," *Journal of Verbal Learning and Verbal Behavior*, Vol. 19, 1980, 705–721; and David Thelen, ed., *Memory and American History* (Bloomington and Indianapolis: Indiana University Press, 1990). This book first appeared as a special issue of *Journal of American History*, Vol. 75, No. 4, 1989, 1115–1280.

15. See William W. Moss, "Oral History: An Appreciation," *American Archivist*, Vol. 40, No. 4, October 1977, 429–439; Caoimhim O'Danachair, "Oral Tradition and the Printed Word," *Irish University Review: A Journal of Irish Studies*, Vol. 9, 1979, 31–41; W. H. Oliver, "Oral and Other History," *New Zealand Journal of History*, Vol. 12, 1978, 99–103; and Jack Goody, *The Interface Between the Written and the Oral* (Cambridge: Cambridge University Press, 1987).

16. See Donald M. Bahr, "On the Complexity of Southwest Indian Emergence Myths," *Journal of Anthropological Research*, Vol. 33, 1977, 317–349; and Jay Miller, *Earthmaker, Tribal Stories from Native North America* (New York: Perigree, 1992).

17. Peter MacDonald with Ted Schwarz, *The Last Warrior* (New York: Orion Books, 1993), 21.

18. Russell Means with Marvin J. Wolf, *Where White Men Fear to Tread: The Autobiography of Russell Means* (New York: St. Martin's Press, 1995), 11.

19. Ibid., 12.

20. As an example, for the Diné (Navajo), see Klara Kelley and Francis Harris, "Places Important to Navajo People," *American Indian Quarterly*, Vol. 17, No. 2, Spring 1993, 151–170.

21. Winifred Gallagher, *The Power of Place: How Our Surroundings Shape Our Thoughts, Emotions, and Actions* (New York: HarperPerennial, 1993), 23 and 96.

22. Melburn D. Thurman, "Plains Indian Winter Counts and the New Ethnohistory," *Plains Anthropologist*, Vol. 27, No. 96, May 1982, 173–175.

23. For insight into the difference of gender in storytelling, see Sherna Gluck and Daphne Patai, eds., *Women's Words: The Feminist Practice of Oral History* (New York: Routledge, 1991).

24. This information is from personal experiences as a native person of Muscogee Creek and Seminole backgrounds of Oklahoma. See also Donald L. Fixico, "The Muscogee Creeks: A Nativistic People," in Arrell M. Gibson, ed., *Between Two Worlds, The Survival of Twentieth Century Indians* (Oklahoma City: Oklahoma Historical Society, 1986), 30–43.

25. Luther Standing Bear, *Land of the Spotted Eagle* (Lincoln: University of Nebraska Press, 1978), originally published 1933, 13.

26. Thomas B. Marquis, ed., *Memoirs of a White Crow Indian (Thomas)H. Leforge* (Lincoln: University of Nebraska Press, 1974), originally published by the Century Company, 1924), 91.

27. Cheryl Crazy Bull, "A Native Conversation About Research And Scholarship," *Tribal College Journal*, Vol. 4, No. 1, Summer 1997, 17; see also John H. Moore, "Cheyenne Names and Cosmology," *American Ethnologist*, Vol. 11, No. 2, 1984, 291–312.

28. Information about the Doris Duke Indian Oral History Project is in Richard Ellis, "The Duke Indian Oral History Collection at the University of New Mexico," *New Mexico Historical Review*, Vol. 48, No. 1, Summer 1997, 259–263.

3

AMERICAN INDIAN CIRCULAR PHILOSOPHY

"Originally the Rabbit was not regarded as a [Muscogee Creek] trickster but as a member of the little animal world. Rabbit came to the ceremonial ground and asked the people to join their circle around a fire. However, suddenly the fire seemed to go out and it became very dark. There was some confusion and people sensed that Rabbit was running away with a large bag. They caught Rabbit, and in that process Rabbit stumbled. When Rabbit stumbled, first the moon came out again, followed by the sun. People from that time on regarded Rabbit as a trickster and his stumbling created the broken, separate rhythms of the lunar and solar cycles which are connected with new energies every eighteen years. But since then, we always have to be aware of the tricky Rabbit when trying to understand the regularities and the intervals in the cosmos."[1]

Jean Chaudhuri (Creek) and Joyotpaul Chaudhuri, 2001

* * *

The circle is a fundamental part of the universe and it is a permanent geometric fixture in beliefs and philosophies throughout the history of cultures.[2] Stonehenge, constructed between 8500 B.C.E–1100 B.C.E., in Wessex on Salisbury Plain in southern England lies in the form of a circle as its builders studied the universe or used it for religious purposes. Born approximately 582 B.C., Pythagoras rejected the idea that the Earth was flat and thought that the Earth and celestial bodies of the sky had a spherical shape. Aristotle hypothesized that the Earth was a sphere due to the nature of gravity and the Earth's shadow eclipsing the Moon helped to prove his beliefs. The Hindus use a mandala, or sacred circle. Jews and Christians incorporate praying circles for healing. Plato wrote "the soul is a circle."[3] Ancient Native American mounds had their bases in the forms of circles and medicine wheels in the West formed a variety of circles to explain the secrets of the universe to native peoples of North America and Canada.

The Circle of Life includes all things and they consist of spiritual energy. All around us are circles and cycles. The migration patterns of animals and cycles of seasons are a part of the Natural Order of Life. The four elements of fire, water, wind, and Earth are a part of the Muscogee Creek ethos and the same four elements are a part of many tribes. From these concepts derives American Indian thought for those Native Americans who believe in their traditions.

The depth of American Indian philosophy has yet to be explored sufficiently by the rest of the world. While most literature about Native Americans attempts to "describe" Indian life, books record the battles of Indian wars, and limited literature focuses on the "thinking" of American Indians and their various tribal philosophies. In order to understand Indian people and their ways of life, it is evident that the "circle" occupies an integral role in the beliefs of American Indians. Patterns and daily norms of American Indian groups involve the circle as a part of their many cultures. In this way, all things are related and they are a part of nature's system that might be called the "Natural Democracy" based on respect for the world and the universe.

Oglala author Ed McGaa described the inner human perspective and the significance of the circle on influencing life. "Inside of us," says McGaa, "within this great Disk of Life that each and every one of us has been bestowed with; within that creation, therein lies our character, our record, our background, our reputation, our knowledge; this mysterious spirit that the dominant culture refers to as the soul . . . You expand, alter and transform this disk, this circle of growing knowledge and related experience."[4] It is a living circle of energy like the Circle of Life that is external to us.

In circular philosophy, all things are related and involved in the broad scope of Indian life. As a part of their life ways, the indigenous peoples of the Americas have studied the Earth, observed the heavenly bodies and contemplated the stars of the universe. The Mayans recorded a calendar based on the number of new moons in a year. The Lakota completed an astronomy about the heavenly bodies, and the Muscogee Creeks incorporated the stars and galaxies into their ethos of the universe. All such things are in a vast continuum that Albert Einstein referred to as circular in form.

A "circular" approach toward life is inherent in Indian cultures since time immemorial. The native world is one of cycles, and observing the cycles provides an order to life and community. Medicine makers, prophets, and wise elders studied the moving world of circularity. Black Elk of the Oglala Sioux reminds all of us about the circularity all around us. He stated, "You have noticed that everything an Indian does is in a circle, and that is because the Power of the World always works in circles, and everything tries to be round." He continued, saying, "Everything the Power of the World does is done in a circle. The sky is round . . . and so are all the stars. The wind, in its greatest power whirls. Birds make their nests in circles, for theirs is the same religion as ours. The sun comes forth and goes down again in a circle. The moon does the same, and both are round. Even the seasons form a great circle in their changing, and always come back again to where they were. The life of a man is a circle from childhood to childhood and so it is in everything where power moves."[5]

For centuries, many indigenous peoples of North America have camped and formed their societies in circles. Indians of the eastern woodlands built their towns around a central point, and plains Indians held summer camps once a year in large camp circles. In their logical reasoning, the circle encompassed all the bands of the same tribe and recognized their presence. The Dakota of the plains is a prime example of this annual circular event of bands coming together.[6] Eastern woodland Indians formed their encampments around a central fire for worship and celebration of the Green Corn harvest.

Numbers help to determine cycles and important events that happen repeatedly. They provide a finite quality to life, and allow Indians to recognize the end of something and the start of its renewal. For example, there are 28 days in the months or moons of many tribes. Then the cycle begins again. The buffalo has 28 ribs, and with the same total days in a month, this number is important in life to many tribes. In the two hands of the human beings, there are 28 joints. Thus, the number 28 is often called sacred as well as the numbers 4 and 7. In the Bighorn Medicine Wheel, built 2,500 years ago by Aztec-Tanoans of the Bighorn Mountains in Wyoming, there are 28 spokes.

Native peoples looked for the constants in life as a part of the universe. They understood life to occur in cycles and those powers of nature formed definite patterns that occurred, repeating themselves. One of these universal constants is the climate. The climate of the world engages land forms in a complex system based on the interaction of the atmosphere, hydrosphere (oceans, lakes, and rivers), biosphere (Earth's living resources), cryosphere (particularly sea ice and polar ice caps), and lithosphere (the Earth's crust and upper mantle).[7] This systematic maze produced the seasons of the year for various parts of the world, and thus assisted in shaping the cultures of peoples and how they viewed life.

The environment and the climate influenced the lives and cultures of native peoples. American Indians seriously observed the weather and lived accordingly. One scholar noted that "Lakota camps did not remain in one spot year-round and did not always have a fixed membership. Validity of composition was due to both internecine struggles and climates. In warmer weather, groups tended to come together; in winter, large groups disbanded into smaller parties. This pattern of aggregation and dispersal reflected, appropriately enough, the exact seasonal behavior of the buffalo, the people's primary subsistence resource."[8]

Seasons and the Earth's rotation governed all life. The seasons of the year, rotation of the Earth, movement of the stars, and the movement of the universe are in flux such that all is in movement. By instinct, the animals innately know the occurrences of these patterns. Plants know this, too. In kindred spirit with the animals, native peoples developed their cultures after studying the ways of animals. Oglala holy man Black Elk observed that "there is much power in the circle, as I have often said; the birds know this for they fly in a circle, and build their homes in the form of a circle; the coyotes know also, for they live in round holes in the ground."[9] Throughout the animal world, the circle is just as fundamental to animals as it is to human beings. Indians have not forgotten its significance to their animal brethren.

Studying the cycles of the Earth and understanding the rotations of the seasons are not unique to American Indians. Other indigenous peoples in the world have done the same in shaping their cultures, according to the Earth's movements. Before the mainstream dependency on the clock, Europeans and Euro-Americans guided their lives according to nature. Many farmers and ranchers continue to live by the cycles and patterns of the Earth, in a non-linear way.

Due to their knowledge of the animals and their living patterns, Native Americans appealed to Nature as well as their great teacher. British scholar Roy Ellen observed that "[indigenous] peoples are still part of nature, and therefore adjusted to natural cycles in ways in which animals are assumed to be. We find this echoed in Germanic conceptions of *Naturvolker* Kropotkin's 'life in a state of nature.'"[10] Nature's way was the way of the American Indian and in his thinking, all life depended upon nature. Indian people did not believe that they were greater than nature, and they altered their cultural norms to fit the cycles of the seasons.

Nothing is transfixed. Nothing is secure or stable or permanent, and Indian people have accepted this situation. We want to believe that nothing has changed, but the reality is that all things change, even the story that we remember being told, but as long as the fabric of the truths of a story are retained, then we can accept it.

The concept of the circle is fundamental to understanding knowledge. This salient point was noted by one native scholar. "In circular thought," he wrote, "if a circle is envisioned and items are placed within it, we realize that each item or element has a relationship with each other in a fixed order within the system." Such entities or particles should be respected and treated equally since they belong to the same universe. In reality some entities are more powerful than others due to their varying strengths, and some of their powers are unknown by nature. They are ranked according to their special qualities and strengths and American Indians have learned about them. Indigenous peoples have treated the unknown with respect since it has a spiritual energy and unknown powers bestowed by the Creator and such power could endanger the people themselves. The circular concept of all things viewed equally is a native philosophy carried forward by generations studying the natural environment involving all of life.[11]

From an opposing point of view, the linear way of thinking and perceiving the world is the non-Indian way that Native Americans have had to learn in schools and while working with other Americans. Charles Eastman, Santee scholar, Luther Standing Bear, Lakota scholar, and others have testified how difficult it was to learn the white man's linear way of thinking. His logic was foreign to their native way of thought. Other literature on Indian boarding schools account for the inhumane treatment of Indian students, but the root of the problem besides cultural and racial differences, proved to be the difference in "thinking" between Indians and whites. Their philosophies, ideologies, logic, and world views proved distinctively different due to the separate evolutions of the human mind set in the Eastern Hemisphere and Western Hemisphere during the pre-Columbia era. Indians in white mainstream schools are addressed in a later chapter.

One young native person concluded that "like the seasons changing in cycles every year and like the day and night in a circular change, the circle of life includes all things, according to Indian belief. The past is a part of the present such that history is a continuum without a beginning or an end in the Indian mind." The young person also said, ". . . the broken circle suggested to me what I felt in my heart and the feelings other people have in their hearts. Because the circle has been around for thousands of years, and now it's coming apart because people are forgetting about the ways of the spirit and the ways of kindness to people. They're greedy and money hungry and want power, and that won't do much when they get to the spirit world. . . . that if people's visions vanish and our way of life isn't like a growing, healthy tree, then we will all vanish . . . That's the philosophy of Indian life. It is centered around the spirits and around the Creator. All of it."[12]

The Circle of Life begins with the cardinal directions. Some tribes have six such directions and some have seven. While recalling his vision, Black Elk remembered that ancient voices of several beings called to him: "Your Grandfathers all over the world are in a council, and they have called you here to teach you. His voice was very kind, but I shook all over with fear now, for I knew that these were not old men, but the Powers of the world. And the first was the Power of the West; the second, of the North; the third, of the East; the fourth of the South; the fifth, of the Sky; the Sixth of the Earth."[13] The Circle of Life also includes the metaphysical beings who influence people of the physical world. Metaphysical powers rule the world. The door to the spiritual world creaked opened, changing Black Elk's life forever.

As a part of his visionary experiences in later life, Black Elk recalled being on top of Harney Peak in the Black Hills. He said, "then I was standing on the highest mountain of them all [Harney Peak], and round about beneath me was the whole hoop of the world. And while I stood there I saw more than I can tell and I understood more that I saw; for I was seeing in a sacred manner these shapes of all things in the spirit, and the shape of all shapes as they must live together like one being. And I saw that the sacred hoop of my people was one of many hoops that made one circle, wide as daylight and as starlight, and in the center grew one mighty flowering tree to shelter all the children of one mother and one father. And I saw that it was holy."[14] Like Moses in the Bible and other religious prophets, the spiritual world allowed Black Elk to see some of its powers. It was beyond his imagination and frightened him.

Living in the sacred way of her people, Jackie Yellow Tail, a Crow woman, philosophized that "life is a circle, the world is a circle." She remarked that the linear way was a part of the Circle of Life. She said, "The Christian way of seeing the world is that within this circle there's a man called Jesus; on the outside is the trees, the rocks, the animals; all around the world are the different things that are on Mother Earth. In the center is man above all things. The Indian way of thinking is that there is this same circle, Mother Earth, and around her are the rocks, the trees, the grass, the mountains, the birds, the four-legged, and man. Man is the same as all those other things, no greater, no less. I mean, it's all so simple; people make it so hard. That's why I say we're like Mother Earth: each one of us has that ability within us to grow spiritually, we're connected with the Creator from the top of our head, our feet walk on Mother Earth. It's within us; and why should we hold that to ourselves when we know, no matter what color that person is, that he has the same spiritual yearning we have? People . . . deserve to be treated with respect."[15]

People naturally want to feel connected to others, to belong to a group, yet most people in Western society have forgotten that they are also connected to nature. All people are a part of the community of life, yet some people try to exclude others.

Oglala spiritual leader of the American Indian Movement (AIM) during the 1970s, Leonard Crow Dog, explained, "we live in a sacred cycle, the sacred hoop. We are born from Mother Earth and we return to Mother Earth. We feed on the deer who, in turn, feeds on the grass which, in turn, is fed by our bodies after we die. It's the story of the biological cycle you learn in school. Everything is harmony and unity, and we fit within that harmony. And when our bodies die, our spirits are freed and will be here. You see, it's not a religion in the white man's sense, but a philosophy of living, a way of living."[16] Such a way of life cannot be rationalized as one part of life such as religion. It is the ethos of how indigenous people believe and live their lives.

The whole is greater than any one of its parts. For example, the family is more important than the individual among tribes who believe in a communal identity. It was meant to be that way for the best means to survive, especially during hard times. Group identity is more meaningful than the identity of one person. Among the Lakota, the *tiyospaye*, or extended family, is the Lakota way of understanding life. Within the family, kinship supports each family member. Yellowtail, Medicine Maker, and Sun Dance of the Crow, stated the relevance of belonging. He noted, "There are thirteen clans among the Crow tribe, and my clan is the Whistling Waters. Each person has relatives through the clan also, so all the members of the tribe can learn a great deal from their relatives both through blood and through the clans. The entire tribe worked together for the benefit of every person in the tribe, and the clan system helped to strengthen the cooperation of every person working toward the common welfare of the tribe."[17]

A Natural Democracy of respect exists in that all things are equal at creation. All things are related in the world and in the universe. Plants and animals are an important part of this Natural Democracy. Each plant and each animal has a role and responsibility. As a result, there is a strong dependency on each thing and all things. Cooperation is highly desired in such a community of togetherness. Anthropologist

Irving Hallowell observed of the Ojibwas that plants and animals were integral to the Ojibwa world. Irving Hallowell's extensive, and extremely sympathetic and reflective work among the Ojibwas, an Algonkian people, provides ample evidence that the Ojibwas regarded animals, plants, and assorted other natural things and phenomena as persons with whom it was possible to enter into complex social intercourse. Animals, plants, stones, thunder, water, hills, and so on may be "persons" in the Ojibwa linguistic organization of experience.[18]

The American Indian mind thinks inclusively. By seeing and believing that all things are related, this natural order is a sociocultural kinship. It is symbolic kinship based on the ethos of totality and inclusion. It includes even the bad and evil things. Kinship is the bonding substance that holds the Natural Democracy system together. Kinships are formed by symbolic relationships and by blood relationships.

This kinship of a Natural Democracy extends to animals and plants. Navajo surgeon, Lori Alvord, described her father's relationship with animals and how he communicated with them. "Almost everywhere we went, on the reservation or off, he knew the dogs, and they recognized him and came running," she said. "Rez dogs. Chocolate and black-splotched or the color of coyote and mesa and riverbed mud. One blue eye, one brown, or two piercing green. They were everywhere on the reservation, used to watch the sheep or guard the Hogan, and when you arrived they appeared magically, just like those annoying friends who materialize at mealtime. My father knew them. Crows also seemed to gather in groups or come and stand on a fence post whenever my father was around. Sometimes I'd turn a corner and find my father standing deep in a philosophical discussion with a crow."[19]

The Navajos believe that all things are connected. Animals are a part of the natural kinship and their presence should be recognized. By learning the ways of animals and making them feel unafraid, a kinship of communication is established with them. Through effective communication, equilibrium is better maintained in the Natural Order of things. But, balance and chaos are in conflict as a part of this continuum of natural order. Within the circle of life, a continual effort for balance is the purpose for individuals and communities. The linear person may not realize the importance of this effort as Western cultured people are often consumed by work or thoughts of getting something done during the day. What Western society does not normally do is to put things in the larger perspective of life. Nor does the linear mind prioritize what is important to him or her as a person in relationship to family and community, thus placing personal needs first.

SE-QUO-YAH.

Philad Published by F. W. Biddle

Drawn & Printed by .... Phil

Sequoyah (Cherokee). (Photograph by McKenney-Hall after painting by Charles Bird King. Courtesy of Archives and Manuscripts Division of Oklahoma Historical Society, Oklahoma City.)

Wilma Mankiller, former Cherokee Principal Chief. (Photograph by C.R. Cowen. Courtesy of Archives and Manuscripts Division of Oklahoma Historical Society, Oklahoma City.)

Gertrude Bonnin "Zitkala-Sa" (Lakota). (Photography by International Newsreel. Courtesy of Archives and Manuscripts Division of Oklahoma Historical Society, Oklahoma City.)

Alexander Lawrence Posey (Creek). (Photograph by F.S. Barde. Courtesy of Archives and Manuscripts Division of Oklahoma Historical Society, Oklahoma City.)

Clock in Cherokee language. (Photograph by C.R. Cowen. Courtesy of Archives and Manuscripts Division of Oklahoma Historical Society, Oklahoma City.)

Shawnee Indian School Children in 1902. (Photograph by Snow. Courtesy of Western History Collections, University of Oklahoma, University of Oklahoma, Norman.)

Alfonso Ortiz, Tewa Pueblo scholar. (Photographer unknown. Courtesy of Beverly Singer, Alfonso Ortiz Center for Intercultural Studies, University of New Mexico, Albuquerque.)

Carlos Montezuma, Yavapai physician. (Photographer unknown. Courtesy of National Archives.)

It is the daily struggle, the moment's effort, to find a comforting state of mind and existence between the two opposites in life. Day and night, right and wrong, good and evil, life and death, man and woman, and the many other polar opposites are the extremities of the balance that constitute life.

Balance is between two things or more and it is the purpose in life for American Indians whose philosophy is inclusive of all things in the universe. At least five kinds of balance exist: (1) balance within one's self, (2) balance within the family, (3) balance within the community or tribe, (4) balance with external communities, including other tribes and the spiritual world, and (5) balance with the environment and the universe.

Balance is equilibrium discovered between opposites such as consistency and change. Both consistency and change are inertia and constants in life. Balance is the compromise when momentum rests in a euphoric state between the two opposite forces. It must always be realized that the greater the opposites, the greater the struggle for balance in this natural dichotomy of life.

An order for life is the purpose for all living things, or else chaos reigns. Disorder becomes a part of one's life or a part of a group, and then it controls the living. The continuous effort is normal—that is finding balance within one's self and within the universe. It is a part of living and evolution of human beings and the universe. When Rabbit temporarily stole the Sun and the Moon, chaos reigned and confused the Muscogee people until they realized what had happened. They captured Rabbit, and balance was restored.

The negativity of life is chaos and disorder. Chaos is frustration in life, anxiety, and disappointment. Such disorder leads to fear, distrust, and, ultimately, to self-destruction. Without effort on our part, it is easy to fall into disorder and chaos. Like evil twins, they are the negativity in the universe.

Without balance in oneself and in one's community, life is more difficult and alarming. Balance is the spiritual beauty of life as exhibited by the innocence of a child as set by nature. In the following years, the child becomes an adult and the struggle for balance is waged even in the twilight years when an elder acts like a child again. As the Muscogees learned from Rabbit's crime, without the Sun and Moon, we have lost balance.

By observing nature and the environment for many generations, American Indians developed tribal philosophies based on the circle. By studying the changes of the seasons and observing the lives of animals and plants as a part of nature, native logic became grounded in the central idea of a continuum of events that seemed familiar. Nature repeated itself in a continuous series of cycles and seasons of circular patterns. Animals and humans live the same various stages of life starting with birth, infancy, puberty, adulthood, old age, then death, and life repeated the same phases with the next generation. Cherokee elder Dhyani Ywahoo observed that "in Tsalagi (Cherokee) world view, life and death, manifestation and formlessness, are all within the circle, which spirals out through all dimensions. The teaching expresses that expansion of the spiral. The same story can be understood in various ways as one is exploring vaster dimensions of mind."[20]

In the white man's world of many kinds of businesses, including academia, people are categorized according to the box that they check on various forms. But when one goes outside the box to think, the person is within the circle of the universe where all beauty and good things exist, able to think new ideas and fresh thoughts, thereby nurturing the soul. The Muscogee Creek, Seminole, and other tribes like the Cheyenne realized that they needed to have a reverent relationship with the Sun and the Moon. They are both light and life to human beings, plants, and animals, including Rabbit.

Outside the box or office is nature and all of its beauty. Indian people viewed themselves as part of nature in a type of Natural Democracy. Because relationships are important, Native people stress the importance of kinship for building positive relationships. In this ethos, the worst that could happen to an individual is to be excluded from the group or community or tribe.

The sources of strength may be a homeland or a place, and perhaps they might be the same. Here is where a person goes for regaining perspective, resting, and giving thought to a major problem, self-examination, contemplating one's vision for leadership, thinking about resources, supporters, and thinking about the big picture to keep things in a real context. This is done in familiar surroundings, and they are a positive influence.

During this return to renewal of spiritual energy, a person asks deep questions of his or her being. One's natural surroundings become like nature's womb for security as the struggle for balance is analyzed by the individual. It is like the Sun providing balance during the day and the Moon supplying balance at night, as both are sources of light. Our original surroundings are best for our soul in providing spiritual strength and renewal to the mentally fatigued.

In addition to the powerful influence of the natural environment is the native concept of time. Native peoples' focus on events and stories about them has deemphasized the measuring of time on the clock of the linear world. To indigenous people, the hands of the white man's clock sometimes feel wrapped around the person's throat, strangling the soul from being free and dictating one's life by deadlines. Ironically many mainstream Americans feel the same way.

Native people have learned to live without the clock for many centuries and kept track of things according to the seasons. Many cultures around the world and other Americans have lived many centuries in the same way. Former Navajo tribal chairman Peter MacDonald recalled that the Bureau of Indian Affairs recorded his birthday as December 16, 1928. But he recalls his parents talking about the intense heat of the midday sun during May. He was born into the Haskonhazohl and Betani clan on that warm day. MacDonald noted that "my people did not track time the way white men did. There was no need to be aware of anything more than the changing seasons. Sometimes your birth was known because of a major event, such as a great blizzard that had made survival difficult for everyone. But when the weather was mild, your birth was marked by the seasons, the exact date remaining unknown, unimportant. We were in harmony with nature—birth, death, and the life that was led in between were all a part of the natural pattern of human existence."[21]

All tribes have their strategies regarding life and survival. It is their life's way and their tribal ethos. The Wintu Indians of California philosophized that a person belonged to the society rather than the person and society being two separate entities.[22] The Wintu people preferred to be a part of a community. In a group, they rationalized that hunting, growing foods, and protection from enemies groomed a communal feeling of security. Strength in numbers became a societal norm, thus causing cultural patterns to develop along this belief. The need for survival became the driving force and common concern, or else as individuals, mass confusion would result, proving the importance of commonality.[23]

In a natural environment, survival was the key issue to life. In community, practical needs were everyone's needs, thereby social behavior and morals of living were defined and redefined by practicality. After practical needs were met, tribal laws, ceremonies, and leadership became important for order in a successful community of cooperation. These nonelemental norms of native society were important, and they evolved as themes for cultural ceremonies, philosophies, art, music, and world view. A cultural genesis is initiated, therefore, with the process of interrelationships of the elements of people, family, and community, thus producing a balance of the themes in the community with nature.[24]

All social-kinship elements function cooperatively for the well-being of the tribe or nation. Traditionalists view an idyllic equilibrium with other nations and the environment, and with all things in their universe. This political-social equilibrium based on kinship including other tribal nations proves more difficult than perceiving one's own tribe in constant balance with nature and the entire universe. Often, one's tribe competed against another tribe for the same hunting areas. The physical reality obviously differed from the idyllic reality as all relations among tribes developed into political situations.

Relations influence reality among Indian peoples in a very deep manner. Ideally, the theory is for "all" to get along in the Natural Democracy, but the basics of life and human desire reestablish the boundaries of such an idyllic democracy where all things are brothers and sisters in a common circular experience. Because obvious size and abilities make animals different from each other, some species are stronger than others, whereas others are faster running or flying, and others have special talents. In the American Indian mind, all of the beings are recognized for their talents with respect.

In this context, American Indians have given human qualities to plants and animals and the learning to relate to all things is a task for life. In the big picture, the relationship of people with all the universe is the most significant, and indigenous peoples have learned how humans view themselves in this role. Thus, it is important for all peoples to comprehend that the essence of life begins with "belief" and understanding "the natural order of things."[25]

In the American mainstream way of thinking, the ego, or the "self," is at the center of life, and the perception of all things surrounding are in relationship to the individual person. For example, Rabbit wanted the Sun and the Moon for himself. He believed that his greed exceeded the needs of the Muscogee people. Rabbit's failure to share disturbed the order of life. Specifically, egocentric Americans perceive themselves as the center of activity, and they act upon and view others from their focal point. Traditionally, Indian people view themselves within the universe as minuscule members of a larger whole meaning that explains existence. In contrast, the Western-minded person refers to him or her "self" as the reference point. When he or she travels, the Western-minded person turns right or left, making reference to direction in this manner. The person is the point of reference. The Wintu of California refer to left and right as the sides of the body. When traveling, the Wintu refer to the four cardinal directions to avoid confusion and becoming lost. For example, if going north, a Wintu would point out that the mountains are to the west. In contrast, some people would say the mountains are on the left. In returning to go south, the Wintu would know the mountains are to the east. A linear person would refer to the mountains being on the right side.[26]

Movement of native people by the cardinal directions stressed the importance of the directions and special meanings were given to the directions. In the Great Lakes, the Huron fishermen offer tobacco and prayers to the waters for taking fish from the streams and rivers. The Hurons believe that designated spirits of the waters had to be appeased, or they would encounter danger from the powers of the spirits.[27] This cultural belief is a part of the philosophy of the Huron. Thus, they recognize animism as a part of their philosophy and the importance of human involvement to produce positive results.[28]

Native peoples treat the natural environment on a social and kinship basis, stressing retribution.[29] Receiving is as important as giving. At a higher level, Indian people developed philosophical explanations for origins and causes of life. Astute native minds have observed the activities of nature for learning lessons and obtaining knowledge. They adopted many of nature's patterns of the four seasons, animal activities, and plant growth as a part of their culture. From most types of animals, native peoples have learned that group behavior is important to life and that social ability is equally significant even in human–animal relationships.[30] In the Natural Democracy of human–animal relations, both parties are equal and mutually respected, thus allowing people to develop respect for life, including the life of plants. All three—human, animal, and plant—possessed life, whose spirits lived within the bodies. Many eastern woodland tribes and some western tribes developed clans represented by animal and plant totems practicing group protection, guardianship, and unity of the group. They preferred the positive side of life, sustained from evil, and at times had to combat negative agents of the dark side of life such as bad medicine makers or witches.

The lesson found in practicing rituals is pertinent to living in beauty. Following traditional practices like their ancestors enabled Indian people to be protected from evil, including evil powers of the supernatural. Dedication to the "good" life of following cultural norms even during hardship corroborated that the ancestors were right and that traditions should not be questioned. This inertia of continuity provided security between the people, compelling them to depend on maintaining traditions.[31] In this type of world view, traditional Indians were more metaphysical than their non-Indian counterparts who eventually adopted various religious beliefs and moved toward science and economic opportunity. Unseen powers of nature in supernatural forms convinced traditional Indians that the laws of nature superseded tribal political laws, thereby compelling native people to subscribe to the laws of nature. Traditional Indians observed and continue to believe in the seen and unseen forces of life. Nature manifested itself through concepts in the ways of native belief, becoming the precepts of many Indian philosophies and therefore unified communities.[32]

The primal relationship between humans and animals dates back to mythical times when both were new members of the created world. In Canada, Cree myths describe an account when a man married certain animals like the beaver, and stories about man's relationship with the animal world developed into stories, legends, parables, and these stories carried forward an oral historical tradition.[33] Waswanipi hunters in the Canadian Boreal forest hunted moose easier after accumulating a large amount of knowledge about the animals' habits, so that the moose "surrendered" its life to the people. One's life was given for another to continue life. The Waswanipi hunter respectfully killed the moose swiftly, without torture, in order to release the animal's spirit easily to return to its life in the other world. In this way, the Waswanipi showed the animal world that they respected the moose. This practice of respect assured successful hunting, with other practices of hunters estimating the animal populations and altering their hunting areas.[34]

Indigenous logic deems that asking for more than a person can use might incur misfortune. Among the Ojibwa and other woodland peoples, hunters shared the game that they killed to insure that they would not be ostracized, criticized, or bewitched by others. They did not hoard materials for fear that others of their community would ridicule them, leading to misfortune.[35] This belief system of such a world view de-emphasized the accumulation of wealth and materialism for they exceeded the needs for life. The Muscogee Creek believe that such excess became the potential for evil, envy, jealousy, and wrongdoing.

Different environmental relations between traditional Indians and non-Indians produced incongruent world views. In the beginning, they were likely the same. Indians developed a respected relationship with nature and early Europeans encountered the same situation in their early settlements in America. As a means of survival based on the family, non-Indians adopted an attitude of individual capitalistic gain. In contrast, the community was emphasized among Indians. Traditional American Indians learned to relate their lives to the natural environment. Euro-Americans thought it best to change the environment. The traditional Indian's natural environment is different from the American man-made environment. The white man domesticated animals and plants, and he preferred to alter the landscape to support an increasing population.[36] Like Rabbit, the white man wanted to change the order of life to meet his imperialistic needs of colonization. Thus, the American value system has colonized many cultures of the world with the introduction of American products such as Pepsi, Coke, designer jeans, and other name brands.

For more than a decade wasteful practices throughout critical parts of the world have caused deserts in parts of the world to grow rapidly and the demanding world capitalism has cut rainforests, for example, threatening the largest rainforest in the world, the Amazon. Without doubt, planet Earth is speeding toward rapid exhaustion of its limited natural resources and animal life.

Human greed practiced by individuals and corporations will certainly cause disastrous consequences for the entire planet.[37] It is a matter of what a person values to be important. Yellowtail, Sun Dance Chief of the Crow, noted "Because of money, many people want to accumulate more things than they really need. The machines and material wealth of this modern world allow people to be able to possess more things. Everyone wants the same thing that someone else has and everyone wants to possess something that he doesn't need. The children want toys that just make them idle their time away. None of the toys teach valuable lessons or skills to the children anymore, and some youngsters have so many toys that they do not respect the gifts that they have been given."[38]

The maturity of human beings has not kept up with the acceleration of advancing technology, thus causing technological progress to work against world conservation. In the disguise of technology, human greed practiced in America has corrupted the world as other nations envy American wealth. It is startling that with a mere population of less than 6 percent of the world, the United States has become the engulfing consumer as the largest producer and consumer of 30 percent of the world's energy.[39] From the indigenous peoples of the Americas, important lessons on conservation and ecology can be learned. But first, linear thinkers should learn about indigenous cultures and the importance of their communities. It is important to learn how the American Indian thinks.

In the late 1800s, ethnographers like John Wesley Powell and entities like the Smithsonian Institution began field work to record the ceremonies and historical information about Indians by visiting reservations throughout Indian Country. The *Bureau of American Ethnology Reports* stand as firsthand observations of Indian life, since ethnographers and anthropologist and much of the public thought the Indian would disappear with the buffalo by the turn of the twentieth century. Even from the native perspective, life seemed at end. In May 1931, Black Elk, the famed sixty-eight year-old Oglala holy man, confessed to John Neihardt, "Now when I look about me upon my people in despair, I feel like crying. . . When I look back from this high hill of my old age, I can still see the butchered women and children lying heaped and scattered all along the crooked gulch as plain as when I saw them with eyes still young. And I can see that something else died there in the bloody mud, and was buried in the blizzard [at Wounded Knee]. A people's dream died there . . . It was a beautiful dream. . . The nation's hoop is broken and scattered. There is no center any longer, and the sacred tree is dead."[40]

The mind of the American Indian and his or her life is unmeasurably complex but in a different way from that of the mainstream American. Writer Mary Roberts noted, "implicitly contrasting Indians with white, the Indian mind is not literal, specific, scientific—it is philosophical, vague, and poetic."[41] One might say that the Indian mind is abstract, and confused with repetition. But another person might say that numerous examples stress the same point as stories told with the same message in mind for teaching the listener. Even these written words may seem repetitious, but in the circular way the purpose is met to prevent misunderstanding. It is a teaching tool like the Suzuki way for learning to play the violin.

Ironically, the study of American Indians has seemingly come full circle. The usage and dependency on computer technology to create images is the same visual imagery that Indian youth have always utilized in traditional learning via stories of the oral tradition. Indian scholars in growing numbers in all academic disciplines and in growing numbers in Indian studies programs are fully participating in the scholarship and sharing knowledge about their people as they did historically many years ago around the campfires. Joseph Bruchac, an Abenaki storyteller, predicted that "If you see things in terms of circles and cycles, and if you care about the survival of your children then you begin to engage in commonsense practices. . . The circle is the way to see. The circle is the way to life, always keeping in mind the seven generations to come, always asking: how will my deeds affect the lives of my children's children's children."[42]

During the early part of the twentieth century as the Lakota nation and other Indian nations sought survival in the white man's world, Lakota holy man Black Elk spoke on the meaning of life and his environmental surroundings of Mother Earth. Black Elk explained "that all things are the works of the Great Spirit. We should know that He is within all things: the trees, the grasses, the rivers, the mountains, and all the four-legged animals, and the winged peoples; and even more important, we should understand that He is also above all things and peoples. When we do understand all this deeply in our hearts, then we will fear, and love, and know the Great Spirit, and then we will be and act and live as He intends."[43] Black Elk explained that all things were interconnected, like it or not: that Indian people, and white people and others were meant to live on Earth in a meaningful way; and that all knowledge, including that about themselves came from the Earth. The Great Spirit had intended it that way, that all things would come full circle such as the life of the American Indian.

The circular ethos permeates many tribes and it offers a lesson for all peoples. The prophetic words of Chief Seattle of the Duamish tribe provide significant insight into the native understanding of the world and the circular universe. For Seattle, all life begins with the Earth and it is threatened by the greed of the white man. He spoke: ". . . If we accept your offer to buy our land, I will make one condition: The white man must treat the beasts of the land as his betters . . . What is man without the beasts? If all the beasts were gone, men would die from loneliness of spirit. For whatever happens to the beasts, soon happens to man. All things are connected. Teach your children what we have taught ours, that the earth is our mother. Whatever befalls the earth soon befalls the children of the earth. This we know, the earth does not belong to man; man belongs to the earth. This we know. All things are connected like the blood which unites one family. So hold in your mind the memory of the land as it is when you take it. And with all your strength, with all your mind, with all your heart . . ."[44]

The Circle of Life is the fundamental philosophy of traditional American Indians and it is integral to their belief system. It is also pertinent to many other cultures throughout the world in the annals of history. The "circle" symbolizes life itself. In this belief system of circularity, the circle encapsulates all of life. Like a Natural Democracy, all things are explained for those who share the same circular philosophy. All things are included in this circular system known to the native mind. Anything outside of the universe has not yet happened and its forthcoming existence becomes a part of the Circle of Life. Such new things are acknowledged and as more information about them occurs they become a part of the natural universe understood by the people.

It is this Circle of Life that American Indians celebrate in many different kinds of ceremonies at various times of the seasons. At pow-wows, the circular drum is at the center like a heartbeat for all of the people participating in unison. The people dance in a circular direction, clockwise to the beat of the drum in celebration of life. Native elder Ed McGaa remarked that "pow wow dancing is social dancing. It is not religious dancing on a par with the Sun Dance. I danced for sheer enjoyment in my early days as a pow wow dancer. The steady drum beat kept us in rhythm as we danced around in a circle. Women and men often danced together but seldom as partners. You were allowed your own freedom of movement as your body seemed to pulsate to the drum beats. I would dance in the afternoon and long into the night, whirling, spinning and keeping my feet in time to the drumming. Bells were attached to our ankles over furred padding. The bells added to the sound of the drums. At a young age, I did not seem to tire. The flow of the rhythm seemed to add to your energy."[45]

To the American Indian mind, time is less relevant for life itself is most important and learning about it is essential for survival and prosperity in life. The main quest for American Indians, as it has remained through the generations, is the quest for survival and balance in life. In the Indian mind, birth and death are a part of the cycle of existence. They are a part of the continuum of the circle within. This is life itself in a dynamic continuity of existence. Jean Hill Chaudhuri observed that "Now, as in the past, Creeks pray for all their relations—seen, unseen, and unknown—a single cosmic string of energy runs through all."[46] All things have spiritual energy.

After survival had been assured, native communities flourished and their cultures developed. But the circle has remained fundamental to the developing native communities and their cultures. It is important to remember that the circle in its perfect form has always been there for all beings in the world, and in the universe, to give meaning to its form in their many diverse cultures. It is a part of the future, the prophecy for all of life and the world. Instead of looking ahead, we as all people should look around us. Examining our environment and all of our relations tells all people much about what is to come. Black Elk reminded us that

> moving around the lodge in a sun-wise manner, the mysterious woman left, but after walking a short distance she looked back towards the people and sat down. When she rose the people were amazed to see that she had become a young red and brown buffalo calf. Then this calf walked farther, lay down, and rolled looking back at the people, and when she got up she was a white buffalo. Again the white buffalo walked farther and rolled on the ground, becoming now a black buffalo. This buffalo then walked

farther away from the people, stopped, and after bowing to each of the four quarters of the universe, disappeared over the hill.[47]

The disappearance of the buffalo is the end of all life for the Lakota, and all people.

The Circle of Life is inclusive of all things, including the physical, metaphysical and time. All things exist in a spiritual energy as said by Muscogee Creek tradition. Within this circle, animal and plant beings live in migration patterns as regulated by the cycles of seasons. This complex system is the natural order of life for Indian people. Nature has given humans, plants, and animals "constants" in life which provide rhythms, celebrated by ceremonies. If Rabbit had succeeded in stealing the Sun and the Moon, some disastrous supernatural chaos would have occurred, thereby destroying the circular continuum of the world.

As the indigenous minds of the Americas became more knowledgeable about life, their initial beliefs about the importance of the circle to human life and to the Earth and universe became confirmed. All things to them were a part of the vast circle known as the American Indian universe as they understood it from their point of view. Their ethos is the full Circle of Life in a Natural Democracy. This idealized concept of such a democratic equality is integral to the mind of the American Indian and it is the responsibility of the people to practice it. Even Rabbit has learned this important lesson.

NOTES

1. Jean Chaudhuri and Joyotpaul Chaudhuri, *A Sacred Path: The Way of the Muscogee Creeks* (Los Angeles: UCLA American Indian Studies Center, 2001), 11.
2. For more information on the fundamental quality of the circle in cultures, see J. L. Coolidge, *A Treatise on the Geometry of the Circle and Sphere* (New York: Chelsea, 1971).
3. For Plato's quote, see http://www.crystlinks.com/healingcircle.html, no date.
4. Ed McGaa, *Native Wisdom: Perceptions of the Natural Way* (Minneapolis: Four Directions Publishing, 1995), 29.
5. Quote of Black Elk, 1933, in Norbert S. Hill, Jr., ed., *Words of Power: Voices From Indian America* (Golden, CO: Fulcrum Publishing, 1994), xi.
6. Ernest L. Schusky, "The Evolution of Indian Leadership of the Great Plains, 1750–1950," *American Indian Quarterly*, Vol. 10, No. 1, Winter 1986, 71.
7. *The Times Atlas of the World*, tenth comprehensive edition, (New York: Random House, 1999), 34.
8. Michael F. Steltenkamp, *Black Elk Holy Man of the Oglala* (Norman: University of Oklahoma Press, 1993), 7.
9. Joseph Epes Brown, ed., *The Sacred Pipe: Black Elk's Account of the Seven Rites of the Oglala Sioux* (New York: Penguin Books, 1971), 92, originally published by University of Oklahoma Press, Norman, 1953.
10. Roy F. Ellen, "What Black Elk Left Unsaid: On the Illusory Images of Green Primitivism," *Anthropology Today*, Vol. 2, No. 6, December 1986, 9.

11. Donald L. Fixico, "American Indians (The Minority of Minorities) and Higher Education," p. 115, in Benjamin P. Bowers, Terry Jones, and Gale Auletta Young, eds., *Toward the Multicultural University* (Westport, CT: Praeger, 1995).

12. Norman Guardipee, "Mending the Broken Circle," in E.K. Caldwell, ed., *Dreaming the Dawn: Conversations with Native Artists and Activists* (Lincoln: University of Nebraska Press, 1999), 28.

13. John G. Neihardt, *Black Elk Speaks: Being the Life Story of a Holy Man of the Oglala Sioux* (Lincoln: University of Nebraska Press, 1973), 21–22.

14. Ibid., 36.

15. Mark St. Pierre and Tilda Long Soldier, *Walking in the Sacred Manner: Healers, Dreamers, and Pipe Carriers—Medicine Women of the Plains Indians* (New York, London, Toronto, Sydney, Tokyo, and Singapore: Touchstone Book, 1995), 14.

16. James Mencarelli and Steven Severin, *Protest 3: Red, Black, Brown Experience in America* (Grand Rapids, MI: William B. Eerdmans Publishing Company, 1975), 150–51.

17. Yellowtail, *Yellowtail Crow Medicine Man and Sun Dance Chief: An Autobiography as Told to Michael Oren Fitzgerald* (Norman: University of Oklahoma Press, 1991), 21.

18. J. Baird Callicott, "American Indian Land Wisdom," in Paul A. Olson, ed., *The Struggle for the Land: Indigenous Insight and Industrial Empire in the Semiarid World* (Lincoln: University of Nebraska Press, 1990), 255–272.

19. Lori Arviso Alvord and Elizabeth Cohen Van Pelt, *The Scalpel and the Silver Bear* (New York: Bantam Books, 1999), 84.

20. Dhyani Ywahoo and Barbara Du Boir, eds., *Voices of Our Ancestors: Cherokee Teachings from the Wisdom Fire* (Boston: Shambhala, 1987), xiii.

21. Peter MacDonald with Ted Schwarz, *The Last Warrior: Peter MacDonald and the Navajo Nation* (New York: Orion Books, 1993), 1–2.

22. Michael Kearney, *World View* (Novato, CA: Chandler & Sharp Publications in Anthropology and Related Fields, 1984), 150–55.

23. See Emile Durkheim, *The Elementary Forms of the Religious Life* (New York: The Free Press, 1967).

24. Morris Oppler also referred to "themes" in cultural development as "affirmations" of cultural practice, Morris Oppler, "Themes as Dynamic Forces in Culture," *The American Journal of Sociology*, Vol. 51, No. 31, November 1945, 198, 199, 202.

25. Durkheim, *Forms of Religious Life*, 41.

26. Dorothy Lee, "Notes on the Conception of Self among the Wintu Indians," *Journal of Abnormal and Social Psychology*, Vol. 45, 1950, 542.

27. Bruce Cox, ed., *Cultural Ecology: Readings on Canadian Indians and Eskimos* (Toronto: McClelland and Stewart Limited, 1973), 30.

28. Sir Edward B. Tylor, *The Origins of Culture* (New York: Harper & Brothers Publishers, 1958), 23.

29. Hans Kelsen, *Society and Nature: A Sociological Inquiry* (London: K. Paul, Trench, 1946), 49–185.

30. Franz Boas, *The Mind of Primitive Man* (New York: Macmillan, 1938), 162.

31. A similarity of Lucien Levy-Bruhl's analysis of primitive societies is applicable to traditional American Indians in their acceptance and belief in traditions and invisible forces, Lucien Levy-Bruhl, *Primitives and the Supernatural* (New York: E. P. Dutton & Co. Inc., 1935), translated by Lilian A. Clare, 20.

32. Durkheim, *Forms of Religious Life*, 41, 62.

33. Stanley Diamond, ed., *Primitive Views of the World: Essays From Culture in History* (New York: Columbia University Press, 1964), 65.

34. Bruce Cox, ed., *Cultural Ecology: Readings on Canadian Indians and Eskimos* (Toronto: McClellan and Stewart), 119–122.

35. A. Irving Hallowell discussed the importance and dangers of greed among traditional Ojibwas, "Ojibwa Ontology, Behavior, and World Views," in Diamond, *Primitive Views*, 75.

36. A. L. Kroeber stated less respect for cultures of small population in his categorical emphasis that small populated societies do not produce rich or advanced cultures. Furthermore, in his discussion on cultural diffusion and intermarginality, he stated that native American cultures were retarded due to their late start from population migrations across the Bering Strait when compared with Old World cultures, see A. L. Kroeber, *Anthropology: Culture Patterns & Processes* (New York and London: Harcourt, Brace & World, Inc., 1963), 195–196, 231–232.

37. *Ibid.*, 31.

38. Yellowtail, *Yellowtail Crow Medicine Man*, 35.

39. *Ibid.*, 130.

40. Neihardt, *Black Elk Speaks*, 180, 270.

41. Margaret D. Jacobs, *Engendered Encounters: Feminism and Pueblo Cultures 1879–1934* (Lincoln: University of Nebraska Press, 1999), 89.

42. Inter Press Service, compiler *Story Earth: Native Voices on the Environment* (San Francisco: Mercury House, 1993), 12–13.

43. Brown, *The Sacred Pipe*, xx.

44. Chief Seattle made this speech to Governor Issac I. Stevens of the Territory of Washington when he surrendered tribal lands to the United States in 1855.

45. McGaa, *Native Wisdom*, 29.

46. Jean Chaudhuri and Joyotpaul Chaudhuri, *A Sacred Path: The Way of the Muscogee Creeks* (Los Angeles: UCLA American Indian Studies Center, 2001), 5.

47. Brown, *The Sacred Pipe*, 9.

4

NATIVE AMERICAN GENIUS AND INDIAN INTELLECTUALISM[1]

"Everything in life is connected. Learn to understand the bonds between humans, spirit, and nature. Realize that our illness and our healing alike come from maintaining strong and healthy relationships in every aspect of our lives. In my culture—the Navajo culture—medicine is performed by a hataalii, someone who sees a person not simply as a body, but as a whole being. Body, mind, and spirit are seen as connected to other people, to families, to communities, and even to the planet and universe. All of these relationships need to be harmony in order to be healthy."[2]

Lori Arviso Alvord, Navajo, 1999

* * *

It can be naturally assumed that genius and intellectualism have existed and still exist among American Indians and other indigenous peoples. Perhaps, the American Indian genius can only be appreciated in indigenous studies. Historically, such genius and native intellectualism have not been viewed as relevant, according to literature written "about" American Indians, but it can be safely acknowledged that all cultures and communities possessed extraordinary "thinking" individuals. The indigenous people of Earth in the Americas were great thinkers and continue to be, although the mainstream culture does not observe them in the intellectual context of mainstream academia.

A dialogue is needed to recognize the native geniuses and indigenous intellectuals of the past and those who deserve recognition now. After more than 500 years of Indian-white relations, the beginning of the twenty-first century is long overdue for recognizing the intellectualism of native peoples, and how they have served their communities.

Like Navajo philosophy, the mainstream needs to see the "big picture" of all people in the United States. Furthermore, the American mainstream needs to acknowledge the native genius and indigenous intellectualism. It has been an uphill battle for native intellects to be recognized by the mainstream academic world. Native intellect is understanding relationships among all things, and this is the American Indian mind, based on tribal values purporting a native ethos.

First, the nature of "genius" and "intellectualism" must be defined, at least for discussion here and for future dialogue. Genius has been defined by *Webster's Dictionary* as "a single strongly marked capacity or aptitude; extraordinary intellectual power especially as manifested in creative activity; a person endowed with transcendent mental superiority; a person with a very high intelligence quotient" with the synonym as "gift."[3]

For the definition of "intellect" and "intellectualism," *Webster's Dictionary* defines intellect as "the power of knowing as distinguished from the power to feel and to will; the capacity for knowledge; the capacity for rational or intelligent thought especially when highly developed; a person of notable intellect" and "intellectualism" as "devotion to the exercise of intellect or to intellectual pursuits."[4] Naturally, this same definition may not be appropriate for identifying knowledgeable and gifted thinkers of traditional Indian societies of the many diverse indigenous communities throughout the Western hemisphere.

The *Webster* definitions apply largely to the American mainstream culture of a linear-thinking mind-set. Thus, these two definitions of "genius" and "intellect" would be different in Native American society, which has its own diverse cultures, although since the nineteenth century many American Indians have been absorbed into the American mainstream culture, and they think less traditionally as indigenous peoples do.

If ideas influence society and thinkers of new ideas offer society significant improvement, then the "acceptability" of such ideas also deserves examination. Ideas influence societal development and thus shape culture of the community. In writing *The Affluent Society*, John Galbraith believed "familiarity" was important for society to accept ideas to ensure stability, which he called "conventional wisdom" of society.[5] This view is shared by the traditional Indian mind.

New ideas and their acceptance by society are called brilliance, especially when society is willing to accept change. This reception might be called societal reform, even though ideas and new ideology are typically accepted slowly by any society. John M. Keynes observed that "we are ruled by ideas and by very little else," in his description of society and economics,[6] and this observation also sheds light on new ideas accepted by Indian people in developing their communities and cultures.

In order to discuss the basic nature of genius and intellectualism, it is necessary to compare the mind-sets of the American Indian and mainstream American. A dichotomy of Indian and linear mind sets separate the two minds.[7] Historically, the minds of the American Indian and the Euro-American are very different due to their evolution in two separate parts of the world. Developing in opposite hemispheres, the American Indian mind and the Euro-American mind are naturally set and steeped in incongruent values that distinguish their separateness. In an earlier publication, I maintained that the Indian mind and Euro-American minds are polar opposites, and that due to cultural developments in different parts of the world, the two races advanced their thinking by developing separate sets of values that remain incongruent in the context of historical Indian–white relations.[8] Geographic distance assisted in creating the polarity of these two opposites. The great length of time before their contact with each other had also caused such a separate development of mind-sets.

In his writing *Individualism Reconsidered*, David Reisman observed "that without consensus on values, our democratic society would not hold together."[9] This would also be true of Indian society in general. Values are pertinent to the shaping of thought and how a person perceives things.[10] As values are reinforced on a daily basis, individual and society norms are established, and culture becomes defined. But, like the Navajo, the native mind considers all things when making decisions. Like the Muscogee Creek concept of *Ibofanga*, "totality," all people should consider the importance of all that exists.

As a result of different hemispheric orientation of the thinking mind, and primarily due to cultural influences and fundamental needs, the brain of the American Indian developed with an orientation to "circular thought" and the brain of the Euro-American developed with an orientation to "linear thought." During the 1970s, some scholars noted this difference in intellect and observed American Indians to be "right-brained" oriented and mainstream individuals to be "left-brained" oriented. The right brain stressed quality performance in the arts and music, emphasizing creativity and imagination. The left brain stressed rationality and scientific reasoning based on laws of physics and math. Naturally, Western society has hoped to merge the two kinds of thinking into one, while it continues to have representation in both groups, and many non-Indians have also showed an orientation toward the right brain of creativity and abstract thought.[11] As stated earlier, some scholars no longer place value on the left and right brain theory, but then "why is the traditional American Indian mind so different from that of the linear mind of the white man?"

One fundamental difference that helps to distinguish American Indian genius and indigenous intellectualism is consideration of "individualism" and "collectivism" as embodiments of both Indian and non-Indian societies. In general, society can be divided into these two categories, yet these two entities tell us how American Indians and mainstream Americans differ greatly. Although Native Americans are individuals, the cultural emphasis is on the group over the individual so that collectivism is more influential; hence collectivism in such communalism is preferred over individualism. For example, the Lakota culture focuses on the *tiyosapaye* as the sociokinship extended family that is the foundation of Lakota society.[12] In a similar collective thinking, eastern woodland peoples like the Muscogee Creeks and Seminoles as well as the Cherokees stressed the importance of "clan" as being central to their societal infrastructures. Clan and togetherness is also important to the Navajo. Navajo surgeon Lori Alvord explained that "Everything in life is connected. Learn to understand the bonds between humans, spirit, and nature. Realize that our illness and our healing alike come from maintaining strong and healthy relationships in every aspect of our lives." Alvord explained the central philosophy of her people. She said that "Navajos believe in *hozho* or *hozhoni*—Walking in Beauty—a world view in which everything in life is connected and influences everything else. A stone thrown into a pond can influence the life of a deer in the forest, a human voice and a spoken word can influence events around the world, and all things possess spirit and power. So Navajos make every effort to live life in harmony and balance with everyone and everything else. Their belief system sees sickness as a result of things falling out of balance, losing one's way on the path of beauty. In this belief system, religion and medicine are one and the same."[13]

Among Indian societies, the natural dichotomy of "individual" and "communalism" creates a balance of cultural norm and behavior expectations. By fate, Rabbit could not steal the Sun and the Moon to fulfill his own greed, and the rooster met his fate. Whereas group collectiveness is preferred for social acceptance and validated by kinship and symbolic kinship relationships, the tribal society acknowledges all members of the community. In writing the early classic, *Social Organization: A Study of the Larger Mind*, Charles Horton Cooley stressed that in Indian society "every peculiarity of temperament was understood, and the individual was respected or despised according to his predominating characteristics."[14] Native peoples acknowledged the individual personalities, but the collective emphasis was greater than individualism that could be achieved by one person.

Such individuality has been championed in Western society, and the American public lauds such individuals as "great minds." For example, individuals who have pioneered frontier development, explored, colonized, and acted were men of "inner direction," a concept coined by David Reisman, and "they were guided by internalized goals and ideals which made them appear to be more individualistic than they actually were."[15] They had discovered their specific roles in life and focused all of their energy toward one goal.

Unlike the Navajos who think about all relationships, the linear mind thinks about all of things related to him with himself being at the center. In an early observation on the development of the United States, Alexis de Tocqueville identified the characteristic of American "individualism."[16] Although Americans found support in communities, they found themselves needing to rely on their own personal strengths and resourcefulness. Why? Perhaps a societal kinship, even symbolic, is struggling to develop within the mainstream community.

In 1893, Professor Frederick Jackson Turner presented his historic "Frontier Thesis" in an essay before the American Historical Association meeting in Chicago. In this address, Turner stressed "individuality" as being a part of the American experience. He mentioned Indians only twelve times, leaving the vivid impression that the continent was conquered by individual Americans, and that Indian people were not imperative to the development of the country.[17]

As the United States entered the twentieth century, a popular trend called Progressivism depicted this modernization of America. Theodore Roosevelt went further to describe a "rugged individualism," which called for American heroes and image building, whether or not the truth was distorted.

Due to the emphasis on "individuality" and the deeds achieved by the individual in America, Native American geniuses and intellectuals have had to work harder in order to be recognized by the American mainstream society. Historic negative stereotypes about Indians incline the public to not recognize the scholarly abilities of native peoples. The struggle for American Indian intellectuals has been great, and even more for native women. The first Navajo woman surgeon, Lori Alvord recalled her personal struggles at Stanford Medical School. She stated, "One day as I was working, he stopped me. 'Lori, have you ever thought about going to medical school?' I'm sure I visibly balked.

A Navajo woman physician. I couldn't remember ever hearing of one in my entire life. 'No, really, I'm serious,' he said. 'Maybe you *should* think about it.' . . . I blushed as I dropped my eyes and turned back to my work. I vividly recalled my dismal brush with the physical and life sciences at Dartmouth [as an undergraduate]. *I don't have what it takes*, I thought. . . . Yet as soon as he spoke the words, I began to take the idea seriously. In traditional Navajo belief, speaking a thought into the air gives it more power."[18]

After being accepted by Stanford Medical School, Alvord recounted her difficulty in perception and logic in trying to look at medicine through the eyes of a white man. She said, "My interest in this scientific way of looking at the world was magnified with each class I took. Biochemistry, chemistry, anatomy, physiology, even calculus had the same internal logic as much Native American cosmology. The way the white blood cells attack an invading virus, the way too much or too little of anything disturbs the body functions, the way tissue defends or repairs itself—it was all *hozho*, the beautiful balance of the universe, rephrased in scientific terms."[19]

Alvord found herself out of balance at Stanford University. She had to struggle to regain her balance within herself. Alvord described her dilemma at this stage of medical school. She said, "Once again I was an outsider—outside the sacred mountains—and it was often lonely and unsettling. I spent my evenings and weekends studying in the Fleischman Learning Center, usually alone. My class of eighty-six students included only two other Native Americans: Robert Fairbanks, a Chippewa from Minnesota, and Miguel Dozier, from Santa Clara Pueblo in New Mexico. The very thought of exhibiting my skills and knowledge before others was disturbing. I could not bring myself to participate in class discussions and debates, or to volunteer answers to professors' questions, although it was expected. The same problems I had encountered at Dartmouth were even more exaggerated here. I didn't feel comfortable raising my hand in class, I wasn't competitive enough about test scores and projects, and I didn't draw attention to myself. I lacked the 'right stuff' that every med student needs: a competitive edge. Yet it was hard for me to behave any other way. Silence is a normal part of Navajo communication; words are used sparingly and weighed carefully. It took me a long time to be comfortable with the non-Navajo style of learning."[20]

Alvord received continuous moral support from Ron Lujan, an accomplished surgeon from Taos Pueblo, New Mexico. He taught her to challenge herself in order to prepare for others who would challenge her. Alvord learned an important lesson about what she would encounter as a surgeon. "As a minority physician, you will be constantly challenged," he said. "Your decisions will be questioned, your authority doubted. To be successful, you will have to have higher standards than everyone else. You will have to study harder, train longer, and know your material backward and forward. In the operating room, you will need to know the anatomy, how to do the operation, and what alternative operations might also work."[21]

Lori Alvord initially doubted her abilities to become a surgeon. She thought about her new relationships with the other medical students. She wondered about her future status in the medical profession, and if she would be accepted. Alvord remarked that "time after time in the years to come, I would encounter skepticism about my abilities. Even after taking all the same classes, passing all the same tests, and meeting the same requirements for graduation as everyone else, I would be eyed sideways and doubted at times. My being a surgeon would be attributed to quota filling, not to the result of hard work and my own merit."[22] In the end, Lori Alvord succeeded in becoming the first Navajo woman surgeon, and her relationships with her friends and relatives were her strength. New relationships became new friendships.

In contrast to the individualistic nature of the American mainstream, the indigenous cultures of America emphasized a collective or communal culture. The social knowledge of the community grew with the thinkers and wise elders of the community, which is a sociological concept of thought. This "sociology of knowledge" that has been described by Karl Mannheim in his work, *Ideology and Utopia*, explains that the "individual" is a product of a group that has influenced the thinking of the individual intellect.[23]

Individualism and collectivism rest within the nature of society and its culture. "Culture relativism" is a borrowed phrase from anthropology that sheds significant light on American Indian genius and indigenous intellectualism. Hence, a group of people or a community live according to certain cultural traits or patterns that have relevant value to the group. This culture relativism defines the identity and what the group or community believes to be important as a body, thus culture and group are synonymous. In writing on "individualism and collectivism," Harry C. Triandis, a psychologist, noted the importance of cultural behavior, stating that "a cultural syndrome is a pattern characterized by shared beliefs, attitudes, norms, roles, and values that are organized around a theme and that can be found in certain geographic regions during a particular historic period."[24]

Within a culture, perception of both the individual and the community is relevant to the defining of the ethos or world view of the indigenous community. The ability of one's perception is germane to the development of one's intellect. Perception is the key to how human beings associate and see the relationships of objects even though their meanings may be incongruent. Hence, the foreseen patterns or connections between objects is kindred association in the mental eye.

Because native people are communally oriented, they have an innate quality of seeing and trying to understand relationships and connections in order to preserve community and unity. Such an order of life is a Natural Democracy. Onondaga scholar Oren Lyons stated, "In our [Iroquois] perception, all life is equal, and that includes the birds, animals, things that grow, things that swim. All life is equal in our perception."[25]

Because the true reality of Indian people is a tandem of physical and metaphysical realities, native thinkers have encountered visions and spirits on a regular basis as a part of life. This aspect of the metaphysical is similar to the dreams of individuals of the Western society, who sometimes find answers to questions that could not be answered by their conscious minds. In the mind of the American Indian, the subconscious and conscious work together in a partnership. This metaphysical dimension of Indian life has led to an easier acceptance of abstract ideas and dealing with abstract thought.

The abstract nature of ideas and abstract thought is more acceptable to tangible items such as place within a physical environment. The sense of "place," usually one's homeland, has a pertinent bearing on the native person and how he or she views the world and the universe. Place is a tangible commodity for reference to one's thoughts, and we easily "see" tangible things on a daily basis in relationship to our tangible place called home. However, "how" we see nontangible things and entertain abstract notions of thought still are better acted upon from a reference to place or homeland. Hence, place is importantly influential in how indigenous people understand the world and the universe. It is all about "seeing" all of our relationships, as the Navajos say. This perspective is their native ethos for realization and adding to their knowledge about life. The place of homeland is germane to the confidence and abilities of anyone, especially to those Indian professionals being challenged by linear skeptics. Lori Alvord recalled her father speaking to her about the four sacred mountains of the Navajos, and how they stood strong as a part of Earth's creation. "Each of the four directions, he said, represented a different part of the day. East, where Blanco Peak is, is dawn; south, where Mount Taylor is, is twilight; west and the San Francisco Peak is yellow evening; and north, where La Plata Peak is, is folding darkness."[26]

One's persona is the basis of Navajo philosophy—how one carries his or herself. "Navajo people," said Alvord, "have a concept called '*Hozhone haaz'dlii*', (Walking in Beauty), but it isn't the beauty most people think of. Beauty to Navajos means living in balance and harmony with yourself and the world. It means caring for yourself—mind, body, and spirit—and having the right relationships with your family, community, the animal world, the environment—earth, air, and water— our planet and universe. . . If a person respects and honors all these relationships," I said, "then they will be Walking in Beauty."[27] Balance and harmony come together at a mental state within the Navajo person and this well being reflects outward as an example to others.

People need a place of reference to remind them who they are, especially when their mental energy is exhausted. Place is important to the mind. It provides substance to life's experiences and how we related to all things. Place is a constant in the universe and one of the undisputed laws of nature. Place provides the physical quality to life, and provides security to mind and body.

Related to the significance of place is the "power" of place. Sacred sites and places empowered significantly influence one's understanding and process of perception. Undoubtedly such sacred places to native people of the Black Hills, Taos Blue Lake, Mackinac Island, Mount Ranier, Mount Taylor, Bear Butte, and other indigenous sites are special in the understanding and learning about life and the universe for native peoples.

In a similar manner, plains Indian people seek hilltops while praying for a vision, other native peoples have special places for prayer, and certain areas were endowed for helping Indian people, especially those who were medicine makers, seers, prophets, and those possessing extraordinary gifts of knowledge. People have special places where they feel more secure and safe, and such places should not be discouraged. This aspect of life is one that indigenous people have understood for a long time and it is a part of their various cultures.

A related and important element is time. How a person understands the concept of "time," however, is less relevant in the basic perception of thought. In making concluding observations about "time" and "order in society," Jean-Louis Servan-Schreiber, in *The Art of Time*, stated, "Once the time structures chosen by us materialize and endure, confusion abates."[28] The increments of time as determined by the measurements of seconds, minutes, hours, and days compels the linear world to run their lives according to the proverbial clock. The fast-paced capitalism of mainstream American society sets up false competition, thus everything is aimed toward accomplishing great deeds within spans of time. Such regulation of life according to time measurements has caused a Western conception of time as a commodity to be dealt with, rather than one of the abstract laws of the universe in the view of Native Americans.

As emphasized earlier, the concept of time for Indian people has been such a continuum that time becomes less relevant and the rotation of life or seasons of the year are stressed as important for understanding life. This is inherent to understanding life for American Indians. It is also inherent to mainstream Americans and the rest of the world, although time is less of a factor for comprehending the changes or phases of life from birth to childhood, to adulthood to old age, and to death.

As "time" is one of the fundamental elements of existence, "space" is another crucial element for understanding life. Space to Indian people is the embodiment of inclusion of tangible and nontangible things in the world and in the universe. All such things have existence and the space between things establishes the beginning of a relationship between two items. For example, any two tangible objects possess a space between them, thus forming a relationship of one object to the other one. Among native people, this relationship was acknowledged with hope that such an arrangement would be positive. Naturally, sometimes the relationship was negative such that history holds records of indigenous communities at war with other native communities known often as historic rivalries.

The space between objects becomes the relationship with intention for harmony. The objects themselves emit an energy, as each possesses a spirit. Among Indian people, it is known that each item has a story about it such as how a bowl of pottery was made, an uncle making a flute for a niece, a father helping his son in making a bow for hunting, and each event encapsulates a story and the object created, giving it life and energy as the source for spirituality. Within the object is soul, which comes alive with each story that is told about the object and retold. It comes alive in the minds of the listeners varying in accordance with the effectiveness of the storyteller.

The counterpart to space is mass. The mass of an object is fundamental to the universe for its weight and constitution of atoms. However, how we perceive mass is entirely a different matter, depending on perspective, and how Indians "see" is acute to realizing and indigenizing intellectualism. Indian people see mass in relationship to other particles of mass; hence, all things are related in light of a big picture of the world and universe.

With individuality de-emphasized, the community of masses (or objects) form a community with human beings that emits a culture of conformity and regular norms that occur in cycles, according to day to night, changing moons, changing seasons, and birth to death. These rhythms are "constants" due to Rabbit's failure to steal the Sun and the Moon and without them the "whole" would be incomplete.

Mass of objects also contain stored energy that upon release, the spirit of an object is manifested such that each object has life. This concept is supported by the native belief that sacred sites exist, trees are living entities, and rivers are believed to be alive. Some empowered sites radiate strong feelings of a positive nature, while others might radiate negative feelings. To believe that only humans, animals, and plants are alive is erroneous.

How atoms, objects, humans, or entities in general are related or associated with each other is imperative to an individual's understanding and comprehension of the world and the universe. According to the Creator, all things are in a sequential order called the Circle of Life. Relationship and order are essential concepts that help to understand the native ethos of Indian people. As mentioned, the relationship of all things in the universe represents an inherent order of life and existence. Understanding the relationships between objects is germane to understanding the Indian world, according to tribal traditions.

In the case of indigenous intellectualism, new relationships are extrapolated in ways that have not been previously realized. Posed as abstract theory, envisioning relationships between objects becomes the catalyst for advancing indigenous intellectualism. Trying to understand relations provokes American Indian thought.

With the foregoing fundamental elements covered, the final element in forming and defining thought is causality. In the indigenous world, the laws of physics do not always apply to explaining "why" something happened. The laws of nature are more appropriate, at least, the natural laws interpreted by the indigenous mind, as linear logic of the Western mind sometimes fails to provide an acceptable explanation. Human-made laws are secondary to the laws of nature.

The causes of action are a part of the physical and metaphysical realities of native people. Furthermore, metaphysical beings can cause things to occur in the physical world, but not vice versa. For this reason, American Indians highly value the metaphysical world, and thus believe that it is more powerful than the physical dimension of their world.

Many indigenous communities of the Western Hemisphere acknowledged that the causality of the "unexplained" resulted from supernatural forces that control the environment, and that a supreme force bestowed life upon the universe. Indigenous thinkers rationalized that the causes of life and historical events were connected and resulted from the actions of positive and negative forces. This natural dualism of the world and the universe superimposed on humans concluded that a balance would produce a harmonious life's experience. Indigenous people accepted this general explanation since "a shortage of [day's] time disallowed scientific investigation (a privilege of bountiful civilizations and later phase of societal development), and their waking hours demanded obtaining and preparing food."[29]

Language is the oral expression of people and a manifestation of their culture. For example, as stated in the earlier chapter on oral tradition, among indigenous communities the native language conveys meaning and culture simultaneously so that the listeners learn much about the values of the speaker and his or her culture. Language served as a two-way communication so that the speaker conveys his or her ideas and the listener receives the same ideas, although the same meaning of the speaker and listener did not always occur. Hence, perception and how one thinks logically due to language becomes a variable or reason for miscommunication and misunderstanding. This is why understanding relationships is so important to disallow miscommunication from harming them.

Within indigenous cultures, certain individuals were viewed as having important roles for their stations as keepers of traditional knowledge. Elders of Indian tribal communities have been viewed as the most knowledgeable people among Indians. Wisdom accumulated over the years from life experiences and observations of historical events and events of other people's lives. Indian elders possess much knowledge that have evolved from early beginnings of their people.

Keepers of traditional knowledge could be listed as native geniuses, although a cutting-edge contribution to science seems to be an important criterion in mainstream academia. A standard profile of an American Indian genius and the profile of an indigenous intellectual have yet to be determined. One suggested profile of the American Indian genius might include a person steeped in traditionalism of his or her people relating to values of the tribal community, and the manifestation of individual expression through individual actions of the person who represents deep inner thought on a frequent basis that also enlighten one's family, relatives, and community.

Hence, the word, "genius" from the English language might not necessarily describe the Indian genius, and it would be helpful to consider that there would likely be more than one kind or level of Native American geniuses. For example, an Indian genius like a theorist or prophet could be a person who might be intuitive about thought, while another native genius, like a war leader, could be both intuitive in thought and in action. Possibly, a native genius could be intuitive about his or her own personal life, but the second person could also influence others or change the course of action, such as on the battlefield or in a classroom, by influencing the learning level of students.

On many occasions, the brilliance of individual Indian people has been demonstrated by the influence of circumstances or situations. Unfortunately, such brilliance has been on the battlefield in war against the United States, as it has been recorded by mainstream observers and written by non-Indian journalists, writers, and scholars. As a result, many outstanding Indian leaders who might have been deemed geniuses have been tested on the battlefield, whereas their true arena may have been in another area. For example, young Chief Joseph of the Nez Perce did not wish to be a military leader. He was a man of peace, but circumstances forced him to exhibit his brilliance leading 700 men, women, and children in four major battles and small skirmishes against 2,000 soldiers of the United States.

It is in these other circumstances that other cases must be considered for Indian intellectualism. Deeds of honor, development of native society in religious thought, philosophical thought, and medicine are other areas that a native genius was likely acknowledged by his or her people. For example, Sanapia, Comanche Eagle Doctor, was a person who earned the respect of her people, even though this came later in life, as she initially avoided the gift of medicine making.[30] Due to the exclusive nature of general focus on what is important to the American mainstream, Sanapia is little known.

Again, native values must be considered when considering indigenous intellectualism. Of the various values that Indian people hold in high esteem, relationships is one of them. As described earlier, relationships are keys to understanding the world and the universe; hence, knowing and gaining new relationships is essential to well-being and existence in the Native American world.

Related to relationships is kinship. Kinship is the bonding element that holds together the entities of the Indian world. This type of spiritual energy is essential for the maintenance of indigenous peoples who depend on collectivism. Thus, relationships are imperative to communal continuity as well as to the understanding of relationships with nonhumans and with the metaphysical entities of life. Appreciation and respect for animals are important values to native people. Native Americans view themselves as being symbolically "related" to animals.[31]

Undoubtedly tradition and native heritage influence a native genius, and form the foundation of their thinking. Early childhood exposure to pertinent values and beliefs would be routine in one's life.

For example, parents and elders teach a child about the differences between things and why such differences are evident. The child would then see the relationships or illogical relationships between things, as first he or she would understand concrete items, then abstract items.

By understanding the relationships between items, the native thinker engages thought to theorize about illogical relationships between items that could relate to each other in an unusual pattern. Such unusual relationships and parallels engaged by the native genius would then become so familiar that theory, idea, familiarity, and permanent relationship would develop to create a philosophy about such relationships and parallels within the world and universe. Such relationships and parallels do not always have to be human to human relationships and parallels. Rather, native thinkers have involved human–animal and human–plant relationships since their earliest oral traditions as their people envisioned a human relationship with all things, tangible and nontangible.

The indigenous understanding of tangible and nontangible things reminds us of the differences between the traditional Indian world and the white world. The native thinker comes from his or her Indian world of values and ethos, and he or she is able to function within the values and ethos of the white world of the Western mind. This dualistic behavior calls for competence and confidence in the abilities of the native genius to operate successfully in both societies. Furthermore, the Indian genius is an amalgamation of both worlds and their sets of values and norms.

However, a true native genius would excel in both societies, although the first level is to demonstrate intuitive knowledge and performance in one's native society. This level of genius performance should be enough, but because native people are in the minority compared to the majority, then the latter is required to accept the superior Indian intellectual functioning in the white world.

The state of action here is the native cyclical mind operating in the Western linear society and being acknowledged at a high level of intelligence. Continued performance at a high level and acknowledgment from the linear society establishes a categorical status of the American Indian genius of indigenous thought.

Specifically, some of the past native leaders were likely indigenous intellectuals and possible American Indian geniuses. For example, Tecumseh, the great Shawnee leader during the War of 1812 envisioned an Indian confederacy based on many alliances. He was a genius for negotiating all of these alliances through the intricate relations with other tribes. He foresaw such relationships while his skeptics and enemies sought to undermine his goal to unite the many tribes of the eastern woodlands against the United States.

The Cherokee genius, Sequoyah, was a quiet individual who invented an 86-character syllabary to produce a written Cherokee language. At the same time, other Cherokees criticized him. Some tribesmen called him a witch for trying to capture spoken words on paper. His invention revolutionized the Cherokee nation, making the Cherokee the most advanced Indian nation during the mid-nineteenth century.[32]

Young Chief Joseph was noted for his resourcefulness in times of war against the United States when his people, the Nez Perce, did not wish to fight. Yet, Joseph was a man of peace. Employing tricks, deception, and resourceful thinking, Chief Joseph outmaneuvered his people and saved them in several battles, until he was forced to surrender just short of leading his people into Canada.

Alexander Lawrence Posey composed humorous satire about the Indian Territory at the turn of the twentieth century. Daniel F. Littlefield Jr., the biographer of Alex Posey, called the Creek intellectual, a poet, journalist, and humorist.[33] A witty young Muscogee Creek, Posey wrote about the wrongdoing of the federal government's treatment of American Indians from a native perspective. In 1902, Posey purchased the *Indian Journal* and quickly established a reputation for his political satire in his "Fus Fixico" letters over the next few years. In 1908, the talented writing Posey tragically died in a drowning accident in the North Canadian River. His writing earned him a national reputation among journalists, and he wrote poetry as well. For the suppressed Indian people of the Indian Territory, his Fus Fixico letters provided humor and hope that better times were ahead during a pressured time that involved land allotment via amendments to the Dawes Act, affecting the Five Civilized Tribes and the push for statehood of Oklahoma, which occurred in 1907.[34]

Charles Alexander Eastman, a Santee Sioux, became a physician in 1890. After serving in Lakota country as a doctor, Eastman lectured across the United States. He wrote several books about his life and that of the American Indian in general at the turn of the twentieth century to enlighten the American public, who grew curious about Indian life. His transition from an Indian world to the white world proved remarkable as he succeeded in both, as well as other notable Indians like Carlos Montezuma, who was a contemporary of Eastman. Montezuma, a Yavapai from Arizona, struggled in a similar way, going to college and medical school. Raised as an orphan, Montezuma had achieved professional recognition in the white man's world.

In modern life in the twentieth century, the American Indian genius and indigenous intellectuals have yet to be properly recognized by the American mainstream. In indigenous communities, the modern Indian genius has been acknowledged by native peoples, according to other names. Deep thinkers and native individuals of traditional knowledge fall into this category of modern Indian geniuses, who also take action in some way. Their thoughts and actions distinguish them usually in leadership positions, although this manifestation does not always have to be in the political arena such as a tribal leader, or leader of an Indian organization.

One such modern American Indian genius is Vine Deloria, Jr. Considered by many as the most articulate Indian spokesperson of the late twentieth and early twenty-first centuries, Vine Deloria Jr., a Standing Rock Sioux, continues to pour out books and articles of his thoughts and ideas that have educated many Indian and non-Indian people. A prolific scholar of more than fifteen books, Deloria is a keen thinker and has produced such work of clever insights that he has led others to see and to understand Indian people from an Indian point of view. This is American Indian genius.

N. Scott Momaday, a Kiowa scholar, became famous when his novel, *House Made of Dawn* (1968), won the Pulitzer Prize for literature in 1969. His gift of writing was recognized by the public, and since then he has provided Indian people and the world with a continuous diet of poetry and novels. He has an inquisitive thirst for understanding and sharing native tradition. His ability to express such traditions and his own interpretation exemplifies the connections between tribal traditions, humor, and understanding which have made his work such a joy to hear and to read.

Ample evidence exists of the American Indian genius being in the past and present. This evidence of the American Indian genius is historic and dates back to the earliest existence of indigenous communities, although such individuals were probably called wise elders or persons of great medicine. An encyclopedia like publication by Gale Publishing, *Notable Native Americans*, edited by Sharon Malinowski, listed 267 notable American Indians in various fields and occupations such as education, tribal leadership positions, as warriors, activists, and as writers.[35] Although this is a low number to recognize, even if a safe guess of 10 percent of these 267 American Indian individuals were considered, then there have been at least 25 American Indian geniuses and some are living today. Furthermore, there are many more notable individuals to mention than the ones just discussed.

During the mid 1970s, educator Dean Chavers completed a survey of American Indians in academia, and found that 191 American Indians held doctorates. His survey also noted that most professional Indian people went into law and education. This is a very low number, and in the year 2000, Chavers projected that there were at least now 1,000 American Indians holding doctorates.[36] The status of indigenous intellectualism has been established thirty years ago.

However, many traditional elders are also Native American intellectuals at various levels, and some might also be geniuses. In their own communities, tribal members acknowledge wise individuals who have exceptional abilities that can provide help and perspective on critical problems. In native society, great thinkers are not given as much respect as those gifted individuals who are able to provide explanations and solution to problems. Practicality is a value that identifies exceptional individuals in Indian society.

In conclusion, undoubtedly more Indian geniuses and native intellectuals have lived and are living now than the American public has ever acknowledged. The point is that American Indians have not been previously thought to be intellectuals or even to be called a geniuses by non-Indians. Until mainstream academia acknowledges the existence of Indian intellectualism and Native American geniuses, then many such brilliant native people will go unnoticed. For too long, American Indian intellectuals have been neglected by the mainstream academic world unless their works directly impact upon the mainstream. It is unfortunate that their work goes unrecognized, as their work is channeled in certain areas unrelated to the needs of the mainstream. For American Indian intellectuals, it has been an uphill struggle in gaining recognition for their work and even for their ideas to be entertained. Due to different kinds of evidence and the logic of the linear mind, only empirical evidence is acceptable to the Western world. In a holistic way, Lori Alvord reminds all of us that everything in life is connected, and this is the basis of traditional knowledge from a tribal ethos. It is a matter of accepting Indian intellectualism. Indian genius is a matter of understanding relationships and the beauty of them. Perhaps Indian people should give recognition to their own native geniuses and indigenous intellectuals. Their contributions should be acknowledged, but ironically this presents a challenge in itself and concordance among various tribal traditions of individuals not wanting to be singled out for attention for fear of ridicule. Although group acceptance has prevailed as a part of the indigenous cultures of this continent, this cultural assumption should not deny the recognition of the American Indian genius and indigenous intellectualism.

NOTES

1. An earlier version appeared as Donald L. Fixico, "Call for American Indian Genius and Indigenous Intellectualism," in *Indigenous Nations Studies Journal*, Vol. 1, No. 1, Spring 2000, 43–59.
2. Lori Arviso Alvord and Elizabeth Cohen Van Pelt, *The Scalpel and the Silver Bear: The First Navajo Woman Surgeon Combines Western Medicine and Traditional Healing* (New York, Toronto, London, Sydney and Auckland: Bantam Books, 1999), 3.
3. *Webster's Seventh New Collegiate Dictionary*, based on *Webster's Third New International Dictionary* (Springfield, MA: G. & C. Merriam Company, Publishers, 1970), 348.
4. Ibid., 440.
5. John Kenneth Galbraith, *The Affluent Society* (Boston: Houghton Mifflin Company, 1958), 9.
6. Ibid., 20, originally stated in John M. Keynes, *Essays in Persuasion: Economic Possibilities for Grandchildren* (London: Macmillan, 1932), 350–360.
7. As examples of the Western mind, see Arthur K. Moore, *The Frontier Mind* (Lexington: University of Kentucky Press, 1957) and Henry Steele Commager, *The American Mind: An Interpretation of American Thought and Character Since the 1880's* (New Haven: Yale University Press, 1950).
8. Donald L. Fixico, "The Struggle for Our Homes: Indian and White Values and Tribal Lands," in Jace Weaver, ed., *Defending Mother Earth: Native American Perspectives on Environmental Justice* (Maryknoll, NY: Orbis Books, 1996), 30–31.
9. David Reisman, *Individualism Reconsidered: And Other Essays* (Glencoe, IL: The Free Press, 1954), 17.
10. A helpful discussion of American values is Donald N. Barrett, ed., *Values in America* (Notre Dame, IN: University of Notre Dame University Press, 1961).
11. Jan Ehrenwald, *Anatomy of Genius: Split Brains and Global Minds* (New York: Human Sciences Press, Inc., 1984), 7–9.
12. I am indebted to Dr. Leonard Bruguier, Director of American Indian Studies at the University of South Dakota, Vermillion, SD, for introducing this Lakota concept to me many years ago.
13. Alvord and Van Pelt, 3 and 14. See also Paul Wileto, "Dine College Struggles to Synthesize Navajo and Western Knowledge," *Tribal College: Journal of American Indian Higher Education*, Vol. 9, No. 2, Fall 1997, 11–15.
14. Originally quoted in F. S. Dellenbaugh, *The North Americans of Yesterday*, 416; Charles Horton Cooley stresses the importance of individual recognition by the clan, and he parallels American Indian tribal communities to the German Teutonic tribes in stating, "In a life that of the Teutonic tribes before they took on Roman civilization, the social medium was small, limited for most purposes to the family, clan or village group. Within this narrow circle there was a vivid interchange of thought and feeling, a sphere of moral unity, of sympathy, loyalty, honor and congenial intercourse. Here precious traditions were cherished . . ." *Social Organization: A Study of the Larger Mind* (New York: Schocken Books, 1962), 107–108, copyright 1909, published in 1937 by Charles Scribner's Sons.
15. Reisman, *Individualism Reconsidered*, 17.

16. See Alexis de Tocqueville, *Democracy in America* (New York: Vintage Books, 1954), 2 vols.

17. In 1893, a young professor Frederick Jackson Turner, a historian, of the University of Wisconsin, Madison, delivered his famed essay "Frontier" at the American Historical Association meeting in Chicago.

18. Alvord and Van Pelt, *The Scalpel and Bear*, 36.

19. Ibid., 37.

20. Ibid., 39.

21. Ibid.

22. Ibid., 50.

23. Karl Mannheim, translated by Louis Wirth and Edward Shils; *Ideology and Utopia: An Introduction to the Sociology of Knowledge* (London: Routledge and Kegan Paul Limited, 1936), 2–3.

24. Harry C. Triandis, *Individualism and Collectivism* (Boulder, CO: Westview Press, 1995), 43.

25. Oren Lyons, "An Iroquois Perspective," in Christopher Vecsey and Robert W. Venables, eds., *American Indian Environments: Ecological Issues in Native American History* (Syracuse: Syracuse University Press, 1980), 173.

26. Alvord and Van Pelt, *The Scalpel and Bear*, 164.

27. Ibid., 186.

28. Jean-Louis Servan-Schreiber, *The Art of Time* (Reading, MA: Addison-Wesley Publishing Company, Inc., 1988), translated by Franklin Philip, third printing, 127.

29. Hans Kelsen professed that the principle of causality was unknown to primitive peoples (and American Indians are often classified as such), and that primitives interpreted nature according to social norms and the norm of retribution; see Hans Kelsen, *Society and Nature, A Sociological Inquiry* (Chicago and London: University of Chicago Press, 1943), vii; and see Donald L. Fixico, *The Invasion of Indian Country in the Twentieth Century: American Capitalism and Tribal Natural Resources* (Niwot, CO: University Press of Colorado, 1998), Chapter 11, 205–218.

30. See David E. Jones, ed., *Sanapia: Comanche Eagle Doctor* (Prospect Heights, IL: Waveland Press, 1984).

31. Howard L. Harrod has described the Indian–animal relationships among twelve northern plains tribal groups in *The Animals Came Dancing: Native American Sacred Ecology and Animal Kinship* (Tucson: University of Arizona Press, 2000).

32. W.C. Carmack, ed., *Indian Oratory: Famous Speeches by Noted Indian Chieftains* (Norman: University of Oklahoma Press, 1971), 101–102; see also Traveller Bird, *Tell Them They Lie: The Sequoyah Myth* (Los Angeles. Westernlore Publishers, 1971); George E. Foster, *Se-Quo-Yah, The American Cadmus and Modern Moses* (Philadelphia: Indian Rights Association, 1885); and Grant Foreman, *Sequoyah* (Norman: University of Oklahoma Press, 1938).

33. The primary biography of Alex Posey is Daniel F. Littlefield, Jr., *Alex Posey: Creek Poet, Journalist, and Humorist* (Lincoln: University of Nebraska Press, 1992).

34. Alexander Posey, Daniel F. Littlefield, Jr., and Carol A. Petty Hunter, eds., *Alexander Posey: The Fus Fixico Letters* (Lincoln: University of Nebraska Press, 1993), xiii–xiv. Additional works about Posey's life are Alexander Posey, edited by Edward E. Dale, "The Journal of Alexander Lawrence Posey, January 1 to September 4, 1897," *Chronicles of Oklahoma* Vol. 45, No. 4, Winter 1967–68, 2–15; Alexander Posey, "Journal of Creek Enrollment Field Party 1905 by Alexander Posey," *Chronicles of Oklahoma*, Vol. 46, No. 1, Spring 1968, 2–15; and Anna Lewis, "Miss Anna Lewis, Teacher of Alexander Posey at Bacone University," *Chronicles of Oklahoma*, Vol. 45, No. 3, Autumn 1967, 332–35; and [no author], "Alexander Posey, the Creek Poet," *Indian School Journal*, Vol. 11, No. 3, June 1911, 11–14.

35. Sharon Malinowski, ed., *Notable Native Americans* (Detroit: Gale Publishing, Inc., 1995).

36. Dean Chavers did the survey for the Ford Foundation during the mid-1970s, and at a conference of directors of American Indian, Native American and First Nations Studies Programs, held at Arizona State University, March 2–3, 2000, Tempe, AZ, he reflected on his survey and estimated that at least 1,000 American Indians held doctorates currently.

5

INDIAN MINDS AND WHITE TEACHERS[1]

"'O-hee-ye-sa!' called my father, and I obeyed the call. 'It is time for you to go to school, my son,' he said, with his usual air of decision. We had spoken of the matter more than once, yet it seemed hard when it came to the actual undertaking. I remember quite well how I felt as I stood there with eyes fixed upon the ground. 'And what am I to do at the school?' I asked finally, with much embarrassment. 'You will be taught the language of the white man, and also how to count your money and tell the prices of your horses and of your furs. The white teacher will first teach you the signs by which you can make out the words on their books. They call them A, B, C, and so forth. Old as I am, I have learned some of them.' As Ohiyesa rode his pony to the boarding school for the first time, he encountered two Indian school boys and they raced their ponies to the mission school. Eastman told of this event of first entering the white man's school. 'By this time we had reached the second crossing of the river, on whose bank stood the little mission school. Thirty or forty Indian children stood about, curiously watching the newcomer [me] as we came up the steep bank. I realized for the first time that I was an object of curiosity, and it was not a pleasant feeling. On the other hand, I was considerably interested in the strange appearance of these school-children. . . The hair of all the boys was cut short, and, in spite of the evidence of great effort to keep it down, it stood erect like porcupine quills. I thought, as I stood on one side and took a careful observation of the motley gathering, . . . When the teacher spoke to me, I had not the slightest idea what he meant, so I did not trouble myself to make any demonstration for fear of giving offense. . . He then gave some unintelligible directions, and, to my great surprise, the pupils in turn held their books open and talked the talk of a strange people. Afterward the teacher made some curious signs upon a blackboard on the wall, and seemed to ask the children to read them. To me they did not compare in interest with my bird's-track and fish-fin studies on the sands. I was something like a

wild cub caught overnight, and appearing in the corral next morning with the
lambs. I had seen nothing thus far to prove to me the good of civilization." [2]

Charles Eastman, Santee Sioux, 1916

* * *

The mind of traditional American Indians is steeped in the traditional
culture of the people. When non-Indian teachers teach American Indian students, a problem arises. The teacher has failed to recognize the
different logic of the Native American and the unique ethos of the
American Indian mind. As a result, federal and mission boarding
schools punished Indian students for their practice of tribal ways and
for speaking their native languages. This treatment has a long history
that has been documented by scholars. Unfortunately, learning the
English language by native students caused them to forget their tribal
languages. Typically, the mainstream sees progress and moving forward, but never actually looks back and reflects upon what has been
lost. In this spirit of progress, the federal government and religious
groups enforced a colonized assimilation of Indian people, especially
the youth. In response, the school officials met a resilience of the
native intellect and the Indian students resisted changing into non-
Indian students. They began to see a dual perspective from a combination of their native logic and linear mind. As a result, the survival of
ideas, perspective, and Indian thinking remained within the mind of
the American Indian. Most of the following experiences are in the tes-
timonies of people who experienced boarding schools. Their words
are powerful like the oral tradition, touching the emotions of many
Indians who will recall their school days like Charles Eastman.

The set purpose of the Indian boarding school experience was to re-
move the native ethos from the mind of the American Indian student.[3]
The idea of such boarding schools for American Indian children dates
back to the beginnings of the College of William and Mary, Harvard University, Dartmouth College and others that included in their purposes
the education of native youth. Arguments and rhetoric for Indian education based on linear thinking have been a prolonged goal of religious
groups and the United States government.[4] The boarding school tradition and its long history documents the earliest Anglo attempts to usurp
native thinking. Carlisle, Haskell, Chilocco, and other schools employed a
missionary zeal to eradicate Indian values and the Indian languages as a
means to "change" young American Indians to "think" as non-Indians for
assimilation into American mainstream society.

The colonizer had altered the minds of many American Indians as
proven in the case of Many Lightnings, the father of Charles Alexander

Eastman, who was thought to have been killed by the soldiers during the Dakota War of 1862 in Minnesota. As a prisoner who was converted to Christianity, Many Lightnings went to Canada to reclaim his son, Ohiyesa (Charles), for him to be educated in the white man's way. Many Lightnings tried to convince his son of the superior way of the white man: "'Our own life, I will admit, it is the best in a world of our own, such as we have enjoyed for ages,' said my father. 'But here is a race which has learned to weigh and measure everything, time and labor and the results of labor, and has learned to accumulate and preserve both wealth and the records of experience for future generations. You yourselves know and use some of the wonderful inventions of the white man, such as guns and gunpowder, knives and hatchets, garments of every description, and there are thousands of other things both beautiful and useful. Above all, they have their Great Teacher whom they call Jesus and he taught them to pass on their wisdom and knowledge of all other races. It is true that they have subdued and taught many peoples, and our own must eventually bow to this law; the sooner we accept their mode of life and follow their teaching, the better it will be for us all."5 Astonishingly, the ways of his former enemy convinced Many Lightnings to prefer the white man's ways. Now he wanted them for his son.

Eastman described the memorable day of his first experience in the white man's boarding school. Unfortunately, similar experiences have plagued the full blood Indian and those like him who are of a native culture and traditional community. Mixed bloods, with some experience with American culture, had less difficulty of being accepted by white society. Being in a linear school with white teachers is the greatest challenge for the traditional American Indian mind. Ironically, these native students were foreigners in their own land due to the fact that once the entire continent was Indian land.

The cultural alienation and panic of being confronted in the classroom, a strange environment, proved overwhelming for many Indian kids in mission schools, boarding schools, and in public schools. Luther Standing Bear described his humiliation of being asked to read aloud in a classroom at Carlisle Indian School when he was a student. Among his people, one person and his or her views were never tested against another person. He described "there being no such thing as 'grades,' a child was never made conscious of any shortcomings."6

At Carlisle, Standing Bear experienced embarrassment and humiliation for the first time. "I can never forget the confusion and pain I one day underwent in a reading class," he said. "The teacher conceived the idea of trying or testing the strength of the pupils in the class. A paragraph in the reading book was selected for the experiment. A pupil was asked to rise and read the paragraph while the rest listened and corrected any mistakes. Even if no mistakes were made, the teacher, it seems, wanted the pupils to state that they were sure they had made no errors in reading. One after another the pupils read as called upon and each one in turn sat down bewildered and discouraged. My time came and I made no errors. However, upon the teacher's question, 'Are you sure that you have made no error?' I, of course, tried again, reading just as I had the first time. But again she said, 'Are you sure?' So the third and fourth times I read, receiving no comment from her. For the fifth time I stood and read. Even for the sixth and seventh times I read. I began to tremble and I could not see my words plainly. I was terribly hurt and mystified. But for the eighth and ninth times I read. I was growing more terrible. Still the teacher gave no sign of approval, so I read for the tenth time! I started on the paragraph for the eleventh time, but before I was through, everything before me went black and I sat down thoroughly cowed and humiliated for the first time in my life and in front of the whole class! Never as long as I live shall I forget my futile attempts to fathom the reason of this teacher's attitude. Out on the school grounds at recess I could not join in the games and play. I was full of foolish fears."[7]

Standing Bear's experience was not about learning in the classroom. It was about cruel torment to undermine the confidence of an Indian youth and to disarm his native intellect so that a teacher could teach him humility and demonstrate that the teacher had power over anyone in the class. The teacher believed that she had to control her students. Native students found themselves challenged in making tremendous cultural adjustments even with sensitive teachers.

Russell Means described his father's experience with boarding schools. It is well documented that the boarding school was harsh, exploitive, and tormenting, additionally colonized the minds of the American Indians and tried to make them think like white children. Angry at what had happened to his father, Means pointed out that kidnaping Indian kids to fill quotas at boarding schools occurred. Indian children, who were vulnerable at young ages, were targeted and the federal government allowed this cruelty to continue for generation after generation of Indian children who attended boarding schools. Boarding schools became their homes as Indian youth became the stepchildren of the federal government and were brainwashed against their traditional ways and homelands. Means stated that "Because our culture is built around the extended family, boarding schools were an important part of the scheme to destroy our society by eliminating its basic social unit—a plan of cultural genocide that has succeeded brilliantly."[8]

Means summarized the impact of boarding schools on Indian youth. "Because they attended boarding schools," said Means, "five or six generations of Indians grew up without getting to know their brothers and sisters, much less their parents, grandparents, cousins, aunts, and uncles. Most of my father's relatives, including his brothers and sister, fled the reservation to survive as families. They were 'breeds,' and they found it easier to live in the white man's world than to struggle under the oppression of the reservation."[9] The brainwashing of Indian students did not stop. It became a continuous experience that permanently changed native communities and compelled their people to begin viewing life differently from their ancestors.

Reuben Snake, the late, noted leader of the Native American Church, recalled his experience with boarding schools. His mother arrived in Wisconsin in 1942 and Reuben Snake and his cousins started at a new mission school in the small town of Neillsville. Jacob Stucki, a German-speaking doctor and an ordained minister of the United Church of Christ, had started the school. With his sister and two brothers, Reuben Snake attended the small school, along with some of his cousins and other Indian children. For the first time in his life, he faced a regimental lifestyle of getting up at an early hour at the boarding school, cleaning himself up, and marching to breakfast to sit at a specific place at the breakfast table. Every child had certain chores to do during the day, washing dishes, peeling vegetables, or mopping hallways. Snake remembered the minister raising his children among the Winnebago so that they could learn to speak Winnebago fluently, but the founder of the school prohibited Winnebago children from speaking their language at school. Snake recalled, "But the rule enforced at the school was that we couldn't speak our own native language. We had to speak English. We couldn't practice any of our cultural activities because they were condemned as pagan, superstitious rituals. When my grandmother came to visit, she and the headmaster would be laughing and carrying on a hilarious conversation in Winnebago. It used to bother me that he could do that but that when we students talked in Winnebago, we were breaking the rules. That was my first experience of hypocrisy, of the Whites preaching one thing and doing another."[10] Not being allowed to speak one's native language was common throughout boarding schools. Ironically, Indian students were punished for trying to learn as strict teachers tried to make the Indian students monolingual of the English language.

Dorothy R. Parker, the biographer of Flathead scholar D'Arcy Mc-Nickle, described McNickle's boarding school experience. His parents tried hard to raise him as a non-Indian. However, the boarding school reinforced Indian ways within young McNickle. His native friends at the mission school in St. Ignatius influenced his young personality, and this became more evident at Chemawa Indian school. Parker wrote, "His lack of interest in competition as an adult, his refusal to participate in a materialistic one-upmanship, his non directive management style, and his emphasis on consensus building, all of which are consistent with a Native American personality profile, reflect his reservation and boarding school childhood. His sense of humor, especially, seemed more Indian than white."[11] Like Charles Eastman and others, Indian students found themselves wanting to resist white ways and retain their tribal traditions. Clashing cultures reflected the polarized state of Indian minds versus white teachers.

Chemawa obviously was not a totally negative experience for Mc-Nickle, although he later commented that it did little to stimulate his love for learning. This was not surprising; off-reservation boarding schools for Indian children were programmed as vocational training schools, and they made little attempts to prepare their students for higher education. McNickle's experience represented a new type of Indian boarding school culture that formed a biculture of Indian and white ways. This binary developed especially among mixed bloods, who more readily adopted the ways of the white schools, while trying to retain traditional ones. Full blood traditionalists found themselves being left behind and becoming ostracized by mixed bloods, who desired white ways of life.

Russell Means described his grandfather in regard to native logic and learning. Means stated, "Grandpa John told me endless stories about young men who had opportunities to live up to their names. One day, he said, 'there was a young man named Looks Twice—really, he was more like a boy—who left his village alone to hunt, hoping to bring back some meat. He wanted to prove that he was a man. It was in the springtime. He went without a bow or a lance, and he killed a deer with his knife.' . . . 'How did he kill the deer, Grandpa?' I interrupted. 'You'd better figure that out,' he said. 'That's what will make you a man.'" This experience exemplifies the Indian way of thought. It is a native logic that is the basis for survival, even in the white man's world. John Means, Charles Eastman, and all Indian students attending such schools realized that thinking like a white man was required by their white teachers.

A lesson is in the story. Grandpa Means noted that "while Looks Twice was gone, it rained and rained. After killing the deer and butchering it, he returned to his village—only to find that the river had risen. The gentle little creek that he had waded [across] days earlier was swollen as wide as the Missouri [River]. It was raging furiously, with tree limbs hurtling by. There was no way he could get across.' That was the end of the story. I said, 'What do you mean Grandpa? How did he get back home? Did he get his meat to the village? Did he become a man?' 'You figure it out,' said Grandpa."12

As a youth, Russell Means realized that he was being taught the Lakota way of thinking. Lakota logic called for looking at the world in a special way. Means stated, "much later in my life, I realized Grandpa John was teaching me the Indian way of thinking, teaching me to use my imagination, to figure things out for myself, to study, and to analyze. He caused my uniform mind to ask questions—and then search out the answers. He also taught me patience. It took years to figure out some of the questions, but still more years to find the answers."13

Realization does not always come immediately. Means stressed that patience is important to understanding the way of thinking of the Lakota. He observed further, asking "but what was the meaning of the story of Looks Twice, who went to hunt alone to prove his manhood? Because it was spring, when the rains always came, he should have consulted with elders about the weather before leaving. He should have known better than to cross a river without planning a route back during a flood. In his haste to prove that he was indeed a man, he acted like a boy—impetuously. Although he stalked and killed a deer, Looks Twice failed to live up to his name."14

Russell Means stated further that, "in the linear, mathematical way of the Eurocentric male society that has long dominated America, that doesn't work. One is expected to *know* things, to *believe* things. Knowing and believing are all in your head—there is nothing in your heart. If you cannot *feel* that the earth is your Grandmother, then of course you will find it easy to rape her, to behave as though she is under your dominion. You will find it easy to believe that we humans are the dominant species, and to act as though the earth and everything on it are ours to do with as we please. . . That is not so. . . . For a millennium, we Indians lived as part of the earth. We were part of the prairies and the forests and the mountains. We knew every blade of grass, every plant, every tree. We knew the wind and the clouds, the rivers and the lakes. We knew every one of the creatures that fly and crawl and burrow and run and swim—all our relatives with whom we share this earth. We are part of the earth, but not the most important part. . . We knew the universe and how it interacts with our Grandmother. Before I was six years old, my grandparents and my mother had taught me that if all the green things that grow were taken from the earth, there could be no life. If all the four-legged creatures were taken from the earth, there could be no life. If all the winged creatures were taken from the earth, there could be no life. If all our relatives who crawl and swim and live within the earth were taken from the earth, there could be no life. But if all the human beings were taken away, life on earth would flourish."[15] The ways of Nature were imbedded in Indian students raised in tribal communities. Naturally, they applied their logic based on environmental relations in the classroom.

Out of balance, human beings can easily corrupt nature and this has been proven with increasing demands on fossil fuels and the awareness of global warming. The linear society can learn much from the American Indian about management of natural resources. Peter MacDonald described that "all Navajo education had a purpose: to teach wisdom, not just knowledge. We gained knowledge from the work we did each day. We learned to care for the animals and the land. We learned to use every part of the sheep and cattle that we slaughtered. We learned to make clothing, tools, and weapons from the materials all around us. We learned how to assist at birthing when necessary, and how to treat injuries in the field. We learned how to develop our bodies, and we studied the plants that could enhance our health. We had no written laws. The rules under which we lived were given to us by the Great Spirit, and thus were fair for all. They were mastered by the elders, who orally passed them from generation to generation. They were applied equally to everyone, and since they were the same laws by which the Great Spirit judged us, we had no problems with mutual respect."[16]

MacDonald stressed the importance of this kind of education. He said, "Education is critical for both children and adults. The basic education is vocational. But the Coyote stories taught to children become more complex as the years pass, providing older children with appropriate cultural guidelines. Other, more sophisticated stories, told by the elders, especially during the harsh winter months when there is less work to do, deal with ever more complex issues of mortality, ethics, history, and religion, which adults must learn and understand. Thus, the creation story, and other stories of our early history, became more involved as the Navajo passed through the different stages of life."[17] According to native logic, Coyote, Rabbit, and other tricksters had a special role in helping to explain fate, irony, and folly in life.

MacDonald summarized a description of the linear world. He stated, "by contrast, the white world seemed strange to my people. White people were given knowledge—the ability to read, to write, to calculate. They were prepared for a trade. They might be given a religious education or they might reject it as unimportant. They might keep track of current events, or their exposure to the world around them might be limited. They did not take time to learn all the survival skills of their culture. Instead, they became specialists and let other specialists help with the necessities."[18]

In retrospect, MacDonald recounted the past in saying, "Looking back, I realize that the BIA program was poorly planned and unrelated to the needs of the Navajo children. The hostile attitude toward my people [in schools] was emotionally devastating, of course. We were taught that we were superstitious savages, and we were forced to go to church without being given an understanding of the Christian religion. . . We were made to feel that our parents, our grandparents, and everyone who had come before us was inferior. It was even worse for those who came to believe these teachings and who still remembered the stories of Coyote. Those stories, so inspirational in so many ways, taught us not only how we came to be the Diné but also that we could never change. The whites were different from us. We were constantly told that we were truly inferior to them and that we would always be inferior. . . The educational program reinforced this attitude. We were taught reading, writing and arithmetic. We were taught English. We were taught white history, which assumed that all Indians were uneducated, superstitious savages, and that the only advances in civilization were made by whites."[19]

Before Indian students could succeed in the classroom, the minds of the American Indian and the mind of the white man had to clash. Afterward, a new beginning occurred for learning in each Indian child. In the case of Charles Eastman, he reconciled the differences between Indian and white logic. For many others, this reconciliation proved very difficult. Luther Standing Bear, wise elder of the Lakota, described this incongruence in his book, *Land of the Spotted Eagle.* He wrote, "White men seem to have difficulty in realizing that people who live differently from themselves still might be traveling the upward and progressive road of life. . . After nearly four hundred years' [now five hundred years] living upon this continent, it is still popular conception, on the part of the Caucasian mind, to regard the native American as a savage, meaning that he is low in thought and feeling, and cruel in acts; that he is a heathen, meaning that he is incapable, therefore void, of high philosophical thought concerning life and life's relations. For this 'savage' the white man has little brotherly love and little understanding. From the Indian the white man stands off and aloof, scarcely deigning to speak or to touch his hand in human fellowship. . . To the white man many things done by the Indian are inexplicable, though he continues to write much of the visible and exterior life with explanations that are more often than not erroneous. The inner life of the Indian is, of course, a closed book to the white man."[20]

This Indian reality is steeped in American Indians, consisting of beliefs in traditions and values of their ancient forefathers from all parts of America. Many tribes carried such beliefs with them during their removals to the Indian Territory and to other parts of the country, thus creating an estimated two hundred reservations during the nineteenth century. This native mind-set is a combination of physical and metaphysical dimensions. Dreams, visions, and aberrations are very much a part of the reality and the "day" consciousness of Indian people. Ghosts, spirits, and witches influence the lives of American Indians who are close to their traditional beliefs. Indian traditionalists believe that these spiritual powers have control over their lives, and they use protective medicines and take precautions to keep themselves safe. It is a life where the metaphysical is more powerful than the physical world, and where certain ceremonies and important rites need to be performed for protection or blessing by those powers greater than all human beings.

Fred McTaggart, who studied the Mesquakie Indians of Iowa and tried to collect their stories for his doctoral dissertation in literature, began to feel the spiritual environment of the Indians. On their reservation during the winter, he wrote, "I was still shivering but I continued to stand there in the wind, listening carefully and looking out across the clearing to my left. The timber was directly behind me and I could feel its presence vividly. By now, the sound that had stopped me was not important. In the land to my left and the woods behind me was a feeling that demanded attention. As anxious as I was to get inside that warm house, I felt compelled to listen and to look. There were spirits in the land, I had been told, the spirits of the people, animals, plants, dreams, and stories that belonged to this piece of ground. I was romantic enough to accept and believe the mysticism of the Mesquakies. But it was still mysticism."[21]

The ways of nature include the spiritual world as well. The metaphysical influences the conscious mind via dreams and visions. American Indian activist, Russell Means, described the reality of Indian spirituality. He noted that "The grassy, gently rounded prairie hills descend almost to the river, nearly into what remains of Greenwood.

Many *Ihanktonwan* are buried here, their graves unmarked, lost forever in a final, loving embrace with their Grandmother. . . You may deny the existence of ghosts or spirits, and I will not quarrel with you. But drop your gaze to this tall grass, raise it again to the vast skies, free all your senses to explore the moment, and it is hard to walk these hills without feeling a presence, *something* that cannot be explained by Eurocentric reasoning."[22] The metaphysical is often among Indian people who believe and it holds the power to convince skeptics.

Often, the presence of the metaphysical, such as spirits, is not always good. Evil comes in the form of witches as N. Scott Momaday, Kiowa Pulitzer-winning author, described in his autobiography, *The Names*, about his young life at Jemez, New Mexico. He writes, "And on that same harrowing night I saw witches. Some children came to tell us that the witches were about. 'Come, we will show you,' they said, and they led us outside and pointed with their chins into the night. There, at ground level and far away, were lights, three or four, moving here and there, back and forth. The children watched very solemnly, without alarm, and I understood at once that they were not playing tricks; neither did they care one way or another what I thought of what I saw; only they imagined that I might find it interesting to see witches. You are deceived, I thought; there are men with flashlights, running around in the distance, that is all. But then one of the lights flew suddenly into the air and, like a shooting star, moved across the whole dome of the sky."[23]

In a similar way of spiritual belief, Peter MacDonald described the metaphysical world of the Diné. He said, "The request was based on our belief that all living things would share their spirit with the Navajo people. Some spirits are good, some are bad, and some are both good and bad. For example, the snake can be protective, but it can also be vicious, and thus it must be approached with great respect. Likewise the spider can be either protective or deadly. The positive characteristics of the spider emerge out of the legend surrounding the construction of the web. When an enemy was coming at the spider, the web could be woven very fast to stop the aggressor, much like a barbed wire fence. If a Navajo was going into battle, he might pray to the spirit of the spider for the ability to spin a web to stop his enemy. Against that power an attacking enemy would suddenly find himself helpless, as though tied up. The Navajo would not expect actually to see the web, only to have its protective power, provided by the spirit of the spider. . . Typically, a Navajo might take some corn pollen as a sacrifice to the spider. He might say something like this: 'I pray to you, spider spirit, that you will accept this sacrifice. And in return, I want your spirit to protect me from my enemy by the use of your web.'"[24]

MacDonald's personal belief in energy within all things is similar to the Muscogee "totality" of all things possessing spiritual energy. Some objects can come alive. Spiritual energy is all about the Earth, and it is meant to be respected. MacDonald said, "Everything we encountered was spiritual. Even enemies were filled with a spirit we had to identify, because identification allowed us to protect ourselves. . . We believed that encountering other tribes in peace or war contaminated us. We frequently engaged in trade with other tribes, an important act of commerce but one that exposed us to spirits that were dangerous for the Diné. As soon as we could after each encounter, we had a Squaw Dance, the important cleansing ceremony that rid us of the influence of the dangerous spirits. . . This was the custom most misunderstood by the Bureau of Indian Affairs. When I eventually went to the BIA school, there were square dances for the children that were intended to help us overcome our shyness. What the school officials did not understand was that touching a girl of the same clan, even though sex was not involved, meant that we would go blind or insane. It was part of an incest taboo. . . Touching someone who was not Navajo, including the white teachers of the BIA, meant that the person's spirit would contaminate us. The spirits of others were safe for them, but could mean death to the Navajo."[25]

This native belief also contains a devotion to family and community such that the "individual" is de-emphasized. A Natural Democracy exists of human beings, including flora and fauna, and the inclusion of the idea that physical creation such as a river, a meadow, a mountain, or a cloud also has a life and a spirit. Man is not above nature. All things are related. Within this Natural Democracy, the Creator made a universe from four elements: Earth, Fire, Water, and Wind. From these elements the Earth gives us life, the fire is the sun for light and warmth, water is the substance necessary for life also symbolized by blood, the air is the oxygen and is also the wind of a tornado or even a song carried on the wings of the wind. Many Indians believe in fate, and that certain things were meant to be since all of this is according to the Creator.

Native logic is guided by the metaphysical and physical forces of life, thinking from a communal perspective, and thinking in a circular philosophy. As nonlinear people, Indians are cyclical by nature. Their concept of time is that their stories via the oral tradition enliven the past, and that prophecies are told that bring the future back to the present in a time continuum. Day changing to night is a cycle as well as the full moon of a month repeating, additionally the seasons, and life itself are rotations of circles. What goes around, comes around. This is Indian reality; this is the thinking of traditional Indians. Native reality and identity are the two powerful themes here.

This reality collided with prejudiced white men who viewed Indians negatively. In regard to racism in schools, Russell Means remembered that "Mom had taught me to read and write at age four. At five, after we got to Huron, I was enrolled in school. Because my birthday is in November and I entered first grade at five, I was always a year younger than most kids in my classes. Also, until well into my teens, I was considered small for my age. Because of those two circumstances, I spent many years having to prove that I was just as tough as my class-mates. . . I attended an all-white school—very few Indians then lived in South Dakota's towns. I remember a redheaded woman, a teacher, telling me. 'You know, kid, you're never going to be *anything*. You're going to be just like the rest of them,' meaning Indian."[26] Russell Means continued to describe his difficult school experiences at Huron and he became aware of racism.

It is natural that an Indian mind would rebel against the linear way of doing things. It is a different kind of logic and it rebels when the linear way of teaching is forcefully imposed in the classroom. Many Indian children became sick at boarding schools. So far from home, many children died at the schools and never had a chance to return home to be buried. Sometimes their parents were informed in time for them to claim the body of their beloved child.

According to Russell Means, "American education has always seemed much like Christianity to me. It doesn't deal with reality. Aside from math, which is usually taught with logic, children are mostly taught to memorize the latest theory—a hypothesis based on what the powers have decided is 'true' at that moment. Of course, all those theories keep changing. Even the way most subjects are taught is illogical. Why should children be isolated by age group? I think that's insane. Why are students forced to sit in rows, looking at the backs of peoples's heads? America's educational system robs people of their individuality while training them to accept whatever the authorities dictate. Instead of learning to reason for themselves, children learn to obey—precisely the quality most valued by a society dependent on mass production. It's no surprise that so many children grow up to be fodder for the industrial machine. It's all they know how to do. I am a human being. Even in high school, I knew that I wanted to remain one, and that I didn't want to become part of a machine, replaced and discarded when I wore out."[27]

Russell Means described his dislike of public schools, yet he realized the importance of education. Means recalled that he "loathed" school, but he had a desire to learn. "I didn't want to end up with a job like my father's, coming home every night with grease under my fingernails," said Means. "My mother and Grandma Twinkle Star had instilled in me the value of an education. Even one of my junior-high teachers, whom I regard as a racist, had taught me to view education in a different way."[28]

Herman Viola, the biographer of U.S. Senator Ben Nighthorse Campbell of Colorado, described Campbell's rebellion against white education. With signs of promising intellect, Ben actually did not do well in high school. He did not get along with the system, and his grades reflected this problem. During his freshman, sophomore, and junior years, all records reflected a student not giving his best effort with ". . . no As, three Bs (art, shop drawing, and woodworking), a smattering of Cs, a preponderance of Ds, but only one F (in U.S. history)." An English teacher noted his lack of trying in the classroom, noting, "Makes no effort. Is conveniently absent when assignments are due." For whatever reasons, Campbell displayed the same effort in other courses. A second instructor evaluated Ben Campbell as good in character, but poor in work habits and class attitude. Gym class did not interest him as well, as the physical education instructor, who was also the assistant principal, noted that "Ben always has an excuse written out to get out of taking gym." She noted also that "I doubt that [he has] been ill so much but due to fact [his] Mother has T.B. [he] may be afraid to take chances."[29]

Ben Nighthorse Campbell described himself as a rebellious kid during those high school years. "I was probably the world's worst student," he said. "I was at odds with just about every teacher at Placer High School except those who taught art, shop, and physical education." Sylvia Besana, the physical education teacher disagreed. "He was Mr. Personality, a very pleasant young man. Why, he even took one of my advanced dance classes." The teacher called Ben a nice boy and not a serious troublemaker. Another teacher who saw merit in Ben was Mr. Gein, a shop teacher: "Born 100 yrs. Too late!" he noted on Ben's transcript in an entry dated June 1, 1950. "Should have been Dan'l Boone's pal. [Has] many abilities not appreciated by modern life or school. A fine boy." The only thing Campbell really enjoyed in school, he says, was art. "I had always done art as a child, and I began using my hands at a very early age. In fact, any toys I ever had I made myself."[30] Ben attributed his interest in art to his dad because he loved to make jewelry. Albert Campbell taught his son the beginning lessons in "shaping, soldering, and piercing metal."[31]

Reuben Snake remembered his difficult days in schools. It was somewhat like being in prison. The pressure was horrific. He said, "Sometimes I talked with my grandmother and relatives about the unpleasant experiences at school. They understood and they commiserated with us. But it was a white man's institution. We were there to be educated, so they said, 'Well, you just have to do what they tell you to do and don't get into trouble. . . Some older guys would get truly upset and frustrated with the system and would run away. And then the local law enforcement people would be informed that some Indian kids had run away from the school. They'd be out hunting them and when they brought them back they used to shave their heads. That was the punishment for running away, to be shaved bald-headed. . . That school was far more restrictive than any public school of today could be.'"[32]

Reuben Snake continued his critical view, saying, "Our teachers were puritanical. We could only have fun in a Christian way. For them, having a good time meant singing hymns. We had vespers every evening. At the vesper service one of the housemothers or teachers would read scripture to us and lead us in singing in Christian hymns such as 'The Old Rugged Cross,' 'Nearer My God to Thee,' and 'How Great Thou Art.' We learned all those hymns. We had to memorize all of them and were coached on how to sing them properly. At that time my favorite subject was reading. I developed a love for reading in that school. I'd pick up anything and read it. I enjoyed reading *Treasure Island* and all of Jack London's books about Alaska. And oh, *The Black Stallion*. That kind of storytelling was really interesting to me. I wasn't too hot in math. But English and History courses interested me. I used to contemplate about how we were taught in American History that George Washington was the father of our country. Whenever I saw a picture of George Washington I couldn't fathom how this White guy with his big nose and his powdered wig could be my father. Absolutely nothing about Native American cultures was taught. There was nothing Indian in our schooling."[33]

Next, Reuben Snake summarized his early education with the following memory. He said, "After we left the mission school in Neillsville we came back to Hastings, Minnesota. Our mother enrolled us in the local public school system. Of course, carrying the name 'snake' in a White society created a provocative situation, and we were often teased—both because we were Indians and because we had this weird name. So my sister and I were obliged to 'educate' a lot of White kids.

We had to give them a knuckle sandwich now and then so they would learn to respect our name. We had to go to 'Duke City' every now and then to defend our identity. We were friendly to everybody and the non-Indian kids were friendly toward us. People weren't openly racist. They were just ignorant. And once they came to know us, they realized that we weren't that much different than they were. And we'd go visit our White friends and they'd come over to our place. We had good relationships. My older brothers played on the local softball teams. They had White girlfriends. So we fit in fairly well with the non-Indian people living around us."[34]

A definite pattern describes many Indian students in high school. Struggling in public schools, Comanche activist and founder of Americans for Indian Opportunity (AIO), LaDonna Harris described her hardship. She said, "While growing up I always wanted to be a wife and a mother with a nice house. That was my great desire. As I got older, it changed somewhat, but I was never particularly ambitious—never wanted to be a professional person. I was probably inhibited by the fact that I am dyslexic and didn't believe that I could go on to higher education because I was so impaired. I limited myself for a long time. I knew I was smart, but I knew I had to do things in roundabout ways, rather than in ways everybody else did. That kept me from wanting to be a professional person. Secretaries weren't even in the Indian vocabulary. Just nurses and teachers. I became very ambitious through my husband, Fred Harris."[35]

Wilma Mankiller, former Chief of the Oklahoma Cherokees described her early education in white schools. She said, "I was uncomfortable. I felt stigmatized. I continually found myself alienated from the other students, who mostly treated me as though I had come from outer space. I was insecure, and the least little remark or glance would leave me mortified. That was especially true whenever people had to teach me something basic or elementary, such as how to use a telephone. I was convinced that they must think it odd to be teaching an eleven- or twelve-year old how to pick up a phone, listen for a tone, and then dial a number. . . In Daly City, [California] I was getting ready to enter the seventh grade. The thought of that depressed me a great deal. That meant having to meet more new kids. Not only did I speak differently than they did, but I had an unfamiliar name that the others ridiculed. We were teased unmercifully about our Oklahoma accents. My sister Linda and I still read out loud to each other every night to lose our accents. Like most young people everywhere, we wanted to belong. Also, there were changes going on inside me that I could not account for, and that troubled me very much. I was experiencing all the problems girls face when approaching the beginning of womanhood. I was afraid and did not know what to do. Besides having to deal with the internal changes, I was also growing like a weed and had almost reached my full adult height. People thought I was much older than twelve. I hated what was happening. I hated my body. I hated school. I hated the teachers. I hated the other students. Most of all, I hated the city."[36]

Mankiller continued describing her public school experience. She found it increasingly difficult to fit in with her non-Indian peers. "Most of the time," she said, "I was only going through the motions of attending classes. I was never much of a scholar, and I do not have many memories from my years in high school. Those I do have are not of much consequence. My grades range from A to F, depending on the subject and my level of interest. Science and math were my downfalls, but I had an affinity for English and literature courses. None of my teachers left enough impact for me even to remember their names. I was not much of a joiner. I did not go in for glee club or the yearbook staff or sports or any of the organizations except Junior Achievement. I did participate in that for a while, and liked it. . . Mostly, I went to the Indian Center. That is still my best teenage memory. Much more was going on at the center than ping-pong games and dance parties. It was in the early 60s, and change was in the air. A person could almost touch it. During that time, many people, including my friends and siblings and I, were aware of the currents of restlessness."[37]

Young native students like Phillip Martin, current Chief of the Mississippi Choctaws, were naive to the many tricks to get Indians students into boarding schools. Such schools were strange to the newcomer Indian children and too often there was a language barrier. In the case of Phillip Martin, his father died tragically by a car in 1937 when Phillip was eleven years old. The local BIA superintendent urged Phillip to attend the Cherokee boarding school in North Carolina. Phillip Martin said that the superintendent "hounded me so much I thought he was going to get a bonus if I went." The young Martin did not want to leave his family, and the superintendent promised him three or four times that he would buy Phillip new clothes if he went to the boarding school. Finally, Phillip agreed and entered the fifth grade, but discovered that the superintendent lied about buying him the clothes. Martin said, "Early on I learned that I couldn't trust government agents." The new school in North Carolina proved difficult as most of the students spoke Cherokee, but were not allowed to speak their native language. An English teacher took an interest in young Philip and taught him English. Phillip stayed for six years, and only visited his home in Mississippi once. After graduation in 1945, he joined the Air Force, following his two older brothers into the service in World War II. His brother, Raymond was killed in battle on April 20, 1945, another tragedy occurring in Phillip's life.[38]

In Hobbs, New Mexico, during his early life, native author, N. Scott Momaday, described his early years as a student. In his autobiography, *The Names*, he writes, "I was not much interested in the process of learning at school. I can only barely remember the sort of work that was put to us; it was a thing that was not congenial to my mind. The evil of recitation was real; I hated to be called upon. And even worse was the anticipation of it. I knew of no relief that was equal to that of the bell. My eyes were very weak, and I had about that time to wear eyeglasses. Eyeglasses conformed in no way at all to any notion that I had of myself, and I did away with them at every opportunity. . . My mother read to me, or she told me stories in which I had the leading part. And my father told me the old Kiowa tales. There were many times more exciting than anything I found at school; they, more than the grammars and arthmetics, [they] nourished the life of my mind."[39]

Given the vast differences between the mind of the American Indian and the mind of the linear American, what might be best for Indian people? For Indian students in public schools? In reality, American Indians and Indian students are in a transitional stage of finding their way into the mainstream educational system. They can no longer remain on their reservations and stay isolated from the rest of the world. N. Scott Momaday noted this transition of becoming educated in the white world. He noted, "it is imperative to consider that the Indian is, for the time being, better off in his own world than in another. It is the only world in which he has a fighting chance. Certainly the Indian cannot remain indefinitely isolated; that is neither possible nor desirable. When the Indian no longer needs the reservation, he will leave it of his own accord."[40] Indian students in high school faced a serious dilemma. They felt uncomfortable due to a curriculum that did not interest them since it reflected the teachings of linear-minded American culture, and their teachers expected them to perform and behave like other American students. This type of promoting Americanism was the colonized message for all schools and their students.

In his propaganda in the early twentieth century for "One America" of basic beliefs and similar values, President Theodore Roosevelt stated, "There is no room in this country for hyphenated Americanism.

... The one absolutely certain way of bringing this nation to ruin, of preventing all possibility of its continuing to be a nation at all, would be to permit it to become a tangle of squabbling nationalities."[41] The outspokenness of the president of the United States worked against the American Indian mind and the values of his or her people. Indigenous intellect came under renewed attack in the early years of the twentieth century and it did not relent. Indian minds and white teachers were at odds as the latter tried to change the native logic and ethos of young Indian minds.

Indian minds in white schools with white teachers experienced punishment for practicing Indian ways as proven in the boarding schools. The loss of native language almost within a single generation resulted with little regard for this tremendous loss of indigenous culture. The colonized effort to educate the Indian child and change the way he thought negatively impacted Indian students. Nonetheless many of them went on to become noted Indian leaders in modern Native American history like Charles Eastman. At the same time, white teachers and administrators underestimated the resilience of the native intellect. With all of the efforts, the students' mind could not be totally changed to white ways. As a result, the native students now saw things in a dual perspective, from their tribal view and from the white world, at least as much of it that they could understand. The national government, even with all of its boarding schools and teachers could not permanently change the Indian mind, as the students continued to think from a native perspective about ideas and new concepts introduced to them. Using their own logic to become a hybrid of their tribal way and the white way. Like a young Charles Eastman more than a hundred years ago, Indian children usually have white teachers and Indian parents want their children to do very well in school. It took until the 1960s for mainstream America to recognize and begin to accept the Indian voice in academia.

NOTES

1. Donald L. Fixico, "American Indian Minds in Public Schools," invited keynote presentation, California Content Standards and American Indian Civics and Government Symposium, Humboldt State University and DQ University, April 5–6, 2001.
2. Charles A. Eastman, *From the Deep Woods to Civilization: Chapter in the Autobiography of an Indian* (Lincoln: University of Nebraska Press, 1936), 21–23, originally published 1916.
3. Carole Barrett, Britton Barrett, and Marcia Wolter, "'You Didn't Dare Try to be Indian': Oral Histories of Former Indian Boarding School Students," *North Dakota His-*

tory, Vol. 64, No. 2, 1997, 4–25; Robert F. Jr. Berkhofer, "Model Zions for the American Indian," *American Quarterly*, Vol. 5, No. 2, Part 1 Summer 1963, 176–190; Sally J. Southwick, "Educating the Mind, Enlightening the Soul: Mission Schools as a Means of Transforming the Navajos, 1898–1928," *Journal of Arizona History*, Vol. 37, No. 1, 1996, 47–66; Frederick J. Stefon, "Richard Henry Pratt and His Indians," *Journal of Ethnic Studies*, Vol. 15, No. 2, 1987, 86–112; Michael G. Kenny, "A Place for Memory: The Interface Between Individual and Collective History," *Comparative Studies in Society and History*, Vol. 41, No. 3, 1999, 420–437; Amy Goodburn, "Literacy Practices at the Genoa Industrial Indian School," *Great Plains Quarterly*, Vol. 19, No. 1, Winter 1999, 35–52; and Jeffrey Hamley, "An Introduction to the Federal Indian Boarding School Movement," *North Dakota History*, Vol. 61, No. 2, 1994, 2–9. Major studies on the Indian boarding school experience include Basil H. Johnston, *Indian School Days* (Norman and London: University of Oklahoma Press, 1989); and see Henrietta Mann, *Cheyenne-Arapaho Education 1871–1982* (Niwot, CO: University Press of Colorado, 1997); Francis Paul Prucha, *The Churches and the Indian Schools 1888–1912* (Lincoln and London: University of Nebraska Press, 1979); Scott Riney, *The Rapid City Indian School 1898–1933* (Norman: University of Oklahoma Press, 1999); Clyde Ellis, *To Change Them Forever: Indian Education at the Rainy Mountain Boarding School* (Norman and London: University of Oklahoma Press, 1996); Donal F. Lindsey, *Indians at Hampton Institute, 1877–1923* (Urbana and Chicago: University of Illinois Press, 1995); Devon A. Mihesuah, *Cultivating the Rosebuds: The Education of Women at the Cherokee Female Seminary, 1851–1909* (Urbana and Chicago: University of Illinois Press, 1993); Jon Reyhner, ed., *Teaching American Indian Students* (Norman and London: University of Oklahoma Press, 1992); Michael C. Coleman, *American Indian Children at School, 1850–1930* (Jackson, MS: University Press of Mississippi, 1993), 1–230; David Wallace Adams, *Education for Extinction: American Indians and the Boarding-School Experience, 1875–1928* (Lawrence, KS: University Press of Kansas, 1995), 1–396; Margaret Connell Szarz, *Indian Education in the American Colonies, 1607–1783* (Albuquerque, NM: University of New Mexico Press, 1988), 1–333; Sally Hyer, *One House, One Voice, One Heart: Native American Education at the Santa Fe Indian School* (Santa Fe, NM: Museum of New Mexico Press, 1990), 1–108; and Robert A. Trennert, Jr., *The Phoenix Indian School; Forced Assimilation in Arizona, 1891–1935* (Norman: University of Oklahoma Press, 1988), 1–256.

4. Robert H. Keller, Jr., "American Indian Education: An Historical Context," *Journal of the West*, Vol. 13, No. 2, April 1974, 75–82; Margaret Connell Szasz, "Federal Boarding Schools and the Indian Child: 1920–1960," *South Dakota History*, Vol. 1, No. 4, Fall 1977, 371–384; Robert A. Trennert, " 'And the Sword Will Give Way to the Spelling Book': Establishing the Phoenix Indian School," *Journal of Arizona History*, Vol. 23, No. 1, Spring 1982, 35–58.

5. Eastman, *Deep Woods to Civilization*, 8.

6. Luther Standing Bear, *Land of the Spotted Eagle* (Lincoln: University of Nebraska Press, 1978, [originally published 1933]), 16–17.

7. Standing Bear, *Land of the Spotted Eagle*, 16–17.

8. Russell Means with Marvin J. Wolf, *Where White Men Fear to Tread: The Autobiography of Russell Means* (New York: St. Martin's Press, 1995), 18; and see Mary Lou Hultgren and Paulette Molin Fairbanks, " 'Long Rides Across the Plains': Fort Berthold Students at Hampton Institute," *North Dakota History*, Vol. 61, No. 2, 1994, 10–36.

9. Means with Wolf, *Where White Men Fear to Tread*, 18.

10. Jay C. Fikes, *Reuben Snake, Your Humble Serpent: Indian Visionary and Activist* (Santa Fe, NM: Clear Light Publishers, 1996), 49. For further discussion on the punishment at Indian boarding schools, see Michael C. Coleman, "The Mission Education of Francis La Flesche: An American Indian Response to the Presbyterian Boarding School in the 1860s," *American Studies in Scandinavia [Norway]*, Vol. 18, No. 2, 1986,

67–82 and Robert A. Trennert, "Corporal Punishment and the Politics of Indian Reform," *History of Education Quarterly*, Vol. 29, No. 4, Winter 1989, 595–617.

11. Dorothy R. Parker, *Singing An Indian Song: A Biography of D'Arcy McNickle* (Lincoln: University of Nebraska Press, 1992), 20.
12. Means with Wolf, *Where White Men Fear to Tread*, 13.
13. Ibid.
14. Ibid., 14.
15. Ibid.
16. Peter MacDonald with Ted Schwarz, *The Last Warrior: Peter MacDonald and the Navajo Nation* (New York: Orion Books, 1993), 16.
17. Ibid., 17.
18. Ibid.
19. Ibid., 48–49.
20. Standing Bear, *Land of Spotted Eagle*, xv.
21. Fred McTaggart, *Wolf That I Am: In Search of the Red Earth People* (Norman: University of Oklahoma Press, 1984), 107.
22. Means with Wolf, *Where White Men Fear to Tread*, 4.
23. N. Scott Momaday, *The Names: A Memoir* (New York: Harper & Row Publishers, 1976), 136.
24. MacDonald with Schwarz, *The Last Warrior*, 22.
25. Ibid., 24–25.
26. Means with Wolf, *Where White Men Fear to Tread*, 25.
27. Ibid., 49–50.
28. Ibid., 57.
29. Herman J. Viola, *Ben Nighthorse Campbell: An American Warrior* (New York: Orion Books, 1993), 30.
30. Ibid.
31. Ibid.
32. Fikes, *Reuben Snake*, 50. Also see Wilbert H. Ahern, "An Experiment Aborted: Returned Indian Students in the Indian School Service, 1881–1908," *Ethnohistory*, Vol. 44, No. 2, Spring 1997, 263–304; and Scott Riney, "Education by Hardship: Native American Boarding Schools in the U.S. and Canada," *Oral History Review*, Vol. 24, No. 2, Winter 1997, 117–123.
33. Fikes, *Reuben Snake*, 54.
34. Ibid., 59.
35. LaDonna Harris with Henrietta H. Stockel, *LaDonna Harris: A Comanche Life* (Lincoln: University of Nebraska Press, 2000), 28.
36. Wilma Mankiller and Michael Wallis, *Mankiller: A Chief and Her People* (New York: St. Martin's Press, 1993), 103.
37. Ibid., 115.
38. Peter J. Ferrara, *The Choctaw Revolution: Lessons for Federal Indian Policy* (Washington, D.C.: Americans for Tax Reform Foundation, 1998), 49–50.
39. N. Scott Momaday, *The Names: A Memoir by N. Scott Momaday* (New York: Harper and Row Publishers, 1976), 88.
40. Matthias Schubnell, *N. Scott Momaday: The Cultural and Literary Background* (Norman: University of Oklahoma Press, 1985), 9, originally quoted in N. Scott Momaday, "The Morality of Indian Hating," *Ramparts*, Vol. 3, No. 1, Summer 1964, 29–40.
41. *Quotations from Our Presidents* (Mount Vernon, NY: The Peter Pauper Press, 1969), 40.

6
RISE OF AMERICAN INDIAN STUDIES

"With us the circle stands for the togetherness of people who sit with one another around the campfire, relatives, friends united in peace while the pipe passed from hand to hand. The camp in which every tipi had its place was also a ring. The tipi was a ring in which people sat in a circle and all the families in the village were in turn circles within a larger circle, part of the larger hoop which was the seven campfires of the Sioux, representing one nation. The nation was only a part of the universe, in itself circular and made of the earth, which is round, of the sun, which is round, of the stars, which are round. The moon, horizon, the rainbow—circles within circles, with no beginning and no end."[1]

John Lame Deer, Lakota, ca. 1972

* * *

The origin of American Indian studies started during chaos in America. The 1960s provided good timing, but the need for American Indian studies had been argued by native peoples and their supporters since the early decades of the twentieth century. The need for the expression of concerns and issues about American Indians by learning about their history and culture became clear to the mainstream and to academia from the protesting of various ethnic groups. During the 1960s, an American Indian studies movement began with programs offering a few courses to meet the need of Native American students. By the end of the twentieth century, one source reported 112 American Indian studies programs, departments, or centers in colleges and universities in the U.S. and Canada. At the dawn of the twenty-first century, American Indian studies continues to thrive and it is multiple in expressions as another form of traditional knowledge. Programs, departments, centers, and institutes teach and research American Indians as a field in academia.

Indians are still of popular interest to the American mainstream society. Recent scholarship and interest in American Indians is flourishing and people want to know more about Native Americans. Since the 1980s, movies like *Smoke Signals* (1999) and earlier films like *The Last of the Mohicans* (1992) and *Dances with Wolves,* (1990) along with the writings of native scholars such as Sherman Alexie, N. Scott Momaday, Leslie Silko, and others have accelerated public interest in Indians. Throughout the United States and in many foreign countries, curious people want to know more about American Indians.

Such public interest developed in the 1980s in spite of Reaganomics and insensitive bureaucrats such as former Secretary of the Interior James Watts, who placed little significance on Indians. This type of federal thinking cut budgets of government-supported Indian programs for the benefit of the rest of the country. The momentum of Indian interests in the 1980s and 1990s carried forward from the hard-fought times of the 1960s and 1970s when an earlier generation of Indian scholars and non-Indian scholars risked their careers and sometimes their lives in speaking against the U.S. government and standing up for American Indian rights.

The decade of the 1960s witnessed radical changes in America. Bell bottoms, the peace sign, Jimi Hendrix, marijuana, Janis Joplin, the invasion of the Beatles in 1964, the Rolling Stones, the New Left, underground protest groups, Vietnam, Civil Rights Movement, NAACP, John Kennedy, LBJ, and more issues and iconic figures symbolized this era. The American Indian conference held in Chicago in 1961, rise of the National Indian Youth Council (NIYC), Indian fish-ins in Washington state, beginning in 1964, the founding of the American Indian Movement in 1968, Red Power, and the Alcatraz takeover in 1969 ushered in a new era of Native American deconstruction and reaction to begin a burgeoning generation of Native American studies and Indian self-determination.

Following the end of the radical 1960s, three provocative books about Indians appeared on the shelves of book stores. These three pertinent books influenced the following decades and provided food for thought, causing a renaissance of scholars and students ready to study Native Americans. These emotionally charged books—Dee Brown's *Bury My Heart at Wounded Knee* (1971), Vine Deloria, Jr.'s *Custer Died for Your Sins: An Indian Manifesto* (1968), and N. Scott Momaday's *House Made of Dawn* (1968) captured the attention of anyone interested or concerned about American Indians. In 1969 Momaday's *House Made of Dawn* won the Pulitzer Prize for literature, the only work written thus far by a Native American to be awarded the Pulitzer. Yet, these three books represented native points of view, and informed the public profoundly that Indians were people too and that they had thoughts of their own, and ideas, dreams, and ambitions. These timely publications changed many people's minds about Indians and frequently drew the attention of some linear thinkers for the first time.

A large part of this scholarly current to study American Indians derived from the political movements of Black Power, Brown Power, and Red Power. Civil rights for minorities and equal rights for women expressed during political protests and activism caused society and institutions of higher learning to reconsider the status and past written histories of ethnic groups and women. The 1960s represented pivotal changes in American society as people contemplated their own lives and the values of the mainstream society and the dominant culture.

Until the 1960s, the mainstream society had refused to listen to or learn from Native Americans. Only a small undercurrent of individuals—students, writers, and scholars, and Indian people continued public interest in Native Americans. Naturally, this rejection by the mainstream provoked the title of Vine Deloria, Jr.'s rhetorical book, *We Talk; You Listen: New Tribes, New Turf.* From an Indian point of view, Deloria predicted in 1972 in this book that "American society is unconsciously going Indian. Moods, attitudes, and values are changing. People are becoming more aware of their isolation even while they continue to worship the rugged individualist who needs no one. The self-sufficient man is casting about for a community to call his own. The glittering generalities and mythologies of American society no longer satisfy the need and desire to belong."[2] The undercurrent of Indian studies had reached an opening, and began to draw the interest of the American public inside this movement to learn about Indians. Following *We Talk; You Listen*, Vine Deloria, Jr. wrote *God Is Red* (1974). In this provocative work, he pointed out that Native Americans identified with place rather than time, unlike white men, and that Indians galvanized toward group identity rather than individuality. Undoubtedly, Americans searched for security in various ways and forms, even looking to Native Americans because of their traditional values of communalism and environmental relationship with the Earth. Due to the self-examining society of the 1960s, people began asking questions about their inner selves, wondering who they were, while many of them entered libraries and archives for the first time to research their roots. They needed something to identify with, and to bring balance into their lives. Many people looked toward Indians and nature for answers. The words of Lame Deer, that people were a part of a circle rang true, that things happen in circles, and that now the white man wanted to learn from the Indian.

Timing proved to be germane to the powerful influence during the 1960s as people needed a link to the past. Turning to Indians, more people began to read the words of Deloria and other books about Indians such as Dee Brown's *Bury My Heart at Wounded Knee*, but their books shocked them, revealing the country's mistreatment of Native Americans. This was not unique; in a similarly stunning way, another book was published ninety years earlier—Helen Hunt Jackson's *A Century of Dishonor* (1881)—an exposé that alerted the public to the plight of the American Indian.[3] As a result of Indian activism in the late 1960s and early 1970s, plus the writings about Indians, journalists, writers, and scholars began to offer new ideas and theories. They introduced new ways to look at their subjects through a broader context and with open minds. Until the 1960s, the dominant society had maintained strict control over learning, forcing Western linear thinking into the minds of Indian students at boarding schools and missionary schools, while public schools berated the ways of Native Americans and demeaned them as inferior to white ways. Inexperienced mainstream teachers continued to colonize the minds of Indian youth with their Amerocentrism as the only way to learn. Decades and generations ignored the native perspective until the unleashing of the 1960s.

In his introduction to *Bury My Heart at Wounded Knee*, Dee Brown wrote, ". . . I have tried to fashion a narrative of the conquest of the American West as the victims experienced it, using their own words whenever possible. Americans who have always looked westward when reading about this period should read this book facing eastward. . . . This is not a cheerful book, but history has a way of intruding upon the present, and perhaps those who read it will have a clearer understanding of what the American Indian is, by knowing what he was."[4] From where one stood physically for this reading was important in order for non-Indians to realize what it might feel like for America to be invaded by a foreign power.

Indians became victims in the words of Dee Brown, but they also became people. By no means did Brown's book convince writers and scholars to write about Indians; American Indians have always remained a popular topic among many readers. But Dee Brown's book reintroduced Indians in a different way—it humanized them.

In 1970, a decade began with numerous books continuing to be published about Indians. In that year, a sum of thirteen Indian books, and probably more, appeared in print. These works included Anson Bert, *The Miami Indians;*[5] Robert C. Carriker, *Fort Supply Indian Territory: Frontier Outpost on the Plains;*[6] Angie Debo, *A History of the Indians of the United States;*[7] Arthur H. DeRosier Jr., *The Removal of the Choctaw Indians;*[8] Richard Ellis, *General Pope and U.S. Indian Policy;*[9] Jess C. Epple, *Custer's Battle of the Washita and a History of the Plains Indian Tribes;*[10] John Philip Reid, *A Law of Blood: The Primitive Law of the Cherokee Nation;*[11] Anthony F. C. Wallace, *The Death and Rebirth of the Seneca: The History and Culture of the Great Iroquois Nation, Their Destruction and Demoralization, and their Cultural Revival at the Hands of the Indian Visionary, Handsome Lake;*[12] Thurman Wilkins, *Cherokee Tragedy: The Story of the Ridge Family and the Decimation of a People;*[13] and Ellen M. Whitney, ed., *The Black Hawk War: 1831–1832, Vol. 1.*[14]

The following year in 1971 with *Bury My Heart at Wounded Knee* in the bookstores, Hazel Hertzberg published *The Search for an American Indian History: Modern Pan-Indian Movements,*[15] thereby indicating that social, cultural, and political history of a minority was important enough to write about, especially in the twentieth century. Other noted books of the early 1970s involving Native Americans that are on book shelves include Francis Paul Prucha, ed., *The Indian in American History* (1971); Joseph G. Jorgensen, *The Sun Dance Religion: Power for the Powerless* (1972); Richard Slotkin, *Regeneration Through Violence: The Mythology of the American Frontier, 1600–1860* (1973);[16] Bernard Sheehan, *Seeds of Extinction: Jeffersonian Philanthropy and the American Indian* (1973);[17] and Red Fox, *Memoirs of Chief Red Fox* (1972).[18]

Although these important books on Indians enabled a growing interest in American Indians, and more books appeared on the horizon; *Bury My Heart at Wounded Knee* had articulated an Indian voice, an Indian version of the history of the American West. Rediscovering the "Indian voice" occurred with Virginia Irving Armstrong, *I Have Spoken: American History Through the Voices of the Indians* (1971);[19] W. C. Vanderwerth, *Indian Oratory: Famous Speeches Told By Noted Indian Chieftains* (1971);[20] Joseph Cash and Herbert Hoover, eds., *To Be An Indian: An Oral History* (1971);[21] and Joseph Epes Brown, ed., *The Sacred Pipe: Black Elk's Account of the Seven Rites of the Oglala Sioux* (1971).[22] These works did not experience the same astonishing success as *Bury My Heart at Wounded Knee,* but they had opened the door and invited curious readers to hear the voices of American Indians. Black

Elk lived again. His words of circular philosophy seemed prophetic about the Indian and white man. The general public, students and scholars were keenly interested in what Indians thought about the history of Indian–white relations. Meanwhile the National Indian Youth Council (NIYC) and the American Indian Movement (AIM) expressed a contemporary Indian voice of multiple opinions during the early 1970s. The First Convocation of Indian Scholars convened in 1970 in California, and the second convocation occurred the following year.

Philosophical interests developed simultaneously with Indian activism and Native American militancy. Indian activists protested that colleges and universities offered very little about American Indians, or incorrect information in their college courses. Non-Indians, too, began to embrace the opportunity to study Native Americans to see the courses they had to offer. This interest in Indian curriculum was not new, rather a renaissance of Native American interest had been born, and a genre of literature with increasing demands. Writings and scholarship changed, and new sources and inspiration pursued answers and insights into the American Indian mind that the linear society had failed to provide.

Due to the emergence of Native American Studies programs, the momentum carried over into the 1970s decade. Even history as an academic discipline began to reexamine its basic approach. In an article, "American Historians and the Idea of National Character: Some Problems and Prospects," historian David Stannard wrote about the American search for national character as a means for writing history, and that historians were looking toward the behavioral sciences as a way of writing history.[23] New ideas about writing history entered the discipline, but the old premise of disregarding Native Americans and other minorities prevailed.

In the early 1970s, the history discipline as practiced by mainstream historians refused to make Native Americans a true part of American history. Simultaneously, the Indian struggled for his place in other academic disciplines as well. In 1970, native scholar Jeanette Henry reprimanded the history profession and American society for denying Native Americans a proper place in the written history of this country. She critically stated, ". . . that every dominant political class in any society attempts to control the ideology of the people most particularly through the learning process in the schools. It is not to be wondered at that 'this' American society does the same. The school boards and curriculum commissions which control the adoption and purchase of textbooks usually adopt books to support the dominant political class.

So, too, do the professors in universities, [and] departments of various disciplines."[24]

During such times of civil rights protests, Indian activism, and AIM militancy, Indian academic warriors like Jeanette Henry and others took on the academic disciplines at various forums of academic conferences, in journals, books, and all forms of the printed word. The number of such warriors was small, drawing from a rank of less than 200 Native Americans holding Ph.D.s by the mid 1970s. This group of academic warriors, which included outspoken Native Americans without doctorates, naturally polarized American academia and Native Americans. The turf battle of the American Indian Movement against the United States had been extended to academia. Leading this Indian attack was Vine Deloria, Jr., whose prolific pen rolled out powerful books as previously mentioned. Deloria's chapter on "Anthropologists and Other Friends" in *Custer Died For Your Sins* became a volleying point for heated discussions, charging writers and scholars who exploited Indians for personal gains and misrepresented Native Americans and their cultures. Deloria insulted anthropologists by writing in his flaming chapter that some people are cursed with plagues and bad luck, "But . . . Indians have anthropologists."[25]

In the middle of the battlefield, native scholars like the late Alfonso Ortiz attempted to reform his own anthropology profession by reexamining Indians and treating them more respectfully. Ortiz realized in one of his writings that he had "taken a position, fully mindful of the dangers of being shot at from both sides." Ortiz observed, ". . . that anthropology is a science born of imperialists and colonial powers and that, at best, all too many of its practioners still approach their tribal and peasant subjects with a neo-colonist attitude."[26] He noted that there were too few Indian scholars to help turn the tide at this time in 1970. Conditions called for a stronger Indian academic voice if indeed, academia aimed to revise its paternalistic views of Native Americans.

Sensitive and open-minded non-Indian scholars began to involve cultural studies in their writings about Native Americans. Hence, cross-cultural studies and cross-disciplinary works became the nature of a growing number of written works. Attempting to understand Indian culture, environment, and community became essential in order to understand Native Americans. This approach, combined with academia contemplating new ideas and theories, urged a reconsideration of the previous means of examining history and the Indian and other minorities.

In 1970, the *Western Historical Quarterly* produced its first issue. The following year, the sixth president of the Western Historical Association, Robert Utley, assessed the field and changes in western history amidst societal changes resulting from the 1960s. He wrote, "Indeed, I shall be surprised if western studies do not gain new life from the intellectual and social ferment now troubling the nation. As attitudes, beliefs, assumptions, and traditions of American life come increasingly under scrutiny, stereotypes begin to disintegrate. . . Does not the current obsession with minority and ethnic studies suggest unplowed western fields? Scholars are already beginning to till these fields . . ."[27]

As an example of Utley's warning, in 1971 Doubleday published William Loren Katz's *The Black West*, a documentary and pictorial history.[28] Seth M. Schultz and Tilden G. Edelstein edited *The Black Americans: Interpretative Readings.*[29] The third edition of Morris U. Schappes's edited book, *A Documentary History of the Jews in the United States, 1654–1875*, reappeared in print.[30] Leonard Dinnerstein published his edited book, *Antisemitism in the United States* in 1971.[31] *The Black Scholar* produced its first issue in November 1969, and other African-American publications appeared such as the *Journal of Black Studies* with its first publication in 1970. The *Journal of Ethnic Studies* released its first issue in the spring of 1973. Other minority journals and publications followed throughout the decade and afterward such as the *Ethnic Forum*, which produced its first issue in the summer of 1981.

In 1971 the late president of the Newberry Library, Lawrence Towner, and other key individuals conceived of the idea to establish a center in the library for studying the history of American Indians. Towner wanted Indian involvement and he contacted D'Arcy McNickle, a Flathead Indian studying anthropology, who had also studied at Oxford University. In September 1972, the Center for the History of the American Indian opened its doors for business with a supporting grant from the National Endowment for the Humanities, the Newberry Library, and eleven supporting universities.[32] D'Arcy McNickle became the first Director of the Center with many scholars becoming research fellows studying Native Americans over the years. During September 12–13, 1997, the McNickle Center celebrated its twenty-fifth year of researching and studying American Indians.

American Indians live in their own way, ever since their people came into existence, and this has been their purpose in life. The human need to express itself in its own particular way has been the "Indian way," according to the 562 federally recognized Native American tribes and other Indian communities. Native Americans exist according to their particular identity and heritage, and this need for freedom of expression involves culture, political concerns, religion, and intellectualism. Although American Indians have sought self-determination since the 1960s, a dominant control of the media, text-book productions, film industry, and the majority of publications suppressed the advancement of Indian people and their communities throughout Indian Country.

A "natural sovereignty" for Indian people has meant that all native communities possessed a heritage of freedom. Indian or tribal communities acknowledged other groups, although intertribal relations also involved warfare. Peaceful alliances and understandings between Indian groups were desired. However, hostilities among Indian people did occur.

A native identity is based on desired segregation from other peoples and their natural right to pursue their own way of life. This is done on reservations throughout Indian Country and in urban Indian areas in most major cities where Native Americans have survived the relocation program of the 1950s and 1960s. More than two-thirds of the total Indian population lives in urban areas, thus Indian Country consists of reservations and urban Indian communities with Los Angeles being the largest urban Indian area.

A history of struggle is common to all nations, and American Indian tribal nations have certainly had this experience. Their effort has been one against European imperialism and the United States. The invasions of these foreign nations have defeated and suppressed Native Americans, and in cases, annihilated Indian people. Euro-American colonization has a history of moving beyond building homesteads and clearing the land for crops. In addition, this colonization experience has been one of deliberate destruction of Native Americans and their culture. In the first 400 years of contact attempts toward coexistence did not work out, and the Indian nations fell before the Euro-American colonization after patriotic resistance in every region of the country.

Aside from attempts of genocide, particularly in the nineteenth century, the survival of Native Americans even against overwhelming odds compelled the United States to assimilate Indian people into the ideological "melting pot." Simultaneously, in order to accomplish this assimilation or desegregation, the United States government and its military sought to suppress the native intellectualism of Indian people. With biased scientific evidence in the late 1800s and attempting to justify the American experience through Frederick Jackson Turner's "frontier thesis," America sought to subordinate Native Americans to a lower level.

Even after the turn of the twentieth century, an insecure American culture believed it necessary to deem Native American knowledge and native intellectualism to be inferior. Undoubtedly, this type of racist intellectualism on the part of mainstream America had not been fully addressed before. The general denial of Indian intellect continued through the early decades of the century. Due to the conservativism of the Eisenhower era of the 1950s, a backlash against this kind of ideology provoked an experimentation with liberalism during the next ten years, and afterward. Native Americans continued to look for themselves in textbooks and in forms of the media. In the early twentieth century, Native Americans had virtually disappeared, and simply were not needed by Turnerian historians to explain the grand history of this country called America. In general, the Indian voice remained lost, except for a handful of writings. Anthropologists studied Indians, writers wrote about Indian wars, and several historians wrote books about Indians.

Following World War II, public interest in Indians began to speak out for more books and college courses about Native Americans. More Indians attended college in the 1950s and an Indian presence emerged on college campuses with the chaotic 1960s. In 1968 a Shoshone–Bannock Indian student enrolled at University of California, Berkeley. Like the boarding school experiences, this sounded familiar, but this was at a leading university, which was among the first schools to introduce American Indian studies. She expressed her frustration at finding her place in the white man's world. She said, "It's hard for me to go to college and eventually be assimilated and never be able to relate to the American Indian and their problems. I feel they're trying to make me into a white person. . . . There is little opportunity to learn anything about my own history. I've tried to take courses in history at the University. I can't find out anything about my people."[33] In 1968, only 181 Native Americans had graduated from college. Twenty years later in 1988 and in 1989, 3,954 Indian students had received bachelor's degrees with 1,086 receiving master's degrees, and 85 graduate students had earned doctorates.[34]

Until the late 1960s, postmodern America continued to move forward with increasingly less interest in American Indians, leaving the issue up to Indians to fight for Indian education. As American Indians were seldom in the path of the daily concerns of the federal government and public concerns, colleges and universities and Indian communities remained as the sources of activity to advance the interests of America's original people. An increasingly curious American public and our nation's leaders needed to be educated about Indian people and Indian issues and concerns. President Lyndon B. Johnson responded sensitively and politically to the concerns of Native Americans and their problems when he gave his "Forgotten American" speech in 1968. In actuality, LBJ proved to be more understanding of Native Americans and their circumstances than his popular predecessor, John F. Kennedy. Following Johnson's Indian reform efforts through the controversial Indian Civil Rights Act of 1968, Richard Nixon continued presidential support of Native Americans.

In 1972, the Indian Education Act authorized public school educational programs for American Indian and Alaskan Native children, and adult-education projects, and the Department of Education provided an Office of Indian Education, thus acknowledging the majority of Indian youth who attended public schools. In addition, the Bureau of Indian Affairs funded educational programs for Native Americans, especially youth enrolled in BIA schools.[35] In 1970 President Richard Nixon called for an end to the termination policy of the 1950s and 1960s and the Kennedy Report of 1969 disclosed an increased need for culturally relevant Indian education. Furthermore, Indian action, especially the militancy of AIM, demanded a new federal Indian policy during the early years of Nixon's presidency. In January 1975, President Gerald Ford signed the Indian Self-Determination and Education Assistance Act. A new federal Indian policy of Indian Self-Determination authorized the development of Indian education and other reform programs. Programs and private foundations like the Ford Foundation and Donner Foundation believed it their task, too, to encourage more Native Americans to earn graduate degrees. Additional granting foundations like Ford and Rockefeller supported the studies about American Indians.

The last decade of the twentieth century witnessed a movement in American Indian intellectualism. In a postmodern America, Indian intellectualism should have been allowed to be expressed. Conservative academic attitudes suppressed or ignored the opportunity for Native American expression, thought, and ideas. Should not American Indian intellectuals have the same right as other intellectuals to express their ideas, philosophies, and theories? Should not American Indian people have the same opportunities to obtain a college education and to succeed as other Americans?

Teaching and discussing Native American studies became important concerns in the late 1960s and 1970s. An American Indian curriculum of courses began with an introduction to American Indian studies, and also offered more related courses for undergraduates. Separate ethnic studies programs began to emerge on college campuses, and the study of American Indians experienced a renaissance.

In 1968, San Francisco State University became the first college to establish a Native American Studies program, which was a partial springboard for the occupation of Alcatraz. Few people know that the first official Indian studies program was attempted at the University of Oklahoma in 1914 when Senator Robert Owen of Oklahoma introduced a resolution in Congress, calling for an Indian Studies Department at the University of Oklahoma. Nothing resulted from Owen's efforts. Another effort in 1937 at the University of Oklahoma also failed.[36] The idea for an American Indian Studies program was premature until after World War II, and better political timing.

In addition to San Francisco State University in 1968, American Indian studies programs emerged at the University of Minnesota; the University of California, Berkeley; and later at the University of California, Los Angeles.[37] They became the flagships of Indian studies in the United States.[38] Less known is the fact that the American Indian Institute began at the University of South Dakota in 1949.

At the University of Minnesota, a committee on American Indian Affairs was formed at the school, and it released its report two years later stating that no native people could be found on the university staff. The report also called for scholarships for Indian students, counseling, tutorials, and other supportive services. A small Indian Affairs Center was formed in 1967 by the Training Center for Community Programs under Professor Arthur Harkins. An Upward Bound program developed and in the fall of 1968 the American Indian Students Association began talks with the University of Minnesota about American Indian Studies, especially after African-American students occupied an administration building and succeeded in forming a black studies program.[39]

In 1969, Trent University in Ontario, Canada, created the first native studies program in Canada.[40] These programs set the precedent for more. Due to the establishing of Native American studies, programs and departments began to develop and flourish during the 1970s. By 1985, 107 colleges and universities had either a program or department of American Indian studies. Many were a part of an ethnic studies program or a unit of an anthropology department. Eighteen Native American studies programs or departments offered majors, and forty of these offered minors.[41] For example, a student could obtain a Ph.D. in the Ethnic Studies Department at the University of California, Berkeley, but Native American studies was under the umbrella of ethnic studies.

By 1995, six Native American Studies units offered graduate programs, including the University of California, Berkeley; the University of Arizona, the University of California, Los Angeles; and Montana State University. Harvard University has a graduate program in American Indian Education, and the University of California at Riverside offers a Ph.D. in Native American Studies.[42] In 1996, the American Indian Studies Program at the University of Arizona announced the end of a seven-year struggle to form the first doctoral program in American Indian studies. With seven core faculty, who are Native Americans, and with a total of 19 faculty participating in the program, American Indian studies at the University of Arizona has set an important new precedent.[43]

By 1976 an estimated 76,000 American Indians had attended accredited colleges and universities. By 1984 some 82,672 Native Americans were enrolled in colleges and universities. Sixty percent of the latter number attended two-year community colleges.[44] The teaching philosophy of Black Elk continued during the 1980s, and American Indian studies was encouraged by the zealous writings of Vine Deloria and growing interests in American Indian literature. On a personal note, when I taught as a visiting professor at San Diego State University in 1984–1985, four separate classes were reading *Black Elk Speaks* in different departments.

The need for more visibility of Native American studies and the other ways of academic advancement is imperative to educate a growing ignorance among other minorities and mainstream Americans about Native Americans and their many diverse cultures. Carter Blue Clark, a Muscogee Creek historian and former Executive Vice-President at Oklahoma City University, stated that "American Indian Studies is trapped in . . . [a] cultural dilemma. . . . American Indian Studies fits no standard academic mold. American Indian Studies is by its nature interdisciplinary. . . . American Indians are unique, and so is their discipline. They stand alone among all of the other ethnic groups because of their history, which involves treaties, tribalism, and other aspects that set them apart."[45]

Another expression of American Indian intellectualism has been via publications in a dozen or more Native American journals. In the mid 1990s, a variety of articles about Native Americans was published in *Akwekon* (1984 Cornell University), *American Indian Culture and Research Journal* (UCLA 1974), *American Indian Education Journal* (at Arizona State University), *American Indian Law Journal* (1975, at the Institute for the Development of Indian Law, Washington, D.C.), *American Indian Law Review* (University of Oklahoma 1973), *American Indian Quarterly* (started in 1974, previously at University of California, Berkeley, currently at Northern Arizona University and published by University of Nebraska Press), *Canadian Journal of Native Studies, Journal of Alaska Native Arts* (1984 at the Institute of Alaska Native Arts, Fairbanks, Alaska), *Journal of Navajo Education* (1983 at Round Rock School at Chinle, Arizona and ceased publication), *Native Studies Review* in Canada, *Tribal College Journal,* and *Wiscazo Sa Review* (1985 at Eastern Washington University).[46] The *Journal of Tribal College: Journal of American Indian Higher Education* began publication during the summer of 1989. The majority of these journals are peer judged and externally refereed. Due to the diversity of Native Americans and their multiple interests, more Indian journals are needed. Yet, human and financial resources are required to operate the necessary number of quality journals as needed by American Indian and non-Indian scholars to publish their works. As a result, the majority of publications appear as single articles in issues of mainstream law journals or ethnic studies journals.

American Indian identity in academia requires increased attention and action. In 1985, Blue Clark stated, "Interest in American Indians will continue as a result of the historic legacy of manifest destiny, yearning for family roots, and a lingering romantic attachment to the glories of a bygone era. The necessities of earning a living with marketable skills will not lessen the need to maintain Indian cultural ties and to learn more about one's Indianness through American Indian studies. Even though some of the attributes of Indian studies will alter with changing demands from society and administrators, American Indian studies will continue to offer insights into America's unique culture and heritage. The basic mission of American Indian studies is to educate and enlighten all students about the diverse and rich cultures that make up American Indian life."[47]

Perhaps it is even sadder that the future of Native American studies and the hope to graduate more American Indians are in the hands of non-Indians who cannot give the same attention that they commit to other minority groups and the mainstream. American Indian studies and Native Americans suffer from the overwhelming concerns and numbers of other minorities and mainstream populations. Throughout all college campuses in the country, the number of Indian students and faculty and administrators are a mere fraction in comparison to the mainstream. American Indians are the smallest minority in numbers in comparison to other minority groups.

This sociocultural alienation is still felt by Native Americans attending colleges and universities even after more than twenty-five years since the beginning of American Indian studies. This individual isolation persists in feeling separated from one's family and one's community. Attempting to form friendships with students of different cultures and different class backgrounds has been observed as an obstacle for Native American students to succeed in college. Since cultural isolation has caused Indian students to drop out of college, this is a strong argument for developing American Indian studies.[48] Charles Eastman, Carlos Montezuma, Lori Alvord, and others have succeeded in the white man's schools, but why were there not sufficient curricula about American Indians for their interests when they went to college?

As an increasing number of books and articles are being written about Native Americans, it is opportunistic and imperative for colleges and universities to offer courses about Native Americans. American Indian studies programs and departments are crucial to defining and shaping the ever growing field of native studies. Originally starting from ethnographic descriptions by travelers, military officers, and early anthropologists, Indian academia was established. Furthermore, the erroneous portrayal of Indians by frontier historians and Western writers sustained an interest in writing "about" Indians. In the late twentieth century, the scholarship of native studies began to be studied for its developmental, methodological approaches of cross disciplines while not neglecting the importance of the oral traditions and oral histories and the perspectives of Indians and their world views.

American Indian studies is coming to fruition, fulfilling the needs of tribes, Indian students, Indian scholars, non-Indian students, mainstream scholars, and public interest. Cheryl Crazy Bull, Sicangu Lakota educator, stated, "We, as tribal people, want research and scholarship that preserves, maintains, and restores our traditions and cultural practices. We want to restore our Native languages; preserve and develop our homelands; revitalize our traditional religious practices; regain our health; and cultivate our economic, social, and governing systems. Our [own] research can help us maintain our sovereignty and preserve our nationhood."[49]

In these early years of the twenty-first century, Indian gaming and repatriation are like a catalyst driving the importance of American Indian studies. The forum for a louder voice of American Indian studies will increase, and it has caused a new generation of American Indian studies programs. Indian scholars, tribal attention, and state and federal interests are a part of this momentum. Whereas founding American Indian studies programs and native departments such as at San Francisco State University, the University of Minnesota, and at University of California, Berkeley reflected the activism of the 1960s and

1970s; a second generation of American Indian studies programs have led to a third generation of American Indian studies programs.

The increasing number of American Indian studies programs has led to more forums hosted at American Indian studies conferences and at annual meetings involving American Indian scholars representing various disciplines. The National Indian Education Association (NIEA) and the American Indian and Alaska Native Professors Association sponsor sessions at their annual meetings that focus on American Indian studies. These forums have aroused debates. Duane Champagne, Turtle Mountain Chippewa and sociologist at UCLA, stated that "debate, nevertheless, is an essential part of the academic process. An open and free forum for discussion among Indian and non-Indian scholars benefits everyone who seeks to produce accurate, substantial, and significant studies of Indian people."[50]

In sum, the origin of American Indian studies grew out of need from the mainstream society and American Indians. The 1960s, when America struggled with its diverse ethnicity, the need to hear from ethnic groups like American Indians drew national attention. Since its developing stages, American Indian studies can be defined as a diverse curricula stressing tribal histories and cultures in a collective manner in order to enlighten linear society and American Indians. American Indian studies reflects a history of struggle in academia and it has fulfilled a need. Yet there is much more progress to be made for its ultimate acceptance by the mainstream academia.

While American Indian studies involves thought and philosophy, it is based on balance found in traditional knowledge of native peoples. The lack of respect and need for fair treatment from academia causes imbalance in American Indian studies. Yet, American Indian studies or native studies moves onward as an increasing number of Indian and non-Indian students want to learn more about indigenous peoples and their cultures. For the present, American Indian studies can be defined as a multidiscipline that is anchored by history, cultural studies, philosophy, literature, political science, and law. It is a study of relationships, such as comparatively analyzing Indian–white relations, and it is holistic and circular, as Lame Deer reminds us, in its methodological approach for examining and understanding all factors, including culture and gender. It is looking at the full circular picture of Indian life and its relationship to nature and the universe. Finally, American Indian studies is an extension of traditional knowledge from an indigenous point of view. Although they have taken a different form, the same historical and cultural values have transcended time and extended into the twenty-first century. As Lame Deer reminded us, all of us are a part of the circle that "has no beginning and no end."[51]

N O T E S

An earlier version was Donald L. Fixico. "Bury My Heart at Wounded Knee and the Indian Voice in Native Studies," *Journal of the West.* Vol. 39, No. 1, January 2001, 7–15.

1. John Lame Deer and Richard Erodes, *Lame Deer, Seeker of Visions* (New York: Touchstone, 1972), 100.

2. Vine Deloria Jr., *We Talk; You Listen: New Tribes, New Turf* (New York: Delta, 1970), 12.

3. Helen Hunt Jackson, *A Century of Dishonor, A Sketch of the United States Government Dealings with Some of the Indian Tribes* (New York: Harper and Brothers, 1881).

4. Dee Brown, *Bury My Heart at Wounded Knee: An Indian History of the American West* (New York: Holt, Rinehart and Winston, Inc., 1971), xii–xiii.

5. Anson Bert, *The Miami Indians* (Norman: University of Oklahoma Press, 1970).

6. Robert C. Carriker, *Fort Supply, Indian Territory Frontier Outpost on the Plains* (Norman: University of Oklahoma Press, 1970).

7. Angie Debo, *A History of the Indians of the United States* (Norman: University of Oklahoma Press, 1970).

8. Arthur H. De Rosier, Jr., *The Removal of the Choctaw Indians* (Knoxville: University of Tennessee Press, 1970).

9. Richard Ellis, *General Pope and U.S. Indian Policy* (Albuquerque: University of New Mexico Press, 1970).

10. Jess C. Epple, *Custer's Battle of the Washita and a History of the Plains Indian Tribes* (New York: Exposition Press, 1970).

11. John Philip Reid, *A Law of Blood: The Primitive Law of the Cherokee Nation* (New York: New York University Press, 1970).

12. Anthony F. C. Wallace, *The Death and Rebirth of the Seneca: The History and Culture of the Great Iroquois Nation, Their Destruction and Demoralization, and Their Cultural Revival at the Hands of the Indian Visionary, Handsome Lake* (New York: Alfred A. Knopf, 1970).

13. Thurman Wilkins, *Cherokee Tragedy: The Story of the Ridge Family and the Decimation of a People* (New York: Macmillan, 1970).

14. Ellen M. Whitney, ed., *The Black Hawk War: 1831–1832*, Vol. 1 (Springfield: Illinois State Historical Library, 1970).

15. Hazel Hertzberg, *The Search for an American Indian Identity: Modern Pan-Indian Movements* (Syracuse: Syracuse University Press, 1971).

16. Richard Slotkin, *Regeneration Through Violence: The Mythology of the American Frontier, 1600–1860* (Middletown, CT: Wesleyan University Press, 1973).

17. Bernard Sheehan, *Seeds of Extinction: Jeffersonian Philanthropy and the American Indian* (Chapel Hill: University of North Carolina Press, 1973).

18. Chief Red Fox, *Memoirs of Chief Red Fox* (New York: McGraw-Hill, 1972).

19. Virginia Irving Armstrong, *I Have Spoken: American History Through the Voices of the Indians* (Chicago: Swallow Press, 1971).

20. W. C. Vanderwerth, *Indian Oratory: Famous Speeches told By Noted Indian Chieftains* (Norman: University of Oklahoma, 1971).

21. Joseph Cash and Herbert Hoover, eds., *To Be An Indian: An Oral History* (New York: Holt, Rinehart and Winston, 1971).

22. Joseph Epes Brown, ed., *The Sacred Pipe: Black Elk's Account of the Seven Rites of the Oglala Sioux* (Baltimore: Penguin, 1971).

23. David Stannard, "American Historians and the Idea of National Character: Some Problems and Prospects," *American Quarterly*, Vol. 23, No. 2, May 1971, 202–220.

24. Jeanette Henry, "The American Indian in American History," in *Indian Voices: The First Convocation of American Indian Scholars* (San Francisco: The Indian Historian Press, 1970), 109.

25. Vine Deloria, Jr., *Custer Died For Your Sins: An Indian Manifesto* (Norman: University of Oklahoma Press, 1988), 78.

26. Alfonso Ortiz, "An Indian Anthropologist's Perspective on Anthropology," in *Anthropology and the American Indian: Report of a Symposium* (San Francisco: The Indian Historian Press, 1970), 89 and 91.

27. Robert M. Utley, "But for Custer's Sins," *Western Historical Quarterly*, Vol. 2, No. 4, October 1971, 361.

28. William Loren Katz, *The Black West* (Garden City: Doubleday, 1971).

29. Seth M. Scheiner and Tilden G. Edelstein, eds., *The Black Americans: Interpretative Readings* (New York: Holt, Rinehart and Winston, 1971).

30. Morris U. Schappes, *A Documentary History of Jews in the United States, 1654–1875* (New York: Schocken Books, 1971), 3rd ed.

31. Leonard Dinnerstein, ed., *Antisemitism in the United States* (New York: Holt, Rinehart and Winston, 1971).

32. Craig Howe et al., *25th Anniversary Conference and Celebration Meeting Ground* (Chicago: D'Arcy McNickle Center for the History of the American Indian, 1997).

33. Troy R. Johnson, *The Occupation of Alcatraz Island: Indian Self-Determination and the Rise of Indian Activism* (Urbana: University of Illinois Press, 1996), 10–11.

34. C. Patrick Morris and Michael O'Donnell, "U. S. Indian Higher Education," in Duane Champagne, ed., *The Native North American Almanac: A Reference Work on Native North Americans in the United States and Canada* (Detroit: Gale Research Inc., 1994), 878.

35. "Interior Provisions," *Congressional Quarterly Almanac, 1993*, Vol. 49, 103rd Congress, 1st sess., 629.

36. W. Roger Buffalohead, "Native American Studies Programs: Review and Evaluation," *First Convocation of Indian Scholars*, 161.

37. Edward Castillo, "California Indians," in Champagne, *Native North American Almanac*, 332; additional information on the development of American Indian or Native American Studies programs and departments include Wilcomb E. Washburn, "American Indian Studies: A Status Report," *American Quarterly*, Vol. 27, No. 3, August 1975, 263–274; Morgan G. Otis Jr., "A Native American Studies Program," *The Indian Historian*, Vol. 9, No. 1, Winter 1976, 14–18; Bea Medicine, "Responsibilities of Foundations in Native American Programs," *Indian Voices: The First Convocation of American Indian Scholars* (San Francisco: The Indian Historian Press, 1970), 357–364; W. Roger Buffalohead, "Native American Studies Programs: Review and Evaluation," *Indian Voices: The First Convocation of American Indian Scholars* (San Francisco: The Indian Historian Press, 1970), 161–167; Russell Thornton, "American Indian Studies as an Academic Discipline," *American Indian Culture and Research Journal*, Vol. 2, Nos. 3–4, 1978, 10–19 and "American Indian Studies as an Academic Discipline," *Journal of Ethnic Studies*, Vol. 5, No. 1, Fall 1977, 1–15; Terry P. Wilson, "Custer Never Would Have Believed It: Native American Studies in Academia," *American Indian Quarterly*, Vol. 5, No. 3, August 1979, 207–227; and Ward Churchill, "White Studies or Isolation: An Alternative Model for Native American Studies Programs," in *American Indian Issues in Higher Education* (Los Angeles: American Indian Studies Center, UCLA, 1981), 19–33.

38. For more discussion on the formation on American Indian studies programs, see Duane Champagne and Jay Stauss, eds., *Native American Studies in Higher Educa-*

tion: Models for Collaboration Between Universities and Indigenous Nations (Walnut Creek, Landham, NY and Oxford: AltaMira Press, 2002) and the *Indigenous Nations Studies Journal*, Vol. 2, No. 1, Spring 2001.

39. John A. Price, *Native Studies American and Canadian Indians* (New York: McGraw-Hill Ryerson, 1978), 8–9.

40. Clifford Trafzer, "Native American Studies," in Frederick Hoxie, *Encyclopedia of North American Indians: Native American History, and Life From Paleo-Indians to the Present* (Boston and New York: Houghton Mifflin Company, 1996), 421.

41. Ibid.

42. Ibid.

43. Tsianiana Lomawaima announced the establishment of the first doctoral program in the United States in her paper, "Changing Paradigms in Ethnography," presented at the annual meeting of the American Society for Ethnohistory, Portland, OR, November 7–9, 1996.

44. C. Patrick Morris and Michael O'Donnell, "U. S. Indian Higher Education," in Champagne, *The Native North American Almanac*, 871.

45. Carter Blue Clark, "America's First Discipline: American Indian Studies," in Clifford E. Trafzer, ed., *American Indian Identity: Today's Changing Perspective* (Sacramento: Sierra Oaks Publishing Company, 1985), 49.

46. Daniel F. Littlefield, Jr., "Newspapers, Magazines, and Journals," in Hoxie, *Encyclopedia of North American Indians*, 428–431.

47. Clark, "America's First Discipline," 50–51.

48. John Reyhner, "The Case for Native American Studies," in Dane Morrison, ed., *American Indian Studies: An Interdisciplinary Approach to Contemporary Issues* (New York: Peter Lang, 1997), 93–99.

49. Cheryl Crazy Bull, "A Native Conversation About Research And Scholarship," *Tribal College Journal*, Vol. 9, No. 1, Summer 1997, 17.

50. Duane Champagne, "American Indian Studies Is For Everyone," *American Indian Quarterly*, Vol. 20, No. 1, Winter 1996, 77.

53. Lame Deer and Erodes, *Lame Deer, Seeker of Visions*, 100.

7

CULTURAL PATRIMONY AND NATIVE SCHOLARS IN ACADEMIA

"One morning many years ago as a young assistant professor, I was lecturing about American history at the University of Wisconsin-Milwaukee. It was a trailer course, a required course taught at 4:30 in the afternoon, the dead zone. This was my first real faculty job, although I had taught part-time or as a visiting lecturer at other universities, and I was putting everything into my efforts to make the class go well. I wrote what I thought was an important point in American history at the very center of the blackboard. One of my female students raised her hand, and asked as she was busily taking notes: 'Professor Fixico, why is it that you don't write on the blackboard in the upper lefthand corner?' I had not realized that I had put my most important point of the lecture in the middle of the board, and I had proceeded to tell why I thought that it was significant to know and for the students to remember by telling a story about it. To me, it was natural to put the most salient point in the middle of the blackboard so that all of the class could focus on it and concentrate on its importance. However, the student was more interested in taking notes in an orderly linear style."
Donald L. Fixico, Creek, Seminole, Shawnee, Sac & Fox, 1982

* * *

Non-Indians have studied American Indians since colonial times. As a result, cultural information about Native American ceremonies, daily life, philosophy, and history have been written "about" by non-Indians in more than 30,000 books and thousands of articles. Due to the lack of original written languages among the indigenous peoples of North America and emphasis on oral tradition, documents reporting Indian history and describing native cultures have been largely produced by non-Indians. Given this one-sided situation, American Indians have been exploited by non-Indians, who have established successful careers, won writing awards, have been called the nation's leading experts on

Indians, and who have fed their families by writing "about" American Indians. A fair question is "what have they given Indian people in return?" This exploitive situation became a serious issue in the late twentieth century and among native scholars it remains a critical concern in the twenty-first century. Since the first American Indian studies programs began in the late 1960s, a steady increase of Indian scholars have become a part of the mainstream academy. Combined with an increasing academic and public interest in Native American culture and history, important questions of cultural ownership, respecting Indian artifacts repatriation, and the need for research protocol in Indian communities have been raised.

At present, there is estimated 300 million indigenous peoples, which is about five percent of the world's population. Indigenous peoples constitute more than 5,000 distinct peoples living in 70 countries. The largest concentrations reside in China and India, estimated at 7 percent or 80 million and 65 million of their respective populations. An estimated 13 million and 15 million people live in Central and South America, ranging from over 15,000 in Belize and 4,000 in Guyana to 8 million in Mexico and 8.6 million in Peru. There are more than 35 million indigenous people living in Africa. In the countries of Australia, New Zealand, United States, and Canada an estimated 0.25, 0.3, 1.5, and 1 million indigenous peoples live, respectively. Over 160,000 Inuit and Saami peoples live in the Arctic and Europe.[1]

A full approach of examining community, culture, history, and environment is needed for studying native peoples, as one scholar remarked, "all these are integral parts of living, dynamic, and adaptive heritage, and of the wider environment, within which communities develop sustainable cultural systems. In short, the perspective is one of holistic preservation and continuation of all aspects of cultural life. Museums should ensure that their practices are grounded in holistic heritage frameworks."[2] Using the Navajo approach of considering all relations and the Muscogee concept of totality is important for studying indigenous people. The next step is cultural patrimony of who owns native cultural evidence and traditional knowledge. To most people, it would seem obvious that native people do, but the academic process of research and publication has caused serious discussion. Who owns the copyright of printed materials about indigenous peoples and their cultures? Who owns the stories which share traditional knowledge even with outsiders?

Phyllis Messenger wrote in the introduction to her book, *The Ethics of Collecting Cultural Property: Whose Culture? Whose Property?* that "one way to organize the various claims which surface in the dispute over cultural properties is in terms of what I call the 3 R's, claims concerning the restitution of cultural properties, and the rights (e.g., rights of ownership, rights of access, rights of inheritance) retained by relevant parties."[3] These areas are relevant for a serious discussion on cultural patrimony and research protocol in working with indigenous communities.

Modern academia excludes the indigenous mind and neglects to infuse it as a part of the American experience in textbooks, films, and in the classrooms. At best, some textbooks, documentaries, and culturally sensitive teachers make an effort. It has placed growing pressure on native communities to protect their traditional knowledge. In the twenty-first century, protecting traditional knowledge is becoming more critical as traditionalists die.

Another scholar observed that the "Western society has been globally dominant over the past three centuries. This has enabled Western views of the world to become widely established. At the same time, economic power has aggrandized archaeology in Europe and North America, providing resources for extensive field work both at home and abroad. Coupled with colonialism, archaeology gave Western scholars the initiative in investigating and interpreting the early remains and antiquities of non-Western cultures. The resultant strongly Eurocentric view of human development only began to be reassessed and modified within the past 30 years."[4] Has academic freedom gone too far? Can scholars of the dominant society do whatever they want with indigenous knowledge?

Typically, scientific scholars study Native American society by examining its natural environment and ecology, including their early historical contact with the United States.[5] This early period of Anglo-Indian relations involved cultural, economic, and political interaction between Europeans and American Indians. This beginning of colonized history spread as early national America subordinated Indians to an inferior status while stressing the importance of the founding of the U.S. and issues related to early America. Amerocentricism invaded throughout Indian Country. The Western mind won the West, according to textbooks. By the late twentieth century, this situation began to change with the increase of more native scholars who challenged mainstream academia for more recognition of their work and American Indian studies.

In New Zealand, one scholar noted that "few Maori graduates or even non-graduates are yet at work in the field of Maori heritage. It will be many years before the community can hope to produce scholars sufficient to dominate Maori studies. Moreover, there is growing hostility among Maoris toward any professional expertise concerning the definition of their past, whether the experts are Pakeha or Maori. This suggests that Maori people in the future will be even less inclined to leave their heritage in the care of scholars, of whatever ethnic descent. All scholars and researchers may have to run some gauntlet of tribal approval."[6]

In regard to traditional Indian knowledge, the United States federal law has provided an area for recourse of protection. For American Indians, one scholar noted "there are three federal laws that protect American Indian cultural property. They are actually under the collection of artifacts: The American Indian Religious Freedom Act (42 U.S.C. §1996), Archaeological Resources Protection Act (16 U.S.C. §407cc(c), (g)) and Native American Graves Protection and Repatriation Act (25 U.S.C. §§3001–13)."[7] More work needs to be done in this area of collecting traditional knowledge, and even more than "collecting" to be done. Because collection and preservation have become pertinent issues to tribal communities and to native scholars, the museum profession has renewed its involvement.

One scholar, Paul Perrot, noted that "the American Association of Museums attempted to codify when it passed its first *Code of Ethics* in 1925, less than twenty years after the Association's founding."[8] Since that time, the federal government has enacted very few legal regulations until the 1970s. During this decade, museums began forming guidelines for researching and preserving Indian artifacts.

The American Association of Museums had not changed any collecting codes or guidelines for nearly fifty years, and were badly outdated. The creation of the United Nations Educational, Scientific, and Cultural Organization (UNESCO) in 1946 and the founding of the International Council of Museums (ICOM) as an independent, non-governmental organization, formed to recognize museums for "the support, governance, and administration of museums."[9] Perrot pointed out that "one of ICOM's first priorities was to deal with the urgent need to protect the patrimony of countries newly freed from colonialism, to establish norms for the protection of archaeological sites, and to prevent a repetition of the wholesale depredation that characterized many prewar excavations whether authorized or not. Years of study, negotiation, and false starts, led to UNESCO's Convention on the Means of Prohibiting and Preventing the Illicit Import, Export, and Transfer of Ownership of Cultural Property adopted in 1970."[10] This effort recognized that nations have a right to their patrimony, and it developed a judicial procedure for the implementing of the antiquities' act and other laws established for protecting cultural artifacts.

American Indians have experienced a prolonged history of exploitation since 1492 when Christopher Columbus introduced colonization in the Western Hemisphere. As American Indian political influence and military strength quickly diminished during the ensuing centuries, European commanders and soldiers set out to annihilate, pillage, plunder, rape, and exploit American Indians in all areas of life. They succeeded. One might think that such a violated history of greed would come to a halt when nothing seemed left, but even in the twentieth and twenty-first centuries, American greed has threatened to seize tribal natural resources, brainwash young Indian minds, convert native souls from their traditional beliefs, rob Indian graves, and claim credit for writing the truth "about" American Indians. The last point, "about" truth, is the issue here.

Throughout the history of the "colonizer" exploiting the native people in America, no one has effectively provided ample protection from this prolonged extortion. Even the Bureau of Indian Affairs as the legal arm to provide federal trust has failed to protect Indian people, their tribes, and their communities from losing properties, natural resources, and Indian children to white society. It is astonishing that American Indians only retain 2.3 percent or 53,633,797 acres of the land in the United States when once all of the continent belonged to Indian people. In regard to cultural patrimony, who owns American Indian studies has become a burning question. A larger question is, who owns the traditional knowledge of indigenous peoples and when does it become a part of the academic process? Since indigenous knowledge derives from oral tradition and oral history, it would seem simple that indigenous people own their own traditional knowledge, but this has not been the case.[11]

The late 1960s witnessed an effort by Indian activists and native scholars to call attention to the fact that books and articles about Indian people were wrong. The prevailing literature about Indians only presented one side of the story of American Indians. The white version of Indian books and articles focuses on Indian–white relations, and are not necessarily about American Indians. In this light, American Indian history and American Indian studies is really the history of Indian–white relations. Hence, non-Indian scholars and writers write about Indian–white relations.

Furthermore, the white version has been a case of the "conqueror writing his history." Americans demonized the so-called Noble Savage to become the Wild Savage—a foe to be conquered, and killed. The frontier attitude leashed its fury against Indians. "The only good Indians I ever saw were dead" was first quoted by General Philip Sheridan, who hunted plains Indians in the West from 1874 to 1877.

The romantic version of Indian wars, which led to the killing of Indians in 1,642 official engagements, was authorized by the United States government. This feat of "Winning the West," as acclaimed by Teddy Roosevelt, and Frederick Jackson Turner's infamous "Frontier Thesis," propagandized Americans into making Americans think about Indians as inferior and as losers in a supreme contest for land. This observation became the impetus for American history and has been the message of textbooks since the late nineteenth century. Historic white stereotypes of American Indians depicted "Indians" as cardboard figures to be knocked down. They were seen as not human.

The public attitude that the Indian was a lost cause made Indian people and their histories and cultures vulnerable to writers and scholars. Frontier historians wanted to tell how Indians had to be defeated, ethnographers intruded into Indian communities to extort cultural information, and people calling themselves archaeologists robbed Indian graves. Until the late 1960s, when American Indian studies programs and Indian scholars began to emerge on the academic scene, the literature continued to pile up with increasingly biased views about Indian people, promotion of misinformation, and gross misunderstanding of Indian people.

The emergence of a collective Indian voice written by native scholars captured national attention in the late 1960s. Indian scholars began to invade mainstream academia during the 1970s. The struggle for Indian scholarship written by Indians ushered in a new era of Indian war. This was a literary fight to present the Indian point of view and to claim ownership of American Indian studies. Up to this point, the writings of Charles Eastman, D'Arcy McNickle, William Warren, and other solitary Indian writers, plus the revealing words of Black Elk, represented limited evidence to the mainstream that there might be another version of Indian–white relations.

The explosion of 112 American Indian studies programs, departments, and centers from the 1970s to the 1990s in the United States and in Canada validated that American Indian studies, and all academic disciplines researching American Indians, were worth studying. But which point of view becomes the issue? By the 1990s, Indian scholars began to ask new questions and Indian students and their tribes opposed the prejudiced books and articles written about them and their cultures.

One scholar asked, "'What is cultural property?' From the many situations considered in the previous chapters, one ought to reconsider firstly the meaning of the term 'cultural property.' It has been said that Anglo-Saxon countries tend to avoid the use of the word 'culture,' except in its limited scientific, ethnological or artistic sense." In this same vein, the point was made that "the rest of the world uses the term more readily, much more generally and without much precision. In Third World countries, for instance, it has a more political meaning equated to anything which heightens national consciousness or identity."[12]

It is only fair to consider that American Indians have something to say about the research and literature about them. Indians have not remained silent, but their voices have been ignored. The control of presses, media, and textbooks in the hands of non-Indians has prohibited Native Americans from sufficiently expressing their points of view.

Furthermore, it is a matter of professionalism, ethics, and courtesy that American Indians and their communities and tribes are approached by scholars with tact and diplomacy. Common courtesy suggests that you obtain the approval from the people whom you want to study. Students who want to study at their choice of institutions must apply for admission, and scholars who want to work at the universities must apply for a faculty position. In both cases, they must be accepted for admission or be offered a job. Thus, it would seem only right that students and scholars ask or apply to a tribal community to study the tribe. By the fall of 1996, the nine tribes of the Apache had adopted a policy to govern the acquisition of cultural property from them, such as images, text, music, songs, stories, symbols, beliefs, customs, ideas, and items connected to history and culture of the tribes. By 1996, the Navajo, Hopi, and Zuni had also adopted research policies for scholars to abide by in researching their tribes.[13]

Unfortunately, anthropologists have set a bad precedent for researching American Indians, and Vine Deloria, Jr. heavily criticized them for exploiting native peoples in his book, *Custer Died For Your Sins*. He writes, "But Indians have been cursed above all other people in history. Indians have anthropologists. . . 'They' are the anthropologists. Social anthropologists, historical anthropologists, political anthropologists, economic anthropologists, all brands of the species, embark on the great summer adventure. . . An anthropologist comes out to the Indian reservations to make OBSERVATIONS. During the winter these observations will become books by which future anthropologists will be trained, so that they can come out to reservations years from now and verify the observations they have studied."[14]

The damage had already been done, and researchers were not to be trusted, as Fred McTaggart experienced while doing his research among the Mesquakie people in Iowa. He wrote about this frustration of being the wolf kept at bay in his noted book, *Wolf That I Am: In Search of the Red Earth People*. In his frustration, McTaggart stated, "I asked the Mesquakie word for 'story,' for 'legend,' for 'tell.' The elder Clouds responded readily with definitions I sought but gave no further information. Even though they were friendly now, I was confronted again and again with a silence that I did not understand. I am shy and quiet myself, but this silence was extremely embarrassing for me. After a few minutes, I excused myself and left. 'Do you know anyone who might be able to tell me some stories?' I asked at the door. Mr. Cloud shook his head. Mrs. Cloud paused, then answered. 'Go talk to our daughter. She lives just down the road, the next house. Maybe she can tell you who to talk to.' It was still early morning when I made my way to Lucille Waters' house. She was not home, but on the front stoop of her house I talked with her husband, John. 'No, she went into town,' he said. 'I don't know when she'll be back.' . . . 'Am I being too nosey?' I expected a quick denial, a polite pat on the back. Instead there was no reaction, either positive or negative. He was waiting to hear what I had to say. 'I really don't want to embarrass people or get too inquisitive about their religion. In fact, I don't want religious stories at all. I'm interested in secular stories—animal stories or whatever. Something people tell to each other for entertainment. But if I'm embarrassing people or disturbing their privacy, I will quit right now. I just don't want to do that.'"[15]

Without realizing it, McTaggart had embarrassed himself. His own insensitivity was not clear to him, and he failed to understand Mesquakie cultural protocol for introducing himself to the community. At this date, there is no defined academic protocol for approaching tribal communities to conduct research.

Anthropologists have developed a bad reputation among American Indians. Russell Means talked about them and heard about them as a child from his grandmother. He stated, "when I was five or six, Grandma Twinkle Star often used a strange word—*anthropologist*. At the time, I didn't know what she was talking about, but she said, more than once, 'If an anthropologist comes around asking about Indian things, don't you say anything. If they insist, then tell them lies'. . . When I grew up, I learned that was because summer, on most reservations, is the swarming season for 'anthros' from academia, determined to win government grants and tenure no matter what it costs the Indians. During the last century, anthros have spent many tens of millions of dollars of government money studying 'the Indians.' If that money had been paid to Indian nations to invest in their future, as *hundreds* of treaties ratified by the U.S. Senate required, most of our problems—disease, unemployment, malnutrition, poor housing, alcoholism, high infant mortality—would not have existed for them to 'study.' . . . Our way of life is sacred to us. To show respect to the Great Mystery, many of our ceremonies have always been private, shared only with those who have earned the right to worship with us. That excludes most anthros, whose chief concern, aside from furthering their careers, is to put Indians under a social microscope, to reduce the people whose lives they study to objects instead of treating them like human beings."[16]

The basic reasons and fundamental rationale for a professional approach to Indian people, tribes, and communities involve first, that native people are tired of being exploited and sickened by the long history of stereotypes that literature and the media have perpetuated. Such a history of mistreatment should no longer be tolerated by both Indians and non-Indians, and they should treat each with mutual respect. Scholars Teresa La Fromboise and Barbara Plake observed that "typically, American Indians are treated as sources of data rather than being invited to contribute to the complete research venture, include problem formulation, interpretation of data, and conclusions. . . This minimal involvement of tribal people has led to the publication of misinformation and a subsequent mistrust of researchers by tribal community members."[17] Essentially, Indians are not a part of the analytical process as scholars. Indian participation in this phase and the native point of view is of little interest to the linear researcher, unless he or she specializes in indigenous peoples or their communities, and invites Indian input. Instead, linear-minded researchers exploit Indian people as guinea pigs or experiments for their own benefit, which is called Western science.

Second, the basic truth about Indian people and their communities is much deeper than the scholars have written. The majority of literature about American Indians only scratches the surface of the inherent depth of native cultures. By not delving deeply enough into the native cultures and learning the socioeconomic infrastructures and meeting the people of Indian communities, outside scholars writing about Indian people have redirected the importance of indigenous peoples and what they are truly about.

Indian people have said frequently that scholars should get to know Indians, and many scholars have invaded Indian communities and reservations. Some anthropologists have done this for years, and some have been successful befriending Indian people, but all scholars should be doing this as well. However, most linear scholars have yet to learn how to behave in Indian Country. With presumed knowledge about the community or no information, scholars and graduate students race to spend their summers and sabbaticals to study an Indian community.

An official protocol or set of guidelines should be established by each tribe for scholars wanting to research and write about them. Some tribes like the Oklahoma Shawnee have established a research policy. A suggestion for such protocol involves instructions for three phases of studying American Indians. The first phase involves contacting the tribe, the second phase is conduct of research and behavior in Indian Country, and the third phase is the postresearch accountability or the follow-up. Within these three phases of research, ethics, responsibilities, the scholar should employ accountability, and professionalism.

During the first phase of research, the visiting scholar should act with respect in contacting the tribe. The executive branch of a tribal community should be contacted with the scholar presenting his or her request to research, showing of credentials, demonstration of purpose or objective of research and publication. The scholar should agree to a statement of sharing the published literature or reporting the results to the tribe. After contacting the tribe's executive branch or leadership, the scholar should patiently wait for a reply. As permission must be received for researching at private libraries and archives, the same patience should be exercised by the scholar researching an Indian community. This permission becomes more imperative due to the fact that various tribes and their communities will likely have different guidelines or rules or regulations for researching, or they may not have any guidelines at all. If a response from the tribe is not received after a month, then another request should be made by the visiting scholar.

In preparation for contacting the tribal communities, the scholar may access the available web pages of the tribes in order to seek appropriate information such as the contact person and how to contact such persons of the tribes. In addition, the web site may also have a set of guidelines or protocol in doing research on the reservation or in the Indian community. On the tribes' part, it is important for certain "ethics" to be defined and announced on tribal web sites for researching and writing about tribes and their people.

For the tribe, an official designated "contact person(s)" should be assigned to the researching scholar. This person would be the liaison to ensure that the researching scholar does not violate a cultural code or tribal law. This role would involve informing the scholar about sensitive areas of research, and the dos and don'ts of researching in the tribal community or Indian community.

The second phase of actual research should involve how the scholar needs to act while researching. Responsibilities of scholars in dealing with indigenous peoples needs to be taken much more seriously, and need to be defined. For example, the dos and don'ts of researching needs to be listed and defined. Whether the scholar is researching in tribal archives or at a tribal library, interviewing tribal members or taking notes on cultural or political activities, the dos and don'ts need to be acknowledged by the scholar.

A code of professionalism needs to be established so that scholars' actions while visiting Indian Country, and researching and writing about American Indians will respect both sides. Such codes and responsibilities need to be taught to undergraduate students and graduate students who want to research and write about Native Americans. Simultaneously, the history of exploitation and its blind nature should be explained to them. Furthermore, information on the ill relationship that has been created between academics and the Indian community at large needs to be shared with new researchers.

Unfortunately, academic freedom has been exploited in the case of American Indians, and it will continue to be this way until cultural guidelines are established. This same academic freedom has licensed the scholar to do as he or she pleases with little or no sensitivity to the impact of the research results or publication on the tribe or Indian community. For the present, such sensitivity is not of high priority among mainstream researchers.

The third phase of postresearch involves accountability and final responsibility for the researching scholar. Accountability is a critical issue in studying American Indians. The first question is "what is the researcher accountable for?" The second question is "to whom is the researcher held accountable?"

Properly crediting the tribe and giving credit by acknowledging the contact person and the individuals in the tribal community or Indian community who assisted the researching is important. In this manner, at least the tribal community and its members are respected for their information that they shared.

A significant cultural difference or cultural incongruence continues between most Americans and American Indians. This difference, as previously mentioned, has resulted from separate development of values and cultural backgrounds, thus causing a different mind set in approaching American Indian studies. A native logic existed and has persisted over the generation in how American Indians think. This logic is the way in which Indian scholars, who are close to their cultural traditions, approach their research and analyze their evidence.

American Indians scholars in recent American Indian history have established a voice that is being heard with increasing respect throughout academia. At this date, we are experiencing the third generation of native scholars who have influenced academia. The first full generation consisted of the periodic writings of Charles Eastman, Willian Warren, Carlos Montezuma, and others like D'Arcy McNickle. Earlier, two isolated native authors were Samson Occom (1723–1792) who wrote Christian sermons from 1772 to 1792 and William Apess (1798–1839) who wrote his autobiography and about his people, the Pequot.

The first generation of native scholars, who have been recognized by academia, were isolated American Indians who wrote about their lives and cultural experiences and about their peoples and tribal traditions. William Warren, the Ojibwa historian, wrote about his people in Wisconsin. His version of the history of his people represented an Indian view of tribal history and later versions written by non-Indians differed in their portrayal of his people.

The second full generation emerged as a small group in the late 1960s and early 1970s, involving Vine Deloria Jr., N. Scott Momaday, Alfonso Ortiz, and Rupert Costo. Jeanette Henry, Cherokee; Elizabeth Cook-Lynn, Lakota; and Bea Medicine, Lakota were among the few women scholars who published in this generation. Senior scholars of this generation also include Jack Forbes; Renape Powhatan, Lenape Delaware.

Present Indian scholars are those who have been writing since the mid 1970s, in the 1980s, and to the present. They are the third generation of Indian scholars. This observation demonstrates two important points: the "native voice" in academia and the "three generations of native scholarship."

The native voice is the collected perspective of many American Indian academics from various tribal traditions and from many academic disciplines. In fact, a natural difference occurs between the views of native scholars in academia and native scholars from traditional cultures, if the native academic is trained in the Western science approach of the American mainstream. As a result of many native minds being taught in white schools, native scholars have been retrained to think as non-Indian scholars. Yet a growing cadre of native scholars is evident today, and they are placed in many faculty positions in American Indian studies programs and departments in the United States and in Canada. Furthermore, many American Indian students of mixed bloods and full bloods are also a part of this growing community of native academia.

The current generation or third generation of Indian scholars is even greater in number. English, specifically literature, has the most native scholars, and they have written about Indian literature. Several of these noted Indian writers are Luci Tapahonso, Diné; Louise Erdrich, Turtle Mountain Chippewa; Linda Hogan, Chickasaw; Leslie Silko, Laguna; Wendy Rose, Hopi and Me-wuk; Joy Harjo, Muscogee Creek; and Susan Powers, Lakota. In anthropology, native scholars of this discipline include Pat Albers, Chippewa; Tsianina Lomawaima, Creek; and JoAllyn Archabault, Lakota. In religious studies it is Michelene Pesantubbee.

In history, David Edmunds, Cherokee; Carter Blue Clark, Muscogee Creek; Terry Wilson, Potawatomi; Ned Blackhawk, Shoshone; Steven Crum, Shoshone; and Brenda Child-McNamara, Red Lake Chippewa, are noted native scholars. There are others coming along as new professors and native graduate students enter the field.

In all of the foregoing fields, there are more native scholars, but limited space here cannot recognize all of them. In surveying all the academia fields, the "American Indian and Alaska Native Professors" directory that President Karen Gayton Swisher and her staff at Haskell Indian Nations University, in Lawrence, Kansas, produced in 1998 for the Association of American Indian and Alaskan Native Professors meeting in Lawrence, the following breakdown is interesting. There is the following number of native scholars in these disciplines: religious studies, 3; criminal justice, 1; counseling, 5; philosophy, 2; biochemistry, 1; biological science, 6; history, 15; urban planning, 1; ecology, 3; psychology, 24; political science, 8; physics, 1; economics, 1; educational administration, 26; English and literature, 26; math, 2; history of consciousness, 1; business management, 3; family/health medicine, 4; liberal arts, 1; architecture, 1; engineering, 1; social work, 13; library science, 5; education, 62; law, 8; sociology, 14; anthropology, 16; American Indian studies/ethnic studies, 15; American studies, 8; building trades, 1; art, 8; communications, 2; genetics, 1; nursing, 1; and soil/earth science, 2. In the Haskell directory there is a total of 345 native scholars listed as of 1999. The numbers in the directory do not accurately represent the total in all fields since many native scholars did not attend these meetings of the American Indian and Alaska Native Professors Association.

The noted presence of a third generation of Indian scholars with more to come, and the increasing presence of tribal governments, representing 562 federally recognized tribes, raises the importance of American Indian research. One important question of cultural patrimony, calling the question, "who owns American Indian research" actually raises more questions. Should there be set guidelines for doing American Indian research on reservations and in Indian communities?

If so, who should establish them? What criteria should be used to set this code of research or guidelines? Should only the tribe or Indian community set them? Should there be input from Indian scholars, especially from those native scholars who are of the tribe defining the guidelines? Should non-Indian scholars be involved in establishing the guidelines? If they are involved, what about employing some of the professional guidelines of the national organization of their disciplines, such as the American Historians Association and the American Association of Anthropologists? Another important question is how will the guidelines be enforced? Who should enforce them? What might be the penalty for breaking the guidelines?

From the point of view of non-Indian scholars, their work is a lonely one in most cases, and they have all of the responsibility of getting it done and publishing their work. Often, they are under the deadlines of a grant when the work has to be completed by a certain date, so they are determined to get their research done. This is an isolated existence, so researchers are committed and focused on their own research and sometimes forget that they are visitors in an Indian community. They see their experience as research, often forgetting that their interaction with native people is just as important. Often they do not have enough time to spend among Indian people, as they usually have families at home. Thus, they live two lives, so to speak. Their job for tenure, or getting hired for a job, or promotion depends on their completing their research and publishing their work.

From the view of the American Indian scholars and tribal communities, in restating some of the early arguments, unkindly non-Indian research on reservations and in Indian communities causes a rise of emotions that are uneasy and discomforting. Insensitivity, exploitation, being taken advantage of, feeling cheated, feeling run over, and feeling that you are treated rudely in your own community is unthinkable.

The history of exploitation and mistreatment is aroused, and the ugly pressure of the mainstream society of white power is felt. Racism, prejudice, discrimination, superiority, and paternalism are all emotional feelings felt by Indians being researched.

Finally, cultural patrimony and the rise of the third generation of Indian scholars are two experiences that will continue to cause lengthy discussions and disagreements with mainstream academia. Forums will need to be held at conferences and position papers will need to be written in order for a dialogue to occur on cultural patrimony of "who owns American Indian research?" In this effort, parameters will need to be acknowledged for this anticipated dialogue with fairness kept in mind. Terms will need to be defined and accepted by both sides. Most important of all is the point that ethics and protocol for researching on reservations and in Indian communities is called forth by the very nature of human respect for other people's ways of life.

The controversy and issue of control continues over Indian artifacts being housed in museums or given back to tribes. It is important to remember to respect indigenous artifacts for they hold the key to understanding traditional knowledge. Furthermore, the issue of repatriation is still at hand and the future holds no answers for the present. In addition, an essential research protocol needs to be worked out.

A new paradigm is required for researching about American Indians. In fact, it is illogical to conduct research without first practicing protocol to contact the Indian community or native people before beginning to conduct research. Teaching professionalism in occupations sometimes mandates protocol and guidelines to be followed before practicing its occupation, which often includes research. Early research practice by scholars studying American Indians is putting the travois (cart) before the horse.

Cultural patrimony is in need of change, and it requires protocol for studying American Indians. By establishing professional protocol for initial contact with the native peoples, trust develops between the researcher and the Indian person and his or her community. With a successful relationship established and based on trust, friendship will likely ensue. Cultural patrimony is the central issue, and it should be recognized now. This is a critical concern for native scholars, and it needs to be written in the middle of the blackboard for critical discussion, so that its importance will be dealt with directly.

In sum, traditional knowledge of the indigenous peoples of North America is at a crossroads, the increase of native scholars has called for reconsideration of certain issues about Indian artifacts and the academic approach toward studying American Indians. Such issues of cultural ownership, respecting Indian artifacts, supporting a fair process for repatriation of artifacts and burial remains, and research protocol of guidelines to research and interview Native Americans are critical points to be resolved so that American Indians will feel comfortable about non-Indians and native scholars researching among them. In this history of American Indian–mainstream relations, American Indians and their cultural rights are in the middle of the black board as the most important point to be addressed.

NOTES

1. Amareswar Galla, "Indigenous Peoples, Museums, and Ethics," in Gary Edson, ed., *Museum Ethics* (New York and London: Routledge, 1997), 147.
2. Ibid., 150–51.

3. Phyllis Mauch Messenger, ed., *The Ethics of Collecting Cultural Property: Whose Culture? Whose Property?* (Albuquerque: University of New Mexico Press, 1989), 2.

4. Peter Gathercole and David Lowenthal, eds., *The Politics of the Past* (London and Boston: Unwin Hyman, 1990), 17.

5. Ibid., 40.

6. Ibid., 99.

7. For a discussion of the three laws related to native American cultural patrimony, see Marilyn E. Phelan, ed., *Museum Law: A Guide for Officers, Directors and Counsel* (Evanston, IL: Kalos Kapp Press, 1994), 293–296.

8. Paul N. Perrot, "Museum Ethics and Collecting Principles," in Gary Edson, ed., *Museum Ethics*, 191.

9. Ibid., 192.

10. Ibid.

11. Various views are reported in Bernard L. Fontana, "American Indian Oral History: An Anthropologist's Note," *History and Theory* Vol. 8, No. 3, October 1969, 366–370; David P. Henige, "'In possession of the author': the Problem of Source Monopoly in Oral Historiography," *International Journal of Oral History*, Vol. 1, 1980, 181–194; Donald A. Ritchie, "The Oral History/Public History Connection," in Barbara J. Howe and Emory L. Kemp, eds., *Public History: An Introduction* (Malabar, FL: Krieger, 1986), 57–69; Thomas Spear, "Oral Traditions: Whose History?" *History in Africa*, Vol. 8, 1981, 165–181.

12. See Chapter 10, "The Return of Cultural Treasures: Some Conclusions," in Jeannette Greenfield, *The Return of Cultural Treasures* 2nd ed. (New York: Cambridge University Press, 1996), 253.

13. James D. Nason, "Tribal Models for Controlling Research," *Tribal College: Journal of American Indian Higher Education*, Vol. 8, No. 2, Fall 1996, 17–20, and for Canadian First Nations' list of 17 guidelines, see Marjane Ambler, "Cultural Property Rights: What's Next after NAGPRA?" *Tribal College: Journal of American Indian Higher Education*, Vol. 8, No. 2, Fall 1996, 8–11.

14. Vine Deloria Jr., *Custer Died For Your Sins: An Indian Manifesto* (Norman: University of Oklahoma Press, 1988), 78–79, originally published by Avon, 1969.

15. Fred McTaggart, *Wolf That I Am: In Search of the Red Earth People* (Norman: University of Oklahoma Press, 1984), originally published 1976, 24 and 37.

16. Russell Means with Marvin J. Wolf, *Where White Men Fear to Tread: The Autobiography of Russell Means* (New York: St. Martin's Press, 1995), 17.

17. Teresa D. La Fromboise and Barbara S. Plake, "Toward Meeting the Research Needs of American Indians," *Harvard Educational Review*, Vol. 53, No. 1, February 1983, 45.

INSTITUTIONALIZING TRADITIONAL KNOWLEDGE[1]

"There certainly can be no doubt in the public mind today as to the capacity of the younger Indians in taking on white modes and manners. . . However, despite the fact that Indian schools have been established over several generations, there is a dearth of Indians in the professions. . . With school facilities already well established and the capability of the Indian unquestioned, every reservation could well be supplied with Indian doctors, nurses, engineers, road and bridge-builders, draughtsmen, architects, dentists, lawyers, teachers, and instructors in tribal lore, legends, orations, songs, dances, and ceremonial ritual. The Indian, by the very sense of duty, should become his own historian, giving his account of the race— fairer and fewer accounts of the wars and more statecraft, legends, languages, oratory, and philosophical conceptions. . . Rather, a fair and correct history of the native American should be incorporated in the curriculum of the public school. . . But the Indian youth! They, too, have fine pages in their past history; they, too, have patriots and heroes. And it is not fair to rob Indian youth of their history, the stories of their patriots, which, if impartially written, would fill them with pride and dignity. Therefore, give back to Indian youth all, everything in their heritage that belongs to them and augments it with the best in the modern schools. I repeat, doubly-educate the Indian boy and girl. . . Why not build a school of Indian thought, built on the Indian pattern and conducted by Indian instructors? Why not a school of tribal art? . . . There were ideals and practices in the life of my ancestors that have not been improved upon by the present-day civilization; there were in our culture elements of benefit; and there were influences that would broaden any life. But that almost an entire public needs to be enlightened as to this fact need not be discouraging. For many centuries the human mind has labored under the delusion that the world was flat; and thousands of men have believed that the heavens were supported by the strength of Atlas. The human mind is not yet free from fallacious reasoning; it is not yet an open mind and its deepest recesses are not yet swept

free of errors. . . But it is now time for a destructive order to be reversed, and it is well to inform other races that the aboriginal culture of America was not devoid of beauty. Furthermore, in denying the Indian his ancestral rights and heritages, the white race is but robbing itself. But America can be revived, rejuvenated, by recognizing a native school of thought." [2]

Luther Standing Bear, Lakota, 1933

* * *

Joel Iacoomis, Charles Alexander Eastman, and Luther Standing Bear. These individuals are three Indian scholars who are little known to the American public. Their deeds were great, their efforts to become educated in the white man's schools were absolute personal dedication, and they were highly motivated. What did they think about? What did they feel as they became educated in the white man's schools? What did they think happened to themselves? Did they become less Indian? Eastman and Standing Bear are well-known figures in American Indian education, but little is known about Joel Iacoomis. Iacoomis was one of two survivors of the twenty Indian youth sent to Elijah Corlet's Latin Grammar School in Cambridge, Massachusetts, which became known as Harvard University. After graduation, Iacoomis died in a shipwreck off Nantucket Island on his way back to Cambridge.[3]

The quote above are the words of Luther Standing Bear. Spoken many years earlier in 1933, Standing Bear's words are most appropriate for American Indian education and scholarship in the twenty-first century. He called for institutions and thoughts from Indian people in education, and his words supply direction for the future. For too long, the idea of "institution" has been a frightening word among American Indians given the long practice of harsh treatment at Indian boarding schools and Indian patients dying in hospitals. The school attempted to brainwash the native mind of Eastman, Iacoomis, and many others, then change the Indian youth into non-Indians and force them to replace their native language with the white man's English. The institutional hospitals seized the lives of Indian people, preying upon them while they were ill, and native people dreaded these places where their sick ones went to die.

Incredibly, the fear of institutions has been overcome in the last quarter of the twentieth century. Simultaneously the progress of American Indian institutions built by Indians is accelerating at an alarming rate and in a positive direction. Most importantly, American Indians and American Indian institutions are exerting ownership over American Indian education. Interestingly, this progress has come about via a compromise of native traditional knowledge and the American system of higher education in promoting the idea of institutionalizing traditional knowledge. Within American Indian higher education, Indian educators wage the struggle to express their inherent academic freedom. The history and the progress of American Indian institutions in promoting traditional knowledge in a transitional emphasis on American Indian studies are young and dynamic. In this manner, American Indian studies is a process for channeling traditional knowledge from tribal communities to the classroom.

The "institutionalizing" of American Indian intellectualism and traditional knowledge continues to be an Indian–white partnership. Indians and institutions have a long history that began in 1618 when the Virginia Company tried to introduce English-style education to American Indians in what became known as the Henrico Proposal. In 1654, Harvard started its Indian college with the goal of educating the Indian and English youth of the new Massachusetts Colony.[4] Dartmouth College opened its doors in 1769 as a school to educate Indian youth. The University of Notre Dame began as a school in 1842 with part of its mission in its original charter to teach Indian youth. Other lesser known schools like Fort Lewis College in Colorado and Ottawa University in Kansas stressed the importance of enrolling American Indians. In some cases, Indian nations opened schools often with the help of missionaries like in Indian Territory (now Oklahoma).

As emphasized earlier, the infamous efforts to educate Indian young people developed into the notorious boarding school experiences. Following Captain Richard Pratt's Carlisle Indian Industrial School in 1879 in Pennsylvania, other boarding schools emerged. Day schools developed on and near Indian reservations. Although obtaining a high school education was a major accomplishment for most people in the early twentieth century, bureaucrats and missionaries established Indian boarding schools as vocational schools.

Haskell Indian Nations University in Lawrence, Kansas is a prime example of Indian self-determination and native institutionalizing of American Indian intellectual growth and preserving traditional knowledge. Haskell began as a boarding school in 1884 and became a land-grant institution in 1994 with a "vision to become a national center for Indian education, research, fine arts, service, and cultural programs that increase knowledge and support the educational needs of American Indians and Alaska Natives." Its instructional goals are to "(1) achieve full university status, (2) provide programs that promote appreciation, support, and preservation of American Indian/Alaska Native cultures, (3) attract, develop, and graduate top quality students in terms of their spiritual, emotional, intellectual, physical, and cultural well-being, (4) support a safe and secure campus environment that combats substance abuse and promotes healthy lifestyles, (5) extend programs and services beyond the physical campus, (6) improve communication and dissemination of information, (7) improve the facilities and infrastructures to meet the educational needs of the university, [and] (8) diversify the financial base by increasing private and public sources of revenue."[5]

The mission statement for Haskell is "as authorized by Congress and in partial fulfillment of treaty and trust obligations, Haskell provides higher education to federally recognized tribal members. This purpose is accomplished through the provision of tuition-free education, culturally sensitive curricula, innovative services, and a commitment to academic excellence."[6] Haskell has become the premier Indian institution of higher learning in academia. Whereas other famous boarding schools like Carlisle and Chilocco have closed their doors, Haskell achieved the impossible of reinventing itself several times by becoming a vocational school, a high school, a junior college, and a university. No other Indian school has achieved such a historic transition. Interestingly, many changes in institutions impacting Indian people have come from external forces. For example, World War II caused drastic changes in America and in Indian Country. In the 1940s and 1950s, junior colleges began opening in common to many communities throughout the United States. The following decade of the 1960s brought even more radical change in education and for American Indians in higher education.

During the Great Depression, the Works Project Administration (WPA) sent workers to interview Native Americans in Oklahoma, thus producing the Indian–Pioneer Papers. Collections of the papers were made available at the University of Oklahoma and at the Oklahoma Historical Society. The Doris Duke Indian oral history collections, placed at various universities, that were produced from oral history interviews during the late 1960s and early 1970s have yielded a corpus of research data. From Duke's support, universities such as the University of Oklahoma, the University of Illinois, the University of Utah, the University of South Dakota, the University of New Mexico, and the University of Florida received funding to start American Indian oral history collections as a means of preserving traditional knowledge of culture and history remembered by Indian elders.

Since the educational movement of the 1960s, other oral history projects began collecting American Indian oral history at such institutions as Princeton University and the University of New Mexico, which still maintains its Doris Duke Collection. After 1970, American Indians and tribes have exerted an ownership over their intellectualism and traditional knowledge in the development of writings, courses taught, programs, tribal colleges, and tribal museums.

In addition to mainstream colleges and universities, tribes and Indian communities began to institutionalize traditional knowledge under the new rubric of American Indian studies. Since the 1970s, Native American communities have begun developing tribal archives, usually housed by tribal governments. Although most of the depositories collected holdings contain written or printed documents by non-Indians, tribal archives have collected oral history interviews. The Cherokees and Chickasaws in Oklahoma are superb examples together with about a dozen other tribal archives in the state. Institutes and organizations continue to expand, such as the Institute of American Indian Studies at the University of South Dakota, which houses the largest Native American oral history collection.

Rough Rock Demonstration School started the modern institutionalizing of traditional knowledge. During the mid 1960s, Rough Rock opened its doors on the Navajo Reservation as a part of the renewed interest in American Indian history and culture due to the political times of this period. This effort was under Indian autonomy.[7]

In 1969, the United Tribes of North Dakota, an intertribal organization, founded the United Tribes Technical College near Bismarck, North Dakota (UTTC)[8]. Located on 105 acres and chartered by the state of North Dakota, the College is a nonprofit corporation and operated by the five tribes in North Dakota: the Three Affiliated Tribes of Fort Berthold, the Spirit Lake Tribes, the Sisseton Wahpeton Sioux Tribe, the Standing Rock Sioux Tribe, and the Turtle Mountain Band of Chippewa.

United Tribes Technical College is guided in its actions by the following statement of its mission: "United Tribes Technical College is a residential educational institution with a commitment to the American Indian individual and family. The role of UTTC is to provide vocational and technical education to American Indians. It is UTTC's mission to provide an environment in which students and staff can discover, examine, preserve, and transmit the technical knowledge, cultural values, and wisdom that will ensure the survival of Indian people in the present and future generations, while increasing individual opportunities to improve the quality of life. The college seeks to initiate and sustain educational and economic programs. These programs are designed to meet the goals of self-sufficiency, realization, and self-determination of the Indian community. UTTC will continue to serve as a focal point for intertribal discussion of tribal rights and economic progress.[9]

Recognizing the need for accreditation, UTTC applied for and was granted candidacy for accreditation status by the North Central Association (NCA) in 1978. In the spring of 1982, United Tribes received full membership in the NCA as a vocational school. In 1987, the institution received authority from the NCA to offer its first associate degree. In 1989, United Tribes Technical College had two more degrees authorized. In March 1993, the college was approved at the Associate of Applied Science level in all of its programs and has maintained its accreditation status. The college has enrolled students from more than 40 tribes in the United States and Canada.[10]

Starting with limited grant funding, the Navajo Community College Act established Navajo Community College in 1968.[11] Changed to Diné Tribal College, this was the first tribal college. Other tribal colleges followed as a trend developed with Navajo Community College serving as a model.

Oglala Lakota College (OLC) is located in Kyle, South Dakota. OLC is a product of the mid 1960s and it is one of the oldest tribally controlled colleges. Oglala Lakota College emerged from a contract with the University of Colorado in November 1967. Previously, Black Hills State College and the University of South Dakota had taught courses on the Pine Ridge Reservation. Birgil Kills Straight, Gerald One Feather, Gerald Clifford, and others envisioned a tribal college for their people and that they needed higher education. Gerald One Feather had worked with Robert Roessel at Navajo Community College in the southwest and had experience with Rough Rock Demonstration School. Befriending Jim Hamm, Birgil Kills Straight and Gerald Clifford joined in the effort to start Oglala Lakota College.[12]

Initially, OLC offered GED courses, then courses with credit from the University of Colorado were added. By the fall of 1969, OLC had volunteer instructors, and the school became first known as Oglala Sioux Community College. Eighty students completed the first courses offered by the summer of 1969 with the majority being older women students. On March 4, 1971, the tribal council chartered OLC as a public corporation under the name of Lakota Higher Education Center with Navajo Community College as a model. By 1978, the new college offered a two-year comprehensive list of programs in agriculture, business, education, general studies, human services, nursing, and Lakota studies.[13] The school's mission involved "to generally coordinate and regulate all higher education on the Pine Ridge reservation. The college is empowered to develop and operate programs granting post-secondary degrees and certificates and/or enter into agreements with public or private agencies to offer higher education on the reservation. Emphasis is put on programs leading to two-year Associate of Arts degrees." By the end of the 1970s, Oglala Sioux Community College enrolled nearly 400 students with 132 full-time and 242 part-time students at nine college centers: (1) Oglala College Center, Oglala, (2) Manderson College Center, Manderson, (3) Pejuta Haka College Center, Kyle, (4) Eagle Nest College Center, Wanblee, (5) LaCreek College Center, Martin, Oglala, (6) Pass Creek College Center, Allen, (7) East Wakpammi College Center, Batesland, (8) Pahin Sinte College Center, Porcupine, and (9) Pine Ridge Center, Pine Ridge.[14] The accreditation of the school and its name change made the school one of the oldest tribally controlled colleges. By 1996, OLC offered six bachelor degree programs and 18 associate degrees, plus a Master of Arts in Lakota Leadership/Management.[15]

Si Tanka Huron University is located at Eagle Butte, South Dakota. As one of the oldest tribal colleges, Si Tanka Huron purchased one of the oldest private universities in South Dakota. Huron University dates approximately back to 1873. With this extraordinary consolidation, Si Tanka Huron was the first off-reservation tribally controlled university in the United States. More than 50 percent of all its students are members of ethnic minorities with 37 percent being American Indian. Si Tanka Huron University offers degree programs in business, education, nursing, and criminal justice.[16]

In 1960, the All Indian Pueblo Council planned a tribal college to serve native peoples in the Southwest. On August 21, 1971, the council held dedication ceremonies, and Southwestern Indian Polytechnic Institute (SIPI) officially opened its doors to begin offering classes. By 1975, SIPI received accreditation status from the North Central Association of Schools and Colleges, and on August 6, 1993, it received community college status. The mission of Southwestern Indian Polytechnic Institute remains "to provide quality technical and higher education opportunities that meet the dynamic needs of federally recognized tribes. This endeavor provides the opportunities for students to: enter the technological workforce as self-sufficient and contributing members of society; acquire higher levels of academic achievement; enrich and enhance student learning and self-esteem by responding to mental, physical, spiritual, and cultural needs."[17]

During the 1970s, there were thirty-one tribal colleges in America, and there are thirty-four in 2002. As Indian communities continued to flourish with much promise for the next century, academic curriculum attempted to keep pace with this progress. Luther Standing Bear's words were answered with the accelerating increase of the number of tribally controlled colleges.

On May 2, 1973, Fort Berthold Community College (FBCC) began as a tribal college after receiving its charter by the Three Affiliated Tribes of Fort Berthold reservation located at New Town, North Dakota. On February 12, 1988, the North Central Association of Schools and Colleges granted accreditation to the tribal college with its mission to address the tribal needs and concerns and perpetuate tribal heritage, history, and education. Fort Berthold Tribal College holds a leadership role in reservation development. The college makes every effort to enable individuals to achieve positive self-image and the clear sense of identity in order for tribal and community members to participate effectively in a multicultural society.[18]

On the national scene, a subcommittee in the U.S. Senate completed a national survey on Indian education. The report became known as "A National Tragedy—A National Challenge," which described the progress of Indian education as deplorable. At the same time, Indians began to take charge.

In 1969, protesting Indians led by Richard Oakes during the Red Power Movement took over Alcatraz Island in California for several months. Other Indian takeovers followed. In 1970, the U.S. Army abandoned several buildings and barracks on 643 acres in Davis, California. In July 1971, a group of Native Americans led by Dave Risling took over the Army's abandoned buildings to start DQ University (DQU). The "D" stands for the name of the Great Peacemaker of the Iroquois, Deganwidah. The "Q" stood for the Aztec prophet, named Quetzalcoatl, who advocated wisdom and self-discipline. On November 7, 1978, DQ University became Indian-controlled. DQ is a two-year college that sponsors teacher training, courses, seminars, conferences, and specialized offerings on American Indian and Chicano history. Arts, crafts, music and dance, philosophy, and culture are the emphasis at DQU. On a rainy warm day on April 6, 2001, the Attorney General of the State of California handed over the deed for the 643 acres and buildings to DQU President Morgan Otis and the Board of Directors of DQU, making the tribal college totally sovereign and land owned by DQU.[19]

As the 1970s began, a collective effort formed officially. In 1972, tribal Colleges organized the American Indian Higher Education Consortium (AIHEC) to assist students in getting a college education. For the rest of the twentieth century, AIHEC became a strong element in American Indian higher education. Tribal colleges and universities, were created to respond to higher education needs of American Indians and geographically isolated populations.

During these years of great effort, the first urban Indian college emerged in the United States. In 1974, Native American Educational Services, Inc. College (NAES) opened its doors. NAES's mission stressed a college education for urban Indians living in Chicago. As a part of this effort, the curriculum involved the students completing required projects that called for working with the Chicago Indian community in some way. NAES was accredited by the Commission of Institutions of Higher Education of the North Central Association of Colleges and Schools on August 18, 1984.[20]

The mission of NAES College states that "NAES is an American Indian college with four campuses located on two reservations and in two urban Indian communities. NAES offers an accredited Bachelor of Arts degree that is individualized and research oriented. The college educates to meet the demands of the new leadership in our rapidly changing society of which the Indian and tribal communities are an integral part. The instructional program, community based in focus and national in scope, integrates tribal knowledge, learning, and intellectual traditions into academic curriculum and process, providing a liberal arts education tribally defined." The purposes of NAES College are "(1) to provide a quality educational environment for the student in order to develop communicative, analytical, and professional technical skills, (2) to provide a quality educational environment for the student to develop, within a historical framework, knowledge and understanding of the social, governmental, economic, scientific, and educational foundations of the student's community, (3) to develop a professional credited leadership accountable to the community and grounded in a philosophy of community service, (4) to develop, within the Indian community, a system of higher education with a degree granting process based upon the intellectual and philosophical traditions of the tribal worlds."[21] NAES's four campuses are at Chicago, Fort Peck Reservation, in Poplar, Montana, Menominee Reservation in Wisconsin, and in the Twin Cities of Minnesota. In June of 2000, NAES College celebrated twenty-five years since its founding.[22]

Tribal colleges received major support when the U.S. Congress passed the Tribally Controlled Community College Act in 1978, thereby providing limited grants for starting these institutions in Indian Country, including any Alaska native village or village corporation approved by the Secretary of the Interior.[23] At an explosive pace, tribes realized the higher educational needs of their people. As community colleges, they base and develop their curriculum to meet the needs of their people, which are more practically oriented such as courses offered in business and administration. By 1989, the Carnegie Foundation for the Advancement for Teaching reported that twenty-four tribal colleges had been started by the tribes.[24]

Bay Mills Community College (BMCC) is located in Brimley, Michigan, and it is a tribally controlled land-grant college. Originally, the college responded to the economic development of the American Indian communities with the original purpose of the college focusing on training eleven students each year for tribal employment.[25] Starting in 1984 with eleven students, Bay Mills had 500 students by the end of 1997.[26] Overlooking Lake Superior, BMCC offers accredited associate degree programs, technical training, and cultural opportunities to native communities in Michigan, and it serves students nationwide through the Internet. Its student profile includes diverse ages, backgrounds, and goals.

The Bay Mills Chippewa Tribe chartered Bay Mills Community College (BMCC) in 1984. BMCC obtained land grant status in 1994 under the Equity in Educational Land Grant Status Act. Control is vested in a Board of Regents that elects the officers of the administration and establishes overall institutional policy. The college moved to its present facility in 1984, with a small library constructed in 1990, and dormitories built three years later. BMCC has expanded its main building three times to include state-of-the-art computer labs with biology and environmental science facilities, and it added more classrooms to meet growing student needs. BMCC is dedicated to providing students with leading-edge technology training.[27]

Turtle Mountain Community College (TMCC) is another early tribal college. Efforts by local Indian citizens for comprehensive, quality, higher education service culminated in the application for, and approval of, a charter from the Tribe to establish Turtle Mountain Community College in 1972. TMCC is located in Belcourt, North Dakota, on 123 acres in north central North Dakota in the scenic wooded, hilly, and lake country known as the Turtle Mountains. TMCC's mission statement includes "(1) . . . to function as an autonomous Indian controlled college on the reservation focusing on general studies and vocational education programs and to direct scholarly research; (2) . . . to create an environment in which the cultural and social heritage of the Turtle Mountain Band of Chippewa can be brought to bear throughout the curriculum; and (3) . . . to establish an administration, faculty, and student body involved in exerting leadership within the community and providing service to it."[28]

The growing awareness that more college-educated tribal people were needed to provide necessary and effective services on the Turtle

Mountain Chippewa Reservation led efforts in the 1960s to bring college courses to the reservation. The college received initial candidacy for accreditation in 1978 by the North Central Association of Colleges and Schools (NCACS). A decade later, the college was granted ten years of accreditation with a focus visit to occur in the spring of 1996. The visit by NCACS resulted in the college receiving full accreditation.

Turtle Mountain Community College is a tribal community college with obligations of direct community service to the Turtle Mountain Chippewa Tribe. Under this unifying principle, the college seeks to maintain, seek out, and provide comprehensive higher education services in fields needed for true Indian self-determination. TMCC was chartered by the Turtle Mountain Band of Chippewa Indians offering courses and service to the residents of the Turtle Mountain area. In August 1984, the college was granted full accreditation status by the North Central Executive Board. TMCC is a member of the American Indian Higher Education Consortium (AIHEC) and a member of the American Indian College Fund (AICF). The fund was established to secure private and corporate donations for use by member colleges. Its primary purpose is to help the colleges achieve financial stability through private fund-raising, resource development, and economic development. AICF maintains offices and staff in Denver, Colorado, and New York City.[29]

Sitting Bull College (SBC) began as Standing Rock Community College in Fort Yates, North Dakota, on September 21, 1973. On that date, the Standing Rock Sioux Tribal Council granted a charter to Standing Rock Community College to operate as a postsecondary educational institution with the authority to grant degrees at the Associate level. At the time the charter was granted, different colleges in the state offered courses on the reservation. Tribal leaders believed that it would be best to operate as one institution, Bismarck Junior College (BJC). As ties with BJC strengthened, tribal leaders discussed whether the Standing Rock Sioux Tribe should join other tribes that were in the process of forming their own colleges. Standing Rock Community College opened its doors officially in July 1973. The first offices and classrooms were in the Douglas Skye Memorial Retirement Complex in Fort Yates with three full-time people on staff. The process of seeking accreditation was initiated in 1975, and the college received full accreditation in 1984. To mark this achievement and progress, the tribe officially changed the college name to Standing Rock Community College. On March 6, 1996, the Standing Rock Sioux Tribal Council voted to officially amend the charter, changing the college's name to Sitting Bull College. Currently, more than forty full-time faculty teach at the college, including administrative and support staff. The original enrollment of 90 students has grown to a number consistently over 250. Vocational programs, general college transfer programs, as well as programs with other colleges are offered. In association with Sinte Gleska University, Rosebud, South Dakota; Salish Kootenai College, Pablo, Montana; and Oglala Lakota College, Kyle, South Dakota, students can earn four-year degrees at Sitting Bull College. The fact that SBC is tribally controlled means that it must also provide services to the Native American community. The North Central Association of Colleges and Schools Commission on Institutions of Higher Education accredited SBC in 1984.[30]

Sisseton Wahpeton Community College (SWCC), a tribally chartered institution, is a tribal school to meet the unique postsecondary educational needs of the members of the Sisseton Wahpeton Sioux Tribe and other residents of the Lake Traverse Region. Courses are offered at its main campus at Old Agency Village on the Lake Traverse Reservation in Sisseton, South Dakota; at several locations in the Seven Districts of the Reservation; and at other sites located within the traditional lands of the Dakota people. Goals of the school include "(1) to provide courses leading to Associate of Arts and Associate of Science degrees and in preparation for baccalaureate degrees, (2) to preserve and extend knowledge of Dakota history, language and culture, (3) to establish a main campus and offer courses at accessible locations throughout the service area, (4) to support and encourage all aspects of education on the Lake Traverse Reservation through providing continuing developmental community and Adult Basic Education, (5) to assist tribal leadership in furthering social and economic development goals."[31]

Sinte Gleska University (SGU) emerged as a response to a systematic education need on the Rosebud Sioux Reservation that ignored the importance of Lakota language and culture. A feasibility study was conducted by a local group in 1968 to determine if there was a need for postsecondary education on the reservation. The study revealed a sufficient number of interested persons to warrant the establishment of a tribal junior college. In 1969, the Rosebud Sioux Tribal Council passed a resolution in support of a junior college, and it contacted the University of South Dakota at Vermillion and Black Hills State College at Spearfish to begin offering selected courses. In 1973, the South Dakota Board of Regents approved the offering of associate degrees at Sinte Gleska College (SGC) in affiliation with Black Hills State College and the University of South Dakota. The first associate degree was awarded in 1973.[32]

Sinte Gleska College awarded the first bachelor's degree in 1980. In January of 1983, SGC received official notification from the North Central Association that it had gained full accreditation status. Thus, SGC became the first tribally chartered college in the nation to become accredited at both the two-year and four-year levels. SGC conferred its first degree under the full accreditation status in August 1984. In spring 1987, SGC received approval from the North Central Association of Colleges and Schools to offer a limited number of courses at the graduate level outside of degree programs. On June 22, 1989, SGC gained accreditation at the masters degree granting level. In August of 1989, nine graduate students earned their Master of Education degrees in Elementary Education through SGC. In February, 1992, Sinte Gleska College officially, through a special Lakota ceremony, became Sinte Gleska University.[33]

Northwest Indian College (NIC) in Bellingham, Washington, is a tribally controlled institution chartered by the Lummi Indian Business Council. Higher education on the Lummi Reservation began with the establishment in 1971 of the Lummi Indian School of Aquaculture, a single-purpose institution designed to provide technicians for employment in Native American owned and operated fish and shellfish hatcheries throughout the United States and Canada.[34]

In the early 1980s, the employment demand for fishery technicians declined dramatically, and concurrently the Lummi tribal leaders felt a need to focus tribal educational services on the educational needs of Native Americans in Northwest Washington. On April 1, 1983, the Lummi Indian Business Council approved the Charter for Lummi Community College. The mission of Northwest Indian College is to provide postsecondary educational opportunities for Northwest Indian people. The college curriculum includes academic, vocational, continuing, cultural, community service, and adult basic education. Specific courses of study and activities will be offered in accordance with identified needs and interests of the various Native American communities. The college also provides in-service training, planning, research, and evaluation services to tribal institutions and departments as needed. The college extends opportunities to individuals to gain self-sufficiency in a rapidly changing, technological world while helping to develop their cultural identity.[35]

Nebraska Indian Community College (NICC), Omaha, Nebraska, began as a multiple effort to help Nebraska tribes. A task force, appointed by the Tribal Council in 1996, studied the higher education component of the total educational plan. A part of this research included evaluating the general education and major programs at NICC, the two-year institution of higher education in which the Winnebagos shared a partnership. After exploring several options, and based on the recommendation of the task force, the Tribal Council decided to withdraw from NICC and to charter its own tribal college, Little Priest Tribal College (LPTC).

Little Priest Tribal College (LPTC), Winnebago, Nebraska, was named after Little Priest, the last true chief of the Ho-Chunk people. The mission of LPTC is to implement two-year associate degree programs, certificate programs, and community education programs, which provide students with (1) the opportunity to learn about Winnebago language and culture so that students are grounded in self-esteem, (2) an academic plan of learning so that students can succeed at four-year institutions, (3) competency in interpersonal skills such as self-discipline, communication, goal setting, problem solving, and critical thinking, and (4) the ability to integrate culture, academics, physical, psychological, and spiritual behavior so that students can interface with a diverse world.[36]

The Leech Lake Band of Ojibwe established Leech Lake Tribal College (LLTC) by tribal resolution in July 1990. In the fall 1992 quarter, LLTC began offering its own courses leading toward the Associate of Arts and Associate of Applied Science degrees for the first time. In spring 1993, the college had its first graduate of the Associate of Arts program in Anishinaabe Language and Culture. By 1995, the number increased to 24. Leech Lake Tribal College includes approximately 40 faculty and administrative staff and 250 students. Approximately 4 percent of the students enrolled at the college are non-Indian. LLTC is located on the Leech Lake Reservation in Cass Lake north central Minnesota. Approximately 8,000 enrolled members of the Leech Lake Band reside on or near the reservation. In fall 1998, through an agreement with Sinte Gleska University in South Dakota, LLTC began to provide the opportunity for students to complete an accredited four-year degree program in elementary education. From its inception, LLTC has understood its mission to center on the transmission of Anishinaabe language and culture. The college provides a space where the Anishinaabe culture is the dominant one. Here, Anishinaabe can come together to speak the language and talk and practice cultural ways in an atmosphere that nurtures understanding of Ojibwe language and culture. LLTC also serves as a bridge, providing access to higher education for Leech Lake tribal members who may wish to continue studies at four-year institutions or in graduate schools. LLTC is a member of the American Indian Higher Education Consortium and receives its base funding from the Bureau of Indian Affairs under the authority of the Tribally Controlled Community College Act (Title I, P.L. 95-471). The college assists all students who wish to transfer to another two-year or four-year school. In 1994, the college obtained status as a land grant institution by Congress. Presently, LLTC includes approximately 40 faculty and administrative staff and 250 students. Most of the students come from Leech Lake Reservation, although tribal members from other reservations also attend.[37]

LLTC is accredited by the North Central Association of Colleges and Schools, Commission on Schools, for its adult and vocational programs. LLTC is approved in all of its courses of instruction by the U.S. Department of Veteran Affairs. The two-year law enforcement program is approved by the Minnesota Board of Peace Officers Standards and Training. The mission of the college is "to provide all persons with a quality education grounded in the spirituality, history, and culture of the Anishinaabe. To nurture knowledge and respect for women as leaders of their clan families, and as traditional and contemporary leaders of the Anishinaabe. To develop Anishinaabe cultural and language studies as an area of study, and to recognize that the Anishinaabe language is the first language of the Anishinaabe. To provide courses leading to fully accredited and transferable Associate of Arts and Bachelor of Arts degrees. To provide opportunities for studies leading to two-year Associate of Applied Science technical degrees and one-year diploma programs. To assist people to be active and creative members of their communities and of the Leech Lake Nation. To provide tribal members with opportunities to improve skills and understanding in the arts and sciences, business, education, health, natural resources, and social services."

In October 1974, the Blackfeet Tribal Business Council chartered the Blackfeet Community College (BCC) by Executive Action to ". . . provide post-secondary and higher educational services . . ." to the Blackfeet Indian Reservation community. The impetus for this action grew from early tribal efforts to provide an educational opportunity to its residents in a physically, climatically, and culturally isolated area. BCC is located near Browning, Montana, on the Blackfeet Indian Reservation. Browning serves as the center for trade and cultural activities with a population of approximately 8,000. Browning is the headquarters of the Tribal Office, Bureau of Indian Affairs, Indian Health Service, and public school systems.[38]

BCC's mission is to provide transfer equivalent academic and relevant vocational programs of high quality that lead to appropriate associate degrees and certificates. BCC provides a core of general education instruction that results in identifiable student competence in written and oral communication, quantitative reasoning, critical analysis, and logical thinking, with literacy achieved in the discourse or technology appropriate to the student's program of study. Because of the changing nature of the demands placed upon members of the Blackfeet tribes in today's tribal society and beyond, BCC maintains a strong commitment to providing opportunities for life-long education including basic skills development, high school completion, GED, continuing education, and high-quality community service programs. This commitment serves the needs of the Blackfeet tribe and includes electronically accessed distance learning. Finally, and most importantly, it is BCC's mission to serve as a living memorial to the Blackfeet tribe in preserving the traditions and culture of a proud and progressive people. BCC is a fully accredited two-year, higher education institution with degree granting power, sanctioned by the North West Association of Schools and Colleges on December 11, 1985.[39]

Cankdeska Cikana Community College (CCCC), formerly Little Hoop Community College, is a tribally chartered college serving the residents and communities on and near the Spirit Lake Sioux Nation, Fort Totten, North Dakota. CCCC was founded in October 1974 and offered its first classes in the spring of 1975. CCCC operated from 1974 to 1981 as a satellite campus of Lake Region Community College. In 1981, Cankdeska Cikana Community College initiated the accreditation process and it became accredited in February 1990. The mission of Cankdeska Cikana Community College is to provide comprehensive postsecondary education, which addresses both traditional and contemporary aspects of learning. CCCC focuses on educating its students to live successfully by assisting each of them in reaching a goal that is desirable and attainable for their needs in this multicultural world. CCCC was named in honor of Cankdeska Cikana (meaning Little Hoop), the Indian name of Paul Yankton, Sr. Private First Class Yankton, the recipient of two Purple Hearts, who died on November 29, 1944, while serving as a rifleman with the Army's 11th Infantry at Lorraine, France.[40]

Located at Keshena, Wisconsin, the College of Menominee Nation's (CMN) mission is to provide quality educational opportunities in postsecondary education to the Menominee and surrounding residents so that they possess the skills and knowledge to be responsible in their chosen professions. As an institution of higher education chartered by the Menominee Tribe, the college also has the responsibility of infusing this education with Menominee values to prepare students for careers and advanced studies in a cross-cultural world; expand information through research; promote, perpetuate, and nurture Menominee culture; and provide outreach workshops and community services.[41]

Chief Dull Knife College (CDKC) is another Montana Indian college. It is located in the Northern Cheyenne Indian Reservation in Southeastern Montana. The college is named after Chief Dull Knife, also known as the Chief Morning Star. In 1876 after forced removal to Indian Territory (Oklahoma), Chief Dull Knife, under great odds and with great courage, led his band of Northern Cheyenne to their homeland in Montana. Dull Knife fought courageously to maintain the sovereignty of the Cheyenne 100 years before the first academic courses were offered in 1978. He and his people were under heavy fire and many Cheyenne died. Survivors were taken to Fort Robinson in Nebraska, and a reservation was created for them later in Montana. CDKC operates in the belief that all individuals should be "Treated with dignity and respect; Afforded equal opportunity to acquire a complete educational experience; Given an opportunity to discover and develop their special aptitudes and insights; Provided an opportunity to equip themselves for a fulfilling life and responsible citizenship in a world characterized by change, while simultaneously studying and enhancing Cheyenne cultural values."[42]

CDKC was originally chartered in September 1975 by tribal ordinance as the Northern Cheyenne Indian Action Program, Inc., and granted funding by the Indian Technical Assistance Center of the Bureau of Indian Affairs. The Northern Cheyenne Tribal Council appointed six directors to manage the affairs of the corporation. CDKC is an open-admission, community-based, comprehensive, tribally controlled community college and land grant institution designed to provide affordable, quality educational opportunities to residents of the Northern Cheyenne reservation and surrounding communities. Reflecting Chief Dull Knife's determination, the college's primary mission is to provide educational and cultural leadership to its constituents.

CDKC's original curriculum aimed to train students for jobs in the developing mining enterprises in communities near the reservation. Due to a recognition on the part of the staff, the Board of Directors, and tribal leadership of the need for continued expansion of the vocational program and incorporation of academic classes, CDKC developed rapidly. CDKC grew from a limited vocational training program toward a broader vocational and postsecondary educational institution. Since 1978, CDKC has expanded its curricular offerings to provide an Associate of Arts Degree in the academic disciplines, an

Associate of Applied Science in the vocational areas, and vocational certificates in various skill areas.

The mission of Fond du Lac Tribal and Community College (FTCC) is to provide higher education opportunities for its communities in a welcoming, culturally diverse environment. FTCC's mission is to promote scholarship and academic excellence through transfer and career education, and provide access to higher education by offering developmental education. Respectfully promote the language, culture and history of the Anishinaabe. Provide programs which will celebrate the cultural diversity of our community and promote global understanding. Promote a sense of personal respect and wellness. Provide opportunity, experience, and access to current technology, preparing students for the future."[43] Located in Wisconsin, FTCC is operated by the Fond du Lac Chippewa Tribe.

Salish Kootenai College (SKC) is located in Montana. In 1973, President Larry Blake of Flathead Valley Community College in Kalispell, Montana, approached the Flathead tribal council on the Flathead reservation and proposed a forestry technology program. Several tribal councilmen expressed concern about forming an agreement with a non-Indian institution, although a bilateral agreement was made between the two sides, thus laying the foundation for Salish-Kootenai Community College. Several years later, Salish-Kootenai Community College and Flathead Valley Community College secured a Title III grant, which included Blackfeet Community College.[44] Located in northwestern Montana on the Flathead Indian reservation, the early mission of Salish-Kootenai Community College stated "to provide quality education to post-secondary Indian residents" and "a comprehensive open-door community" was later added, "to assist in tribal development, to assist in cultural development of the Salish and Kootenai communities, to develop student academics, [and] to promote Indian self-determination."[45]

On November 8, 1984, the Fort Belknap Community Council charted Fort Belknap College (FBC). Less than a decade later, FBC received full accreditation through the Northwest Association of Schools and Colleges. The mission of FBC is "to provide quality post-secondary education for residents of the Fort Belknap Indian Reservation and surrounding communities. The college will help individuals improve their lives by offering them an opportunity to maintain the cultural integrity of the Gros Ventre and Assiniboine as well as succeed in an American technological society."[46] Located in north-central Montana, Fort Belknap is one of several reservations in the state, covering 675,147 acres. It is the fourth largest reservation in Montana, with the

Milk River bordering the northern section and the Little Rockies resting in the southern section. This is the home of the Assiniboine and Gros Ventre tribes, whose reservation was created from a treaty in 1855 when Governor Isaac I. Stevens of Washington Territory negotiated a peace between the U.S. and the Blackfeet, Flathead, and Nez Perce tribes. The Gros Ventre signed the treaty as a part of the Blackfeet Nation, thereby hunting grounds included the Assiniboine. Act of Congress on May 1, 1888 (Stat., L., XXV, 113) involved all the tribes ceding 17,500,000 acres in return for three reservations, now known as Blackfeet, Fort Peck, and Fort Belknap reservations. Fort Belknap was named for William W. Belknap, who was Secretary of War.[47]

The campus of Fort Peck Community College (FPCC) rests in northeastern Montana and dates back to 1969 when it offered courses by Dawson Community College on the Fort Peck Reservation. The tribal council believed that it was time to start its own tribal college after making a bilateral agreement with Miles Community College and securing a Title III grant. During the 1970s, Robert McAnally provided necessary leadership with the tribal council's appointed education committee, which became the board of trustees.[48] FPCC's mission is stated: "Fort Peck Community College serves the people of the Fort Peck Reservation and northeastern Montana as a vehicle of Indian awareness, as well as self-awareness. The College offers an academic program that enables students to earn credits in college courses transferable to other institutions of post-secondary and higher education. FPCC serves its clientele by maintaining an occupational training program based on the needs of the people living on and near the reservation and on jobs presently available in the region. FPCC serves the people by initiating and supporting community activities and organizations based on the needs and wishes of community members."[49] Tribal officials chartered FPPC during the spring of 1978. The average age of the Fort Peck college student is 27 years, and women make up 60 percent of the college population. Tribal members attend as the majority, with a large number of non-Indians also attending.[50]

Located on the southeastern edge of the Navajo Nation at Crownpoint, New Mexico, is Crownpoint Institute of Technology (CIT). CIT began offering technical skills as a center in July 1970. Facilities at CIT reflected the natural surroundings of the Chaco Canyon mesa and high plateaus. In the following years, Crownpoint developed into a technical-vocational education center. In 1981, the Navajo Nation designated CIT as an independent tribal school to be governed by its five-member Board of Directors and the state of New Mexico. As the school expanded quickly by offering eleven programs, the Board of Directors changed the name of the school to Crownpoint Institute of Technology in 1985. Presently, students select from 17 different programs. CIT's emphasis is to equip students with technical-vocational skills, counseling, career guidance, job placement assistance, and continuing education.[51]

The Institute of American Indian and Alaska Native Arts (IAIANA) is located in Santa Fe, New Mexico. Visionaries and artists had in mind the need for a school to further the talents of young native artists and to continue the artistic traditions of native peoples. In 1962, the Bureau of Indian Affairs began IAIANA as a high school. In 1975, the school became a two-year college offering an associate degree. Located near the plaza in downtown Santa Fe, the institute includes a contemporary Indian art museum. In 1998, Congress transferred the school from the supervision of the Bureau of Indian Affairs to become an independent, public, and private partnership, which continues to receive some federal support. The Institute is one of the three congressional chartered higher education institutions. In its nearly forty years of history, the school has enrolled more than 3,500 students from most of the 562 federally recognized tribes in the U.S.[52]

Keweenaw Bay Ojibwa Community College (KBOCC) is located in Baraga, Michigan. The college received its charter on July 12, 1975 with the goal to provide programs in higher education on the L'Anse Indian Reservation to promote the rich Ojibwa culture and traditions of the people. With its cultural emphasis in its curriculum, the mission of the school is to graduate students who will be lifetime scholars who will understand and possess the skills, attitudes, and abilities for achieving success in the twenty-first century. The college provides a professional, dedicated, open-minded, and enthusiastic faculty that is committed to teaching.[53]

Lac Courte Oreilles Ojibwa Community College (LCOOCC) is located at Hayward, Wisconsin, with its mission "to provide, within the Indian community, a system of post-secondary and continuing education with an associate degree and certificate granting capabilities, while maintaining an open door policy."[54] The college stresses the importance of Ojibwa culture and tribal self-determination while providing opportunities for individual self-improvement. In this rapidly changing world of technology, the college believes it is important to maintain the cultural heart of the Anishinaabe.

Little Bighorn College (LBC) is located at Crow Agency in southeast Montana. Beginning under the name of Crow Central Education

Commission, LBC opened its doors with its goal focused on (1) vocational training, (2) vocational agriculture, (3) vocational business, (4) secretarial science, and (5) media. In 1978, LBC expanded its curriculum with its principal goal: "The preservation and enhancement of the Crow language and Culture while providing an up-to-date higher education opportunity to its students."[55] By the early 1980s, LBC had developed bilateral agreements with higher education institutions in the state university system of Montana, thereby allowing dual enrollment of its students to receive appropriate credits for their courses. Under the leadership of Janine Pease-Pretty-On-Top as the president, LBC made important strides in its development toward accreditation and as a tribal college and member of the American Indian Higher Education Consortium.[56]

Stone Child College (SCC) is located at Rocky Boy Agency, fourteen miles from Box Elder, Montana. SCC is a tribally controlled college operated by the Chippewa–Cree Tribe. On May 17, 1984, the Chippewa–Cree Business Committee chartered the school to preserve the Chippewa–Cree culture and for the training of its people. SCC is dedicated to meet the multiple needs of the community, and tribal members while promoting pride among the Chippewa–Cree. SCC offers Associate of Arts and Associate of Science degrees and certificates, and it is a member of the American Indian Higher Education Consortium.[57]

White Earth Tribal and Community College (WETCC) is located at Mahnomen, Minnesota. It is an Anishinaabe, tribally controlled college with its purpose "dedicated to educational excellence through the provision of a culturally relevant curriculum, in partnership with students, staff, community and industry." Starting in 1979, the White Earth Tribe began an initiative to provide local higher education services to its people. The White Earth Reservation Tribal Council established the WETCC on September 8, 1997. In its charter, the College was established to "promote scholarly research, preserving Anishinaabe language, history, and culture, and other educational activities to serve the people of the White Earth Reservation and surrounding communities."[58]

Founded in 1986, Red Crow Community College (RCCC) is located at Cardston, Alberta, Canada. Postsecondary education became increasingly important with more employment opportunities occurring on and off the Blood Reserve. The school operates under the direction of the Blood Tribe Education Committee. Initially, RCCC began as an adult education center and provided educational training opportunities to its tribal members. The mission statement of RCCC is "to provide quality educational training opportunities to adult Indian and

non-Indian residents and employees of the Blood Reserve and surrounding areas. The curriculum will reflect identified needs and interests of these residents by providing adult basic education, vocational
education, academic, cultural, and community interest programs,
courses, seminars, workshops, activities, and events. Assistance will be
provided to tribal institutions and departments in staff planning, research, and evaluation services according to identified needs. The edu-
cational/training system will provide opportunities for individual
self-improvement for survival in a rapidly changing and technological
world, and yet maintain the integrity of the Blood people." The philosophy of the college is "the Red Crow Board of Governors proposes a
comprehensive plan with curriculum designed to meet the special
needs of the Kainaiwa of the Blackfoot Nation. While the system does
not intend to exclude anyone, and maintains an 'open door' policy, its
primary purpose are to meet the needs of the Blackfoot population."[59]

During the fall of 1994, President Bill Clinton signed the Elementary and Secondary Education Act that gave 29 tribal colleges land
grant status. The legislation enabled the tribal colleges to receive funding from $4.6 million between 1996 and 2000. An additional $1.7 million allowed the tribal colleges to apply for funding for buildings,
laboratories, and other major facilities.[60]

In January 1998, the Legislative Council of the Tohono O'odham
Nation chartered the Tohono O'odham Community College (TOCC).
Located at Sells, Arizona, the new tribal college offered courses in the
Sells, San Xavier Mo'o, and Gu Achi districts. In 2002, Bob Martin became the new president of TOCC to advance the college vision "to enhance greater participation of the Tohono O'odham Nation in the
local, national, and global community." TOCC projects an enrollment
of 500 students in the next three to five years, following its mission "to
enhance the unique Tohono O'odham by strengthening individuals,
families, and communities through holistic, quality services. These
services will provide a variety of academic, life, and development
skills."[61]

During the mid 1990s, thirteen research centers and institutions ex-
isted with their objectives focusing on American Indians. They in-
cluded the American Indian and Alaska Periodicals Research
Clearinghouse at the University of Arkansas in Fayetteville; American
Indian Culture Research Center at Blue Cloud Abbey in Marvin, South
Dakota; American Indian Research Opportunity at Montana State
University in Bozeman, Montana; American Indian Studies Center at
UCLA; American Indian Studies Research Institute at Indiana Univer-

sity, Bloomington; The Amerind Foundation, Inc., at Dragoon, Arizona; Anthropology Film Center Foundation at Santa Fe, New Mexico; D'Arcy McNickle Center for the History of the American Indian at the Newberry Library in Chicago; Center for Pacific Northwest Studies in Bellingham, Washington; Center for Studies of Ethnicity and Race in America at the University of Colorado, Boulder; Institute for American Indian Studies in Washington, Connecticut; The National Center for American Indian and Alaska Mental Health Research in Denver, Colorado; and the Institute of American Indian Studies at the University of South Dakota, Vermillion.[62]

At the University of Kansas in Lawrence, a collective effort formed from native scholars from various backgrounds that include Canadian interests, the United States, and Latin America. At the University of Kansas, one of the nation's premier Latin American Studies Centers exists. For several months in 1997, the native scholars at the University of Kansas debated at length the possible name of their new master's degree program—American Indian Studies, Native American Studies, First Nations Studies, and Indigenous Nations Studies.

The terms "American Indian Studies," "Native American Studies," and "First Nations Studies" all carry meaning and largely negative implications of what foreign colonialism has had on the native communities of the Americas. It seems as if we take the very name of "Indian" from our conquerors and try to give it new definition from a native perspective, to give it our own meaning. Even the term "Native" has equal negative connotations that "native" is something less than the "status quo" of equality, below standard, being primitive, and so forth.

With the urging of the Indian faculty coming from Professors Luci Tapahonso, Ray Pierotti, Michael Yellow Bird, Rob Porter, and other key University of Kansas faculty like Professors Rita Napier of History, Don Stull of Anthropology, Bud Hirsch of English, and Peter Mancall of History, the movement had the support from former President Bob Martin of Haskell Indian Nations University. In the summer of 1996, Provost David Shulenburger with the support of Chancellor Bob Hemenway, launched a Native American Studies Task Force following two years of lobbying by the faculty.[63] At the time in 1996, 253 native students were enrolled at the University of Kansas, although they represented only 1 percent of the student population. The Indian students organized the Native American Student Association (NASA), which changed to First Nations Students Association (FNSA).

The mission of the new master's program at the University of Kansas is that the program "will attract motivated, enthusiastic, and devoted graduate students to KU, promote interdisciplinary basic and applied research on problems confronting indigenous communities, and initiate KU's service to these communities. The Program will also produce trained experts and professionals who are capable of assuming leadership and policymaking positions in Indigenous government, education, community development, and entrepreneurial sectors. The Program will also produce graduates who will be able to serve Indigenous people through service with the federal, state, and local governments, and in the off-reservation private sectors."[64]

More than twenty faculty at the University of Kansas were interested in the development of this new program, and they had a wide-ranging scope of interests. Themes, parallels, concepts, and related interests attracted the various faculty members to monthly discussions of indigenous issues. Such discussion flowed toward themes and concepts of "Colonialism," "Identity," "Victimization," "Sovereignty," "Genocide," "Survival," "Paternalism," and most of these (which were pejorative in nature) had happened in the United States in the past, but they were continuing in other parts of the world, certainly in other parts of the Western Hemisphere. In addition, historic stereotypes continued to berate Indian people in other parts of the world, with the presumption of freezing "Indians" in time. That Indian people have not advanced at all, and that their cultures and communities had disappeared in the nineteenth century is an ongoing concept.[65]

The example at the University of Kansas exemplified a developing trend for the twenty-first century throughout Indian academia of more Indian studies program and Indian studies departments being started. The University of California at Davis's graduate program in indigenous studies started in 1998. Montana State University in Bozeman started a new graduate program with its first class entering in the fall of 2000. Northern Arizona University in Flagstaff started a new Applied Indigenous Nations Studies Program for undergraduates in 2000.

During March 2–3, 2000, Arizona State University held the "First Peoples, First Nations: Voices and Perspectives of American Indian Studies into the 21st Century" conference at Tempe, Arizona. Over one hundred Indian and non-Indian scholars, program directors, and students attended the successful conference.

During the American Indian Studies Directors' Consortium conference at Arizona State University, Dean Chavers projected that the number of American Indians holding doctorates had quintupled the 191 Indian doctorates counted in his survey study during the mid 1970s. No longer did American Indians have to feel like the "Lone Ranger" Indian scholar in their departments instead of feeling like "Tonto." Although the number of Indians in faculty positions was growing, many Indian scholars feel alone as the "Lone Ranger" on their campuses.

As a part of this institutional movement, Indian museums and tribal museums have operated since the 1980s. The Field Museum in Chicago, Denver Public Museum, Milwaukee Public Museum, and the Heard Museum in Phoenix, Arizona have long been places for exhibiting American Indian artifacts. The Buffalo Bill Historical Center in Cody, Wyoming, has been one of the representations of plains Indian culture and history.[66] On July 4, 1927, the original Buffalo Bill Museum, a log building, was dedicated in Cody. Today, the Buffalo Bill Historical Center is an elaborate complex housing four major collections, including the Plains Indian Museum devoted to the cultural traditions of American Indian life in the West.

Founded in 1929, Dwight B. and Maie Bartlett Heard opened the Heard Museum in Phoenix, Arizona to house their personal collection of cultural and fine art. With its mission "to educate the public about the heritage and the living cultures and arts of Native peoples, with an emphasis on the peoples of the Southwest," the Heard Museum also houses the Billie Jane Baguley Library and Archives with materials on Native American art and culture on the American Southwest, including indigenous arts of Oceania, Africa, Asia, and the Americas.[67]

The interest in American Indians, their history and cultures, continued to capture public curiosity throughout the twentieth century. In 1959, Harry and Jeannette Ayer gave the Mille Lacs Indian Museum and trading post to the Minnesota Historical Society. The Ayers had moved to Mille Lacs circa 1918, established a trading post, and opened a fishing resort with cabins, a restaurant, and fishing expeditions. The museum contains more than 1,500 Indian artifacts, including many photographs.[68]

The Eiteljorg Museum opened its doors for operation on June 24, 1989 in Indianapolis. Harrison Eiteljorg (1903–1997) worked with city officials of Indianapolis to house his collection of American Indian objects and Western paintings and sculptures. A businessman and philanthropist, Eiteljorg envisioned a museum of this nature for the midwest of America to enjoy as a part of the White River State Park along the Central Canal in Indianapolis. The mission statement of the Eiteljorg Museum of American Indians and Western Art is "to inspire an appreciation and understanding of the art, history, and cultures of the American West and the indigenous peoples of North America. The Eiteljorg Museum collects and preserves Western art and Native American art and cultural objects of the highest quality, and serves the public through engaging exhibitions, educational programs, cultural exchanges, and entertaining special events."[69]

On August 11, 1998, the cassino-rich Pequot of Connecticut opened the Mashantucket Pequot Museum and Research Center, a 308,000-square-foot complex. Costing $193.4 million, the complex presents multisensory dioramas, exhibits eastern woodland and Mashantucket Pequot cultural history, and uses films, videos, interactive programs, archival materials, and ethnographic and archaeological collections. A state-of-the-art museum and complex includes a library, a children's library, reading rooms, stacks, a research department, storage facilities, and conservation laboratories.[70]

The National Museum of the American Indian emerged from federal legislation to be constructed in three parts with the main one being a part of the Smithsonian complex of museums. Headed by Rick West, a Cheyenne, the NMAI promises much for the future preservation and correct exhibiting of Native American artifacts.

The Oklahoma Indian Museum and Cultural Center is being constructed in Oklahoma City at Interstate 40 and Interstate 35. It calls for Oklahoma congressmen and the public as well as the private sector to fund an institution that will proudly display and respectfully exhibit the Oklahoma Indian experience. One outspoken native person said, "We want to show the world that we are an organized people. In the future, we don't want to end up engraved in a museum's exhibit. We want our music and dance, our songs to nature, to our homes, and to our motherland performed by our people themselves while they are alive. We don't want to be thought of as dead people to be exhibited in a museum, and described in a book, or recorded on film—that is not our tradition. We are a community like any other community in the world. When we go back to our communities, we will tell them that at the museum, we have seen the work of our parents and grandparents who—maybe naively—handed over these sacred objects, which are our people's property, heritage, and patrimony. They handed them over without fully realizing the implications. That is our message, and that is why our participation in this project is so important. We want to share our thoughts, philosophy, and principles as an organization so our fellow indigenous peoples of the Americas and the world will know that we have the capacity to get organized and defend ourselves. The industrialized world wants to destroy our land and contaminate the atmosphere in which we live, which will kill our people and many others. Today, the entire world should be worried about protecting the few remaining Amazonian forests. That is why we got organized—we know that we have to be organized in order to survive and defend our rights. Nobody will save us but our own people."[71] In all, there are 150 tribal museums throughout Indian Country in the United States, and more are being planned.

In Canada, the Vancouver Museum is the largest civic museum in the country. It was previously known as the Centennial Museum until 1981. The museum dates back to 1894 when it was founded. Exhibitions and educational programs focus on the natural, cultural, and human history of the Vancouver region, especially demonstrating the rich cultural history of the Northwest Coast First Nations.[72]

The impact of linear education on Indian people has had severe consequences, although this has not suppressed native intellect and the achievement of American Indian individuals. Cultural discrimination has persisted in white school systems since the boarding school years, in mission schools, and in public schools, which Native Americans have attended.

The work of this generation and the two previous ones have formed a cadre of native scholars, who serve as the foundation of American Indian and indigenous studies programs and departments throughout the United States and Canada. More non-Indian scholars teach in these programs and departments, so that more non-Indians are in the majority as teaching faculty.

The nature of native studies or American Indian studies or indigenous studies is one that has not developed into a discipline of its own. Instead, it draws on the analyses of more than one academic discipline. For example, ethnohistory is one means that might be called an area and a methodology for studying American Indians. Due to the fact that one academic discipline of Western science is inadequate to understand American Indians fully, American Indian studies have come to rely on more than one academic discipline employed by native scholars.

Without a recognized discipline of their own, native studies scholars have been able to establish programs, departments, and centers, but remain isolated and/or dependent on other academic programs and disciplines. It has become important that American Indian studies programs and departments form partnerships with other programs and departments in colleges and universities. Unfortunately, the present reality is that native studies do not wield sufficient political power in academia, even on their own campuses, to operate independently. Operational funding is the obstacle and challenge for native studies now that a sufficient number of students at the undergraduate and graduate levels, and an increasing number of native scholars occurs, and a growing interest in native issues and studies continues.

It has become the responsibility of native studies programs and American Indian scholars to take a proactive stance in "reaching out" to native and non-native scholars and non-native programs. This action implies a sense of ownership and self-determination in an endeavor for native programs and tribes to define their own future of American Indian studies and preservation of traditional knowledge in a proper way.

Establishing forums at tribal colleges to start dialogues would foster native self-determined intellectualism and institutionalism. Such forums created and hosted by native scholars and Indian administrators need to be held on a frequent basis, and they need to be institutionalized for permanency and securing traditional knowledge of the American Indian.

American Indian educators in each institution, whether a tribal college or an American Indian studies program, need visions for the future. Their destinies and success depend on each vision and mission of the program. As the tribal college movement grows in momentum, a new curriculum with native intellectuals is at the forefront of this change. It is a new age as traditional knowledge is in the hands of native intellectuals while others seek to continue their studies of American Indians. Traditional knowledge has become less traditional with each new generation of American Indians who know less and less about tribal values. Simultaneously, tribal values at present are based on modern needs and cultural change, unlike past conditions.

At the dawn of the twenty-first century, Luther Standing Bear would be impressed with the progress made by American Indian academicians and administrators in building institutions. American Indians have overcome most of their fear of institutions that boarding schools had once instilled in them. They now accept them and embrace the idea of them as long as they control them through an Indian academic freedom. Such Indian and/or tribal institutions are new places of traditional knowledge. Ironically, the "institution" once feared is now an important part of the Indian–white partnership in advancing the scholarship of the American Indian mind. Luther Standing Bear would be proud if he saw today's progress of tribal colleges and the many American Indian studies programs and departments at universities.

Most importantly, the American Indian mind has changed and it has become less traditional. The majority of the Indian population is represented by mixed bloods, and the mixed blood thinks differently from the traditional full blood and he or she thinks more like the linear white man due to attending schools with white teachers. What is gained is at the loss of traditional knowledge and the disappearing of the true American Indian mind of the full blood as he observes his people becoming more mixed blooded and urbanized in association with the linear world.

NOTES

1. Donald L. Fixico, "Institutionalizing American Indian Intellectualism and Traditional Knowledge," Annual Conference, "In Partnership," May 31–June 3, 2001, Saskatchewan Indian Federated College, Saskatoon, Saskatchewan, Canada.

2. Luther Standing Bear, "The Future of the Indian," in Charles Hamilton, ed., *Cry of the Thunderbird: The American Indian's Own Story* (Norman: University of Oklahoma Press, 1972), 245–247.

3. Wayne J. Stein, *Tribally Controlled Colleges: Making Good Medicine* (New York: Peter Lang Publishers, 1992), 3, and see Margaret Connell Szasz, *Indian Education in the American Colonies, 1607–1783* (Albuquerque, University of New Mexico Press, 1988).

4. Ibid.

5. Mission Statement for Haskell Indian Nations University, Approved by National Board of Regents, Haskell Indian Nations University, May 11, 2000 <http://www.naes.indian.com/catalog/schools.htm>.

6. Ibid.

7. See Thomas R. Reno, "A Demonstration in Navajo Education," *Journal of American Indian Education*, Vol. 6, No. 3, May 1967, 1–5.

8. United Tribes Technical College Website, n.d., Bismarck, North Dakota <http://www.unitedtribes.tech.com>.

9. Ibid.

10. Ibid.

11. Clifford E. Trafzer, "Native American Studies," in Frederick Hoxie, ed. *Encyclopedia of North American Indians: Native American History. Culture, and Life From Poleo-Indians to the Present.* Boston and New York: Houghton Mifflin, 1996), 421.

12. Wayne Stein, *Tribally Controlled Colleges: Making Good Medicine* (New York, San Francisco, Bern, Baltimore, Frankfurt am Main, Berlin, Wien and Paris: Peter Lang, 1992), 41–53.

13. Ibid.

14. Ibid.

15. Marjane Ambler, "Oglala College Outlasts Skeptics," *Tribal College: Journal of American Indian Higher Education*, Vol. 7, No. 2, Fall 1996, 24–25.

16. "First National American Indian University," *Educational Update Online,* New York City, October 15, 2001 <http://www.educationupdate.com/oct01/oct01_articles/col indian.html>.

17. Website for Southwestern Indian Polytechnic Institute, April 16, 2001 <http://www.sipi.bia.edu/history.htm>.

18. Website for Fort Berthold Community College, April 16, 2001 <http://www.fortbelknap.cc.mt.us>.

19. Stein, *Tribally Controlled Colleges,* 27–40.

20. Donald L. Fixico, *The Urban Indian Experience in America* (Albuquerque: University of New Mexico Press, 2000), 158; see also NAES College Website, n.d., Chicago, Illinois <http://naes.indian.com/naes.html>.

21. NAES College Information, Website, May 29, 2001 <http://www.naes.indian.com/catalog/schools.htm>.

22. Fixico, *The Urban Indian Experience in America*, 158, NAES College Website, n.d., Chicago, Illinois <http://naes.indian.com/naes.html>.

23. "Tribally Controlled Community College Act," P. L. 93–471, October 17, 1978, *U. S. Statutes At Large*, 92:1325–31.

24. "Tribal Colleges: Shaping the Future of Native America," The Carnegie Foundation for the Advancement of Teaching, 1989.

25. Bay Mills Community College Website <http://www.bmcc.org/nish/toc/Generalinfo.html>, April 16, 2001.

26. Mary L. Underwood, "Bay Mills Focuses on Students," *Tribal College: Journal of American Indian Higher Education*, Vol. 7, No. 4, Spring 1997, 32.

27. Bay Mills Community College Website <http://www.bmcc.org/nish/toc/Generalinfo.html>, April 16, 2001.

28. Turtle Mountain Community College Website, May 20, 2002, Bellcourt, North Dakota <http://www.turtle-mountain.cc.nd.us/> and see Logan J. Davis, "Turtle Mountain Celebrates Another Milestone," *Tribal College: Journal of American Indian Higher Education*, Vol. 9, No. 2, Fall 1997, 48–50.

29. Turtle Mountain Community College Website, May 20, 2002, Bellcourt, North Dakota <http://www.turtle-mountain.cc.nd.us/>.

30. Sitting Bull College Website, May 20, 2002, Fort Yates, North Dakota <http://www.sittingbull.edu/History.htm>.

31. Sisseton Wahpeton Community College Website, May 20, 2002, Sesseton, South Dakota <http://www.swcc.cc.sd.us/>.

32. Sinte Gleska University Website, May 20, 2002, Sinte Gleska, South Dakota <http://www.sinte.indian.com/history.html>.

33. Ibid.

34. Northwest Indian College Website, May 20, 2002, Bellingham, Washington <http://www.nwic.edu/>.

35. Ibid.

36. Nebraska Indian Community College Website, May 20, 2002, Winnebago, Nebraska <http://www.thenicc.org/>.

37. Leech Lake Tribal College Website, May 20, 2002, Leech Lake, Minnesota <http://www.lltc.org/>.

38. Stein, *Tribally Controlled Colleges*, 137.

39. Ibid.

40. Cankdeska Cikana Community College Website, May 20, 2002, Fort Totten, North Dakota <http://www.littlehoop.cc/>.

41. College of Menominee Nation Website, May 20, 2002, Keshena, Wisconsin <http://www.menominee.com/newcmn/Intro.htm>.

42. Dull Knife Memorial College Website, May 20, 2002, Lame Deer, Montana <http://www.montana.edu/~wwwai/DKMC.html>.

43. Fond du Lac Tribal and Community College Website, n.d., Cloquet, Minnesota <http://www.fdl.cc.mn.us/>.

44. Stein, *Tribally Controlled Colleges*, 137.

45. Ibid.

46. Mission For Fort Belknap College, Website, n.d. <http://www.fortbelknap.cc.mt.us/mission.html>.

47. "Tribe Connections in the Pacific Northwest," Fort Belknap Agency, Website, May 20, 2002 <http://www.montana.edu/~wwwse/fbc/FBCHIST.HTML>.

48. Stein, *Tribally Controlled Colleges*, 140.

49. Ibid.

50. Ibid., 140–141.

51. "A Bridge to Our Future: Crownpoint Institute of Technology," n.d. <http://www.cit.cc.nm.us/location_and_history.html>.

52. Institute of Indian Arts Website, n.d. <http://www.iaiancad.org/institute.htm>; see also Joy L. Gritton, *The Institute of American Indian Arts: Modernism and U.S. Indian Policy* (Albuquerque: University of New Mexico Press, 2000).

53. Keweenaw Bay Ojibwa Community College Website, March 20, 2002, <www.kbocc.org>.

54. Lac Courte Oreilles Ojibwa Community College Website, March 20, 2002, <www.lco-college.edu>.

55. Stein, *Tribally Controlled Colleges*, 136.

56. Ibid., 136–137.

57. Stone Child College Website, May 20, 2002, Rocky Boy Agency, Montana <http://www.montana.edu/wwwscc/index.html>.

58. White Earth Tribal and Community College Website, May 20, 2002, Mahnomen, Minnesota <http://www/.wetcc.org/charter%20bylaws.htm>.

59. Red Crow Community College Website, May 20, 2002, Alberta, Canada <http://www/.redcrowcollege.com/mission.htm>.

60. Robert Bigart, "Tribal College Land-Grant Future: Promise and Peril," *Tribal College: Journal of American Indian Higher Education*, Vol. 7, No. 4, Spring 1997, 36–37.

61. TOCC–History of Tohono O'odham Community College Website, May 20, 2002, Sells, Arizona <http://www.tocc.cc.az.us/history.htm>.

62. Duane Champagne, ed., *The Native North American Almanac: A Reference Work on Native North Americans in the United States and Canada* (Detroit, Washington, D.C., and London: Gale Research Inc., 1994), 911.

63. Chris Lazzarino, "Talk of the Nations," *Kansas Alumni* (May 1996), 20.

64. Mission Statement from proposal that designed the Indigenous Nations Studies Program, University of Kansas, submitted March 6, 1997 to Provost David Shulenburger by the Indigenous Nations Studies Task Force of the University of Kansas, Lawrence.

65. James H. Howard, *The Native American Image in Western Europe* (Hurst, TX: Society for American Indian Studies & Research, 1978), 33–56.

66. For sources on the Buffalo Bill Historical Center, see Jane Tompkins, "At the Buffalo Bill Museum—June 1988," *South Atlantic Quarterly*, Vol. 89, No. 3, Summer 1990, 525–545; Gene Ball, "Preserving the Western Legacy: The Buffalo Bill Historical Center," *Journal of the West*, Vol. 20, No. 1, Spring 2, 66–71; Peter H. Hassrick, "Yesterday's West Lives on at the Buffalo Bill Historical Center," *American West*, 1977, Vol. 14, No. 3, 16–29.

67. Heard Museum Website, May 20, 2002, Phoenix, Arizona <http://www.heard.org>.

68. Sarah Libertus, "The New Mille Lacs Indian Museum," *Minnesota History* Vol. 55, No. 1, Spring 1996, 32–39.

69. Eiteljorg Museum of American Indians and Western Art Website, May 20, 2002, Indianapolis, Indiana <http://www.eiteljorg.org/>.

70. Mashantucket Pequot Museum and Research Center Website, May 20, 2002, Mashantucket Pequot Tribe, Mashantucket Pequot Reservation, Mashantucket, Connecticut <http://www.mashantucket.com>.

71. National Museum of the American Indian, *All Roads Are Good: Native Voices on Life and Culture* (Washington: Smithsonian Institution Press, 1994), 184.

72. Vancouver Museum Website, May 20, 2002, Vancouver, British Columbia <http://www.vanmuseum.bc.ca/inside/history.htm>.

9
THE FULL CIRCLE
AND ITS CENTER

"Our Grandfather, Wakan-Tanka, You are everything, and yet above everything! You are first. You have always been. This soul that we are keeping will be at the center of the sacred hoop of this nation; through this center our children will have strong hearts, and they will walk the straight red path in a wakan manner. . . Remember this my relatives: that the power of this pure soul will be with you as you walk, for it, too, is the fruit of Mother Earth; it is as a seed, planted in your center, which will in time grow in your hearts, and cause our generation to walk in a wakan manner."[1]
Black Elk, Oglala Lakota, ca. 1933

* * *

Toward the end of one's life, many things make sense and one begins to realize that things come full circle. These realizations are learning from one's life experiences. Indigenous people who are circularly oriented already know this to be true as it is a part of the circular philosophy that has been the point of this book.

By nature, we stand at one point and look at life all around us. But this is not the heart of the circle. As individuals, all of us sometimes think of ourselves as the center since our personal lives and our own perception is 360 degrees in all directions, but we should remind ourselves to look up and down as well. In this instance, our view has taken on a three-dimensional perspective so that the universe from one's reference point is a sphere instead of a circle. Next, we should contemplate the center of our existence, that is our very being. In the Muscogee Creek ethos of *Ibofanga* "totality," the seventh direction is the center. It is well being and the balance of life.

For the Crow people of Montana, the center is being connected to the Creator. Thomas Yellowtail, the famed Medicine Man of the Crow, said, "When we hold ceremonies in this sacred manner, we show our respect not only to the Medicine Father who has passed on the power to us, but also to all of creation. By observing our prayers and performing the ceremonies, the Crow maintain the sacred center that connects us to Acbadadea [the Creator]."[2]

The center of the circle is the momentum of good feeling, the beauty of life. For example, Navajo philosophy is based on "walking in beauty." This center of good feeling is the balance in that happiness of feeling connected with all relatives and all things. It is the balance that we struggle for throughout our lives.

The center is the realization and finally the true understanding of life with a mature perspective. It is not how we want certain things in any given direction and reach for them as a child might do, but rather it is the ability to look in all directions and appreciate and respect all things. The linear person, who is goal oriented, is a part of the mainstream of looking ahead, keeping one's head down and working hard, or not looking back for someone might be gaining on you. In such a view of only looking ahead, a person does not see what or who is to either side of him or her. Perhaps this is why so many people experience stress in the modern American society.

The center of the Circle of Life is symbolized by certain items like the fire and the drum of the plains people. Black Elk reminded us about the importance of the drum in this central position by saying, "Since the drum is often the only instrument used in our sacred rites, I should perhaps tell you here why it is especially sacred and important to us. It is because the round form of the drum represents the whole universe, and its steady strong beat is the pulse, the heart, throbbing at the center of the universe. It is as the voice of *Wakan-Tanka*, and this sound stirs us and helps us to understand the mystery and power of all things."[3]

In another example, Black Elk stated that the importance of the center of the circle is not man, but it is sacred, stating, "The first peace, which is the most important, is that which comes within the souls of men when they realize their relationship, their oneness, with the universe and all its Powers, and when they realize that at the center of the universe dwells *Wakan Tanka*, and that this center is really everywhere."[4]

For the plains Indian people, like the Crow, the Sun Dance is the central traditional ceremony. Yellowtail described the Sun Dance and the importance of the center, saying, "The rafter poles link the sacred circle to the Center Pole, which is the sacred point where all three worlds are connected: the physical world of the [Crow] tribe, the spiritual world of our Medicine Fathers [Givers], and the pure world of

Acbadadea [Creator]. There are other meanings also; the lodge is round, and that represents the Earth, which is round. The twelve poles, leading from each forked pole to the center, represent the twelve months of the year. The twelve months represent another circle, because in it we are brought back to a new beginning. Each of the twelve poles represents a month of the year when we must have our monthly prayer meeting, when the moon is full and up in the air, and we should continue prayers each day between the twelve appointed monthly Sun Dance prayer meetings. The drum which we use to help carry our songs to Acbadadea is also round. All things in Nature's way are round."[5] Black Elk described the Sun Dance among the Oglalas in the following way. He said, "I should tell you here that in setting up the Sun Dance lodge, we are really making the universe in a likeness; for you see, each of the posts around the lodge represents some particular object of creation, so that the whole circle is the entire creation, and the one tree at the center, upon which the twenty-eight poles rest, is *Wakan-Tanka*, who is the center of everything. Everything comes from Him, and sooner or later everything returns to Him."[6]

Among plains Indians, many things are round like a circle such as the base of a tipi, shape of a shield, a drum, and the Sun Dance ceremony. In the center, the people feel the spiritual energy of all people of the circle.

The full circle and its center is that stage of life that one sees in all directions. According to Lori Arviso Alvord, "Navajos believe in *hozho* or *hozhoni*—'Walking in Beauty'—a world view in which everything in life is connected and influences everything else. A stone thrown into a pond can influence the life of a deer in the forest, a human voice and a spoken word can influence events around the world, and all things possess spirit and power. Navajos make every effort to live in harmony and balance with everyone and everything else. Their belief system sees sickness as a result of things falling out of balance, of losing one's way on the path of beauty. In this belief system, religion and medicine are one and the same."[7] Finding such balance is powerful and good, and it is an effort to continue to be at such a place in one's heart. "In order to know the center of the heart," said Black Elk, "where the Great Spirit dwells you must be pure and good, and live in the manner that the Great Spirit has taught us. The man who is thus pure contains the Universe in the pocket of his heart."[8]

During the summer of 2001, my father, my six-year-old son, and I left a little after eleven o'clock on a Saturday night to attend a stomp dance at Tallahassee deep in rural Muscogee Creek country of Oklahoma. Having not been there in many years, my father, who had been raised in the traditional way and who had become a Southern Baptist minister later in life, drove us in his pickup. It was a still night and the Moon was full, like a huge white circle in the night's sky. A third try of various wrong turns in the night while running out of road, and asking directions at one person's house finally enabled us to find Tallahassee a little after midnight. As we pulled up, the dance was in full progress, and full of relatives. Hearing the songs rang of my childhood when we attended stomp dances in the early years of my life. The dance circle was full of men, women, and children dancing counter clockwise with the fire in the middle. The fire crackled as if to sing its own song into the night. That special night, my father led a song for the first time in more than thirty years, his grandson danced during the song, and a proud father danced the same song—three generations at once with the full Moon, hearing my father singing, hearing the women's shaking shells, and feeling the Earth beneath my feet, as it empowered all of us to dance. That night a wind, a fox, and a wolf danced. One could feel the ancient power of Nature's way to respect the Giver of Breath for the gift of life as such a feeling at the stomp dance seemed to take on a life of its own. The enclosed circle of Creeks dancing to the fire lived a life of its own. This was feeling the Circle of Life as it was meant to be. All of the Muscogees there continued to dance through the night until streaks of pinks, reds, then oranges began to show in the East. Like the people coming out of the misty fog from the Earth at the time of creation, we welcomed the light of a new day, and during this summer of the Green Corn in this year we welcomed the twenty-first century.

At the center, the person is at peace like the eye of a hurricane when all things are storming, much like in battle when a war leader needs to be clear minded and strong. The commander or war leader must calmly act quickly in decision-making for he is the balance of the storm while people are dying around him. The center of this existence is the peaceful calm like being in a lodge or house while listening to a teeming rainstorm outside. It is the violence of the life outside of one's sanctuary of being inside of the circle, at the center. This is the center of our existence in balance with life and the universe. For the center of the circle of life is within all of us as we seek to find it, and we should seek the balance in our lives with all of our relations. For if we do not strive to find the balance of beauty and well-being in our lives, we will be stressed and lost in a misty fog of confusion.

NOTES

1. Joseph Epes Brown, ed., *The Sacred Pipe: Black Elk's Account of the Seven Rites of the Oglala Sioux* (New York: Penguin Books, 1971), p. 13, originally published University of Oklahoma Press, Norman, 1953.

2. Yellowtail, *Yellowtail Crow Medicine Man and Sun Dance Chief: An Autobiography as Told to Michael Oren Fitzgerald* (Norman: University of Oklahoma Press, 1991), 13.
3. Brown, *The Sacred Pipe*, 69.
4. Brown, *The Sacred Pipe*, 114–115.
5. Yellowtail, *Yellowtail Crow Medicine Man and Sun Dance Chief*, 150.
6. Ibid., originally quoted in Brown, *The Sacred Pipe*, 157.
7. Lori Arviso Alvord and Elizabeth Cohen Van Pelt, *The Scalpel and the Silver Bear: The First Navajo Woman Surgeon Combines Western Medicine and Traditional Healing* (New York, Toronto, London, Sydney and Auckland: Bantam Books, 1999), 14.
8. Yellowtail, *Yellowtail Crow Medicine Man and Sun Dance Chief*, 105, originally quoted in Brown, *The Sacred Pipe*.

BIBLIOGRAPHY

Government Documents

"Interior Provisions." *Congressional Quarterly Almanac 1993*. Vol. 49, 103rd Congress, 1st sess., 629.

"Tribally Controlled Community College Act," P.L. 93-471, October 17, 1978, *U.S. Statutes At Large*, 92:1325–1331.

Books

Adams, David Wallace. *Education for Extinction: American Indians and the Boarding-School Experience, 1875–1928*. Lawrence, KS: University Press of Kansas. 1995.

All Roads Are Good: Native Voices on Life and Culture. Washington: Smithsonian Institution Press. 1994.

Alvord, Lori Arviso and Elizabeth Cohen Van Pelt. *The Scalpel and the Silver Bear: The First Navajo Woman Surgeon Combines Western Medicine and Traditional Healing*. New York, Toronto, London, Sydney and Auckland: Bantam Books. 1999.

Armstrong, Virginia Irving. *I Have Spoken: American History Through the Voices of the Indians*. Chicago: Swallow Press. 1971.

Barrett, Donald N. ed. *Values in America*. Notre Dame, IN: University of Notre Dame University Press. 1961.

Basso, Keith H. *Western Apache Witchcraft*. Tucson: University of Arizona Press. 1969.

———. *Western Apache Language and Culture: Essays in Linguistic Anthropology*. Tucson: University of Arizona Press. 1990.

Berkhofer, Robert F. Jr. *The White Man's Indian: Images of the American Indians from Columbus to the Present*. New York: Alfred A. Knopf. 1978.

Bert, Anson. *The Miami Indians*. Norman: University of Oklahoma Press. 1970.

Bird, Traveller. *Tell Them They Lie: The Sequoyah Myth*. Los Angeles: Western Lore Publishers. 1971.

Boas, Franz. *The Mind of Primitive Man*. New York: The Macmillan Company. 1938.

Boas, Franz and J. W. Powell. *Introduction to Handbook of American Indian Languages and Indian Linguistic Families of America North of Mexico*. Lincoln: University of Nebraska Press. 1966.

Bowers, Benjamin P., Terry Jones and Gale Auletta Young. eds. *Toward the Multicultural University*. Westport, CT: Praeger. 1995.

179

Brill de Ramirez, Susan Berry. *Contemporary American Indian Literatures and the Oral Tradition.* Tucson: University of Arizona Press. 1999.

Brown, Dee. *Bury My Heart At Wounded Knee: An Indian History of the American West.* New York: Holt, Rinehart and Winston, Inc. 1971.

Brown, Joseph Epes. ed. *The Sacred Pipe: Black Elk's Account of the Seven Rites of the Oglala Sioux.* New York: Penguin Books. 1971. Originally published by University of Oklahoma Press, Norman, 1953.

Caldwell, E.K. ed. *Dreaming the Dawn: Conversations with Native Artists and Activists.* Lincoln: University of Nebraska Press. 1999.

Carmack, W.C. ed. *Indian Oratory: Famous Speeches by Noted Indian Chieftains.* Norman: University of Oklahoma Press. 1971.

Carriker, Robert C. *Fort Supply, Indian Territory: Frontier Outpost on the Plains.* Norman: University of Oklahoma Press. 1970.

Cash, Joseph and Herbert Hoover. eds. *To Be An Indian: An Oral History.* New York: Holt, Rhinehart and Winston. 1971.

Champagne, Duane. ed. *The Native North American Almanac: A Reference Work on Native North Americans in the United States and Canada.* Detroit, Washington, D.C. and London: Gale Research Inc. 1994.

Champagne, Duane and Jay Stauss. eds. *Native American Studies in Higher Education: Models for Collaboration between Universities and Indigenous Nations.* Walnut Creek, Landham, New York and Oxford: AltaMira Press. 2002.

Chaudhuri, Jean and Joyotpaul Chaudhuri. *A Sacred Path: The Way of the Muscogee Creeks.* Los Angeles: UCLA American Indian Studies Center. 2001.

Coleman, Michael C. *American Indian Children at School, 1850–1980.* Jackson, MS: University Press of Mississippi, 1993.

Commager, Henry Steele. *The American Mind: An Interpretation of American Thought and Character Since the 1880's.* New Haven and London. Yale University Press. 1978.

Cooley, Charles H. *Social Organization: A Study of the Larger Mind.* New York: Schocken Books. 1962.

Coolidge, J.L. *A Treatise on the Geometry of the Circle and Sphere.* New York: Chelsea. 1971.

Costo, Rupert. ed. *Indian Voices: The First Convocation of American Indian Scholars.* San Francisco: The Indian Historian Press. 1970.

Cox, Bruce. ed. *Cultural Ecology: Readings on Canadian Indians and Eskimos.* Toronto: McClelland and Stewart Limited. 1973.

Davidson, Gustav. *A Dictionary of Angels Including the Fallen Angels.* New York: The Free Press. 1967.

Debo, Angie. *A History of the Indians of the United States.* Norman: University of Oklahoma Press. 1970.

———. *The Road to Disappearance: A History of the Creek Indians.* Norman: University of Oklahoma Press. 1941.

Dedrick, John M. and Eugene H. Casad. *Sonora Yaqui Language Structures.* Tucson: University of Arizona Press. 1999.

Dellenbaugh, F.S. *The North-Americans of Yesterday: A Comparative Study of North-American Indian Life, Customs, and Products, on the Theory of the Ethnic Unity of the Race.* New York: G.P. Putnam's Sons. 1900.

Deloria, Vine Jr. *Custer Died For Your Sins: An Indian Manifesto.* Norman: University of Oklahoma Press. 1988. Avon 1969 original edition.

———. *We Talk; You Listen: New Tribes, New Turf.* New York: Delta. 1970.

De Rosier, Arthur H. *The Removal of the Choctaw Indians.* Knoxville: University of Tennessee Press. 1970.

de Tocqueville, Alexis. *Democracy in America.* New York. Vintage Books, 2 vols. 1954.

Dhyani Ywahoo, Barbara Du Boir. ed. *Voices of Our Ancestors: Cherokee Teachings from the Wisdom Fire.* Boston: Shambhala. 1987.

Diamond, Stanley. ed. *Primitive Views of the World: Essays From Culture in History.* New York: Columbia University Press. 1964.

Dinnerstein, Leonard. ed. *Antisemitism in the United States.* New York: Holt, Rinehart and Winston. 1971.

Durkheim, Emile. *The Elementary Forms of the Religious Life.* New York: The Free Press. 1967.

Eastman, Charles A. *From the Deep Woods to Civilization.* Lincoln: University of Nebraska Press. 1936. Originally published 1916.

Edson, Gary. ed. *Museum Ethics.* New York and London: Routledge. 1997.

Ehrenwald, Jan. *Anatomy of Genius: Split Brains and Global Minds.* New York: Human Sciences Press, Inc. 1984.

Ellis, Clyde. *To Change Them Forever: Indian Education at the Rainy Mountain Boarding School.* Norman and London: University of Oklahoma Press. 1996.

Ellis, Richard. *General Pope and U.S. Indian Policy.* Albuquerque: University of New Mexico Press. 1970.

Epple, Jess C. *Custer's Battle of the Washita and A History of the Plains Indian Tribes.* New York: Exposition Press. 1970.

Farella, John R. *The Main Stalk: A Synthesis of Navajo Philosophy.* Tucson, Ariz.: University of Arizona Press. 1984.

Ferrara, Peter J. *The Choctaw Revolution: Lessons for Federal Indian Policy.* Washington, D.C.: Americans for Tax Reform Foundation. 1998.

Fikes, Jay C. *Reuben Snake: Your Humble Serpent.* Santa Fe: Clear Light Publishers. 1996.

Finnegan, Ruth. *Oral Traditions and the Verbal Arts: A Guide to Research Practices.* New York: Routledge. 1991.

Fixico, Donald L. *The Invasion of Indian Country in the Twentieth Century: American Capitalism and Tribal Natural Resources.* Niwot, CO: University Press of Colorado. 1998.

———. *The Urban Indian Experience in America.* Albuquerque: University of New Mexico Press. 2000.

Foreman, Grant. *Sequoyah.* Norman: University of Oklahoma Press. 1938.

Foster, George E. *Se-Quo-Yah, The American Cadmus and Modern Moses.* Philadelphia: Indian Rights Association. 1885.

Fuchs, Estelle and Robert Havighurst. *To Live on This Earth: American Indian Education.* Garden City: Anchor Press. 1973.

Galbraith, John K. *The Affluent Society.* Boston: Houghton Mifflin. 1958.

Gallagher, Winifred. *The Power of Place: How Our Surroundings Shape Our Thoughts, Emotions, and Actions.* New York: HarperPerennial. 1993.

Gans, Herbert J. *Middle American Individualism: Political Participation and Liberal Democracy.* New York: Oxford University Press. 1988.

Gathercole, Peter and David Lowenthal. eds. *The Politics of the Past.* London: Unwin Hyman. 1990.

Gluck, Sherna Berger and Daphne Patai. eds. *Women's Words: The Feminist Practice of Oral History.* New York: Routledge. 1991.

Goodwin, Grenville. *The Social Organization of the Western Apache.* Tucson: University of Arizona Press. 1969.

Goody, Jack. *The Interface Between the Written and the Oral.* Cambridge: Cambridge University Press. 1987.

Green, Michael. *The Politics of Indian Removal: Creek Government and Society.* Lincoln: University of Nebraska Press. 1982.

Greenfield, Jeannette. *The Return of Cultural Treasures.* New York: Cambridge University Press. 1996. Second Edition.

Grele, Ronald J. ed. *Envelopes of Sound: Six Practitioners Discuss the Method, Theory and Practice of Oral History and Oral Testimony.* Chicago: Precedent Pub. 1975.

Gritton, Joy L. *The Institute of American Indian Arts: Modernism and U.S. Indian Policy.* Albuquerque: University of New Mexico Press. 2000.

Grosswirth, Marvin, Abbie F. Salny, Alan Stillson, and Members of the American Mensa, Ltd. *Match Wits with Mensa.* Cambridge, MA: Perseus Books. 1981.

Gudschinsky, Sarah. C. *How to Learn an Unwritten Language.* New York: Holt, Rinehart and Winston. 1967.

Guie, Heister Dean. ed. *Mourning Dove Coyote Stories.* Lincoln and London: University of Nebraska Press. 1990.

Haile, Berard. ed. *Navajo Coyote Tales: The Curly To Aheedliinii Version.* Lincoln and London: University of Nebraska Press. 1984.

Hale, Duane Kendall. *Researching and Writing Tribal Histories.* Grand Rapids, MI: Michigan Indian Press and Grand Rapids Inter-Tribal Council. 1991.

Hamilton, Charles Hamilton. ed. *Cry of the Thunderbird: The American Indian's Own Story.* Norman: University of Oklahoma Press. 1972.

Harris, LaDonna with Henrietta H. Stockel. *LaDonna Harris: A Comanche Life.* Lincoln: University of Nebraska Press. 2000.

Harrod, Howard L. *The Animals Came Dancing: Native American Sacred Ecology and Animal Kinship.* Tucson: University of Arizona Press. 2000.

Henige, David P. *Oral Historiography.* London, New York: Longman. 1982.

Hertzberg, Hazel. *The Search for an American Indian Identity: Modern Pan-Indian Movements.* Syracuse: Syracuse University Press. 1971.

Highwater, Jamake. *The Primal Mind.* New York: Harper & Row. 1981.

Hill, Jane H. and Judith T. Irvine. eds. *Responsibility and Evidence in Oral Discourse.* New York: Cambridge University Press. 1993.

Hill, Norbert S. Jr. *Words of Power: Voices From Indian America.* Golden, CO: Fulcrum Publishing. 1994.

Howard, James H. *The Native American Image in Western Europe.* Hurst, TX: Society for American Indian Studies & Research. 1978.

———, in collaboration with Willie Lena. *Oklahoma Seminoles, Medicine, Magic and Religion.* Norman: University of Oklahoma Press. 1990.

Howe, Barbara J. and Emory L. Kemp. eds. *Public History: An Introduction.* Malabar, FL: Krieger. 1986.

Hyer, Sally. *One House, One Voice, One Heart: Native American Education at the Santa Fe Indian School.* Santa Fe, NM: Museum of New Mexico Press, 1990.

Inter Press Service. *Story Earth: Native Voices on the Environment.* San Francisco: Mercury House. 1993.

Jackson, Helen Hunt. *A Century of Dishonor, A Sketch of the United States Government Dealings with Some of the Indian Tribes.* New York: Harper and Brothers. 1881.

Jacobs, Margaret D. *Engendered Encounters: Feminism and Pueblo Cultures, 1879–1934.* Lincoln: University of Nebraska Press. 1999.

Johnson, Troy R. *The Occupation of Alacatraz Island: Indian Self-Determination and the Rise of Indian Activism.* Urbana: University of Illinois Press. 1996.

Johnston, Basil H. *Indian School Days.* Norman and London: University of Oklahoma Press. 1989.

———. *The Manitous: The Supernatural World of the Ojibway.* New York: HarperPerennial. 1995.

Jones, David E. ed. *Sanapia: Comanche Eagle Doctor.* Prospect Heights, IL: Waveland Press. 1984.

Josephy, Alvin M. ed. *Red Power: The American Indians' Fight for Freedom.* New York: McGraw-Hill. 1971.

Katz, William Loren. *The Black West.* Garden City: Doubleday. 1971.

Kearney, Michael. *World View.* Novato, CA: Chandler & Sharp Publications in Anthropology and Related Fields. 1984.

Kelsen, Hans. *Society and Nature: A Sociological Inquiry.* London: K. Paul, Trench, Trubner and Co., Ltd. 1946.

Keynes, John M. *Essays in Persuasion: Economic Possibilities for Grandchildren*. London: Macmillan. 1932.

Kroeber, Alfred L. *Anthropology: Culture Patterns & Processes*. New York and London: Harcourt, Brace & World, Inc. 1963.

Lame Deer, John and Richard Erdoes. *Lame Deer, Seeker of Visions*. New York: Touchstone. 1972.

Leitch, Barbara A. *Chronology of the American Indian*. St. Clair Shores, MI: Scholarly Press. 1975.

Levison, Andrew. *The Working-Class Majority*. New York: Coward, McCann and Geoghegan. 1974.

Levy-Bruhl, Lucien. *Primitives and the Supernatural*. New York: E.P. Dutton & Co., Inc. 1935.

Levy, Jerrold E.; Raymond Neutra and Dennis Parker. *Hand Trembling, Frenzy Witchcraft, and Moth Madness: A Study of Navaho Seizure Disorders*. Tucson: University of Arizona Press. 1987.

Linderman, Frank B. ed. *Old Man Coyote: The Authorized Edition*. Lincoln and London: University of Nebraska Press. 1996. Originally published 1931.

Lindsey, Donal F. *Indians at Hampton Institute, 1877–1923*. Urbana and Chicago: University of Illinois Press. 1995.

Littlefield, Daniel F. Jr. *Alex Posey: Creek Poet, Journalist, and Humorist*. Lincoln and London: University of Nebraska Press. 1992.

Lukes, Steven. *Individualism*. Oxford: Blackwell. 1973.

Lummis, Trevor. *Listening to History: The Authenticity of Oral Evidence*. Totowa, N.J.: Barnes and Noble Books. 1988.

MacDonald, Peter with Ted Schwarz. *The Last Warrior: Peter MacDonald and the Navajo Nation*. New York: Orion Books. 1993.

McGaa, Ed. *Native Wisdom: Perceptions of the Natural Way*. Minneapolis: Four Directions Publishing. 1995.

McNeley, James. *Holy Wind in Navajo Philosophy*. Tucson: University of Arizona Press. 1981.

McTaggart, Fred. *Wolf That I Am: In Search of the Red Earth People*. Norman: University of Oklahoma Press. 1976.

Malinowski, Sharon. ed. *Notable Native Americans*. Detroit: Gales Publishing Ins. 1995.

Malotki, Ekkehart and Michael Lomatuway'ma. eds. *Hopi Coyote Tales: Istutuwutsi*. Lincoln and London: University of Nebraska Press. 1984.

Mankiller, Wilma and Michael Wallis. *Mankiller: A Chief and Her People*. New York: St. Martin's Press. 1993.

Mann, Henrietta Mann. *Cheyenne–Arapaho Education 1871–1982*. Niwot, CO: University Press of Colorado. 1997.

Mannheim, Karl. *Ideology and Utopia: An Introduction to the Sociology of Knowledge*. Trans. by Louis Wirth and Edward Shils. New York. Harcourt, Brace. 1936.

Marquis, Thomas B. ed. *Memoirs of a White Crow Indian (Thomas) H. Leforge)*. Lincoln: University of Nebraska Press, 1974. Originally published by the Century Company, 1924.

Means, Russell with Marvin J. Wolf. *Where White Men Fear to Tread: The Autobiography of Russell Means*. New York: St. Martin's Press. 1995.

Mencarelli, James and Steven Severin. *Protest: Red, Black, Brown Experience in America*. Grand Rapids, MI: William B. Eerdmans Publishing Company. 1975.

Merton, Robert K. *Social Theory and Social Structure*. Glencoe, IL: Free Press, revised and enlarged edition. 1957.

Messenger, Phyliss Mauch. ed. *The Ethics of Collecting Cultural Property: Whose Culture? Whose Property?* Albuquerque: University of New Mexico Press. 1989.

Mihesuah, Devon A. *Cultivating the Rosebuds: The Education of Women at the Cherokee Female Seminary, 1851–1909*. Urbana and Chicago: University of Illinois Press. 1993.

Miller, Jay. *Earthmaker, Tribal Stories from Native North America*. New York: Perigee Books. 1992.

Momaday, N. Scott. *The Names: A Memoir.* New York: Harper & Row. 1976.

Moore, Arthur K. *The Frontier Mind.* New York: McGraw-Hill Book. 1957.

Morrison, Dane. ed. *American Indian Studies: An Interdisciplinary Approach to Contemporary Issues.* New York: Peter Lang. 1997.

Neihardt, John. ed. *Black Elk Speaks: Being the Life Story of a Holy Man of the Oglala Sioux.* New York: Pocket Books. 1973, seventh printing.

Oppelt, Norman T. *The Tribally Controlled Indian Colleges: The Beginnings of Self-Determination in American Indian Education.* Tsaile, AZ: Navajo Community College Press. 1990.

Ortiz, Alfonso. ed. *New Perspectives on the Pueblos.* Albuquerque: University of New Mexico Press. 1972.

Painter, Muriel Thayer. *With Good Heart: Yaqui Beliefs and Ceremonies in Pascua Village.* Tucson: University of Arizona Press. 1986.

Parker, Dorothy R. *Singing an Indian Song: A Biography of D'Arcy McNickle.* Lincoln: University of Nebraska Press. 1992.

Perdue, Theda. *Nations Remembered, An Oral History of the Five Civilized Tribes, 1865–1907.* Westport, CT: Greenwood Press. 1980.

Phelan, Marilyn E. ed. *Museum Law: A Guide for Officers, Directors and Counsel.* Evanston, IL: Kalos Kapp Press. 1994.

Posey, Alexander, Littlefield, Daniel F. Jr., and Carol A. Petty Hunter. eds. *The Fus Fixico Letters.* Lincoln: University of Nebraska Press. 1993.

Price, John A. *Native Studies: American and Canadian Indians.* New York: McGraw-Hill Ryerson. 1978.

Prucha, Francis Paul. *The Churches and the Indian Schools 1888–1912.* Lincoln and London: University of Nebraska Press. 1979.

Quotations from Our Presidents. Mount Vernon, NY: The Peter Pauper Press. 1969.

Radin, Paul. ed. *The Trickster, A Study in American Indian Mythology.* London: Routledge. 1955.

Red Fox, Chief. *Memoirs of Chief Red Fox.* New York: McGraw-Hill. 1972.

Reid, Phillip John. *A Law of Blood: The Primitive Law of the Cherokee Nation.* New York: New York University Press. 1970.

Reyner, Jon. ed. *Teaching American Indian Students.* Norman and London: University of Oklahoma Press. 1992.

Ritchie, Donald A. *Doing Oral History.* New York, Oxford, Sydney, Singapore and Toronto: Twayne Publishers. 1995.

Reisman, David. *Individualism Reconsidered, and Other Essays.* Glencoe, IL: Free Press. 1954.

Riney, Scott. *The Rapid City Indian School, 1898–1933.* Norman: University of Oklahoma Press. 1999.

St. Piere, Mark and Tilda Long Soldier. *Walking in the Sacred Manner: Healers, Dreamers, and Pipe Carriers—Medicine Women of the Plains Indians.* New York, London, Toronto, Sydney, Tokyo, and Singapore: Touchstone Book. 1995.

Schappes, Morris U. *A Documentary History of Jews in the United States, 1654–1875.* New York: Schocken Books. 1971. 3rd ed.

Scheiner, Seth M. and Tilden G. Edelstein. eds. *The Black Americans: Interpretative Readings.* New York: Holt, Rhinehart and Winston. 1971.

Schubell, Matthais. *N. Scott Momaday: The Cultural and Literary Background.* Norman and London: University of Oklahoma Press. 1985.

Servan-Schreiber, Jean-Louis. *The Art of Time.* Reading, MA: Addison-Wesley. 1989. 3rd printing, translated by Franklin Philip.

Sheehan, Bernard. *Seeds of Extinction: Jeffersonian Philanthropy and the American Indian.* Chapel Hill: University of North Carolina Press. 1973.

Slotkin, Richard. *Regeneration Through Violence: The Mythology of the American Frontier, 1600–1860.* Middletown, CT: Wesleyan University Press. 1973.

Smith, Alan. ed. *Directory of Oral History Collections.* Phoenix: Oryx Press. 1988.

Standing Bear, Luther. *Land of the Spotted Eagle.* Lincoln: University of Nebraska Press. 1978. Originally published 1933.

Stein, Wayne J. *Tribally Controlled Colleges: Making Good Medicine.* New York, San Francisco, Bern, Baltimore, Frankfurt am Main, Berlin, Wien and Paris: Peter Lang. 1992.

Steltenkamp, Michael F. *Black Elk Holy Man of the Oglala.* Norman: University of Oklahoma Press. 1993.

Suzuki, David and Peter Knudtson. *Wisdom of the Elders: Honoring Sacred Native Visions of Nature.* New York: Bantam Books. 1992.

Swanton, John R. *Early History of the Creek Indians and Their Neighbors.* Bureau of American Ethnology Bulletin 73. Washington: Government Printing Office. 1922.

———. "The Social History and Usages of the Creek Confederacy," *Forty-Second Annual Report of the Bureau of American Ethnology.* Washington: U.S. Government Printing Office. 1928.

Szasz, Margaret Connell. *Indian Education in the American Colonies, 1607–1783.* Albuquerque: University of New Mexico Press. 1988.

———. *Education and the American Indian: The Road to Self-Determination Since 1928.* Albuquerque: University of Mexico Press. 1999. 3rd ed. Originally published 1974.

Terkel, Studs. *"The Good War": An Oral History of World War Two.* New York: Ballantine Books. 1984.

Thelen, David. ed. *Memory And American History.* Bloomington and Indianapolis: Indiana University Press, 1990. Collection first appeared as special issue of *Journal of American History* Vol. 75, No. 4, 1989.

The Times Atlas of the World, 10th comprehensive edition. New York: Random House. 1999.

Thomas, Rosalind. *Oral Tradition and Written Record in Classical Athens.* Cambridge and New York: Cambridge University Press. 1989.

Thompson, Paul. *The Voice of the Past: Oral History.* Oxford and New York: Oxford University Press. 1978.

Tonkin, Elizabeth. *Narrating Our Pasts: the Social Construction of Oral History.* Cambridge and New York: Cambridge University Press. 1992.

Trennert, Robert A. Jr. *The Phoenix Indian School: Forced Assimilation in Arizona, 1891–1935.* Norman: University of Oklahoma Press. 1988.

Triandis, Harry C. *Individualism and Collectivism.* Boulder, CO: Westview Press. 1995.

Tylor. Sir Edward B. *The Origins of Culture.* New York: Harper & Brothers Publishers. 1958.

Vanderwerth, W.C. *Indian Oratory: Famous Speeches Told By Noted Indian Chieftains.* Norman: University of Oklahoma Press. 1971.

Vansina, Jan. *Oral Tradition as History.* Madison: University of Wisconsin Press. 1985.

———. *Oral Tradition; A Study in Historical Methodology.* Chicago: Aldine Pub Co. 1965.

Viloa, Herman J. *Ben Nighthorse Campbell, An American Warrior.* New York: Orion Books. 1993.

Walker, Deward E. Jr., in collaboration with Daniel N. Matthews. eds. *Nez Perce Coyote Tales.* Norman: University of Oklahoma Press. 1998.

Wallace, Anthony F.C. *The Death and Rebirth of the Seneca: The History and Culture of the Great Iroquois Nation, Their Destruction and Demorization, and Their Cultural Revival at the Hands of the Indian Visionary, Handsome Lake.* New York: Alfred A. Knopf. 1970.

Weaver, Jace. ed. *Defending Mother Earth: Native American Perspectives on Environmental Justice.* Maryknoll, NY: Orbis Books. 1996.

Webster's Seventh New Collegiate Dictionary. Based on Webster's Third New International Dictionary. Springfield, MA: G. & C. Merriam Company, Publishers. 1970.

Whitney, Ellen M. ed. *The Black Hawk War: 1831–1832,* Vol. 1. Springfield: Illinois State Historical Library. 1970.

Wilkins, Thurman. *Cherokee Tragedy: The Story of the Ridge Family and the Decimation of a People.* New York: Macmillan. 1970.

Wright, J. Leitch Jr. *Creeks and Seminoles, The Destruction and Regeneration of the Muscogulgee People.* Lincoln: University of Nebraska Press. 1986.

Yellowtail. *Yellowtail Crow Medicine Man and Sun Dance Chief: An Autobiography as Told To Michael Oren Fritzgerald.* Norman: University of Oklahoma Press. 1991.

Ywahoo, Dhyani and Barbara Du Boir. eds. *Voices of Our Ancestors: Cherokee Teachings from the Wisdom Fire.* Boston: Shambhala. 1987.

Articles

"Alexander Posey, the Creek Poet" [no author], *Indian School Journal,* Vol. 11, No. 3, June 1911, 11–14.

Ahern, Wilbert H. "An Experiment Aborted: Returned Indian Students in the Indian School Service, 1881–1908," *Ethnohistory,* Vol. 44, No. 2, Spring 1997, 263–304.

Ambler, Marjane. "Cultural Property Rights: What's Next after NAGPRA?" *Tribal College: Journal of American Indian Higher Education,* Vol. 7, No. 2, Fall 1996, 8–11.

———. "Oglala College Outlasts Skeptics," *Tribal College: Journal of American Indian Higher Education,* Vol. 7, No. 2, Fall 1996, 24–25.

Apodaca, Paul. "Powerful Images: Portrayals of Native America," *American Anthropologist,* Vol. 101, No. 4, December 1999, 818–823.

Bahr, Donald M. "On the Complexity of Southwest Indian Emergence Myths," *Journal of Anthropological Research,* Vol. 33, No. 3, Fall 1977, 317–349.

Ball, Gene. "Preserving the Western Legacy: The Buffalo Bill Historical Center," *Journal of the West,* Vol. 20, No. 1, 1981, 66–71.

Barrett, Carole Britton and Marcia Wolter. "You Didn't Dare Try to be Indian": Oral Histories of Former Indian Boarding School Students, *North Dakota History,* Vol. 64, No. 2, Spring, 4–25.

Berg, S. Carol. "Arthur C. Parker and the Society of the American Indian, 1911–1916," *New York History,* Vol. 81. No. 2, 2000, 237–246.

Berkhofer, Robert F. Jr. "Model Zions for the American Indian," *American Quarterly,* Vol. 5, No. 2, Part 1, Summer 1963, 176–190.

Bieder, Robert E. "The Collecting of Bones for Anthropological Narratives," *American Indian Culture and Research Journal,* Vol. 16, No. 2, 1992, 21–35.

Bigart, Robert. "Tribal College Land-Grant Future: Promise and Peril," *Tribal College: Journal of American Indian Higher Education,* Vol. 7, No. 4, Spring 1997, 36–37.

Blatz, Perry K. "Craftsmanship and Flexibility in Oral History: a Pluralistic Approach to Methodology and Theory," *Public Historian,* Vol. 12, Fall 1990, 7–22.

Bond, Constance. "An American Legacy," *Smithsonian,* Vol. 20, No. 7, 1989, 42–55.

Boyer, Paul. "Tribal College of the Future," *Tribal College Journal,* Vol. 7, No. 1, Summer 1995, 15.

Bradshaw, J. "Oral Transmission and Human Memory," *Expository Times,* Vol. 92, 1981, 303–307.

Buffalohead, W. Roger. "Native American Studies Programs: Review and Evaluation," in Rupert Costo, ed., *First Convocation of Indian Scholars.* San Francisco: Indian Historian Press. 1970.

Butterfield, Fox. "Why They Excel." *Parade Magazine,* South Bend, *Tribune,* Indiana. January 21, 1990.

Callicott, J. Baird. "American Indian Land Wisdom," in Paul A. Olson, ed., *The Struggle for the Land: Indigenous Insight and Industrial Empire in the Semiarid World.* Lincoln: University of Nebraska Press. 1990.

Campisi, Jack and Laurence M. Hauptman. "Talking back: the Oneida Language and Folklore Project, 1938–1941," *Proceedings of the American Philosophical Society*, Vol. 125, No. 6, 1981, 441–448.

Champagne, Duane. "American Indian Studies Is For Everyone," *American Indian Quarterly*, Vol. 20, No. 1, Winter 1996, 77–82.

Churchill, Ward. "White Studies or Isolation: An Alternative Model for Native American Studies Programs," in *American Indian Issues in Higher Education*. Los Angeles: American Indian Studies Center, UCLA. 1981.

Castillo, Edward. "California Indians," in Duane Champagne, ed., *Native North American Almanac: A Reference Work on Native North Americans in the United States and Canada*. Detroit: Gale Research Inc.

Clark, Carter Blue. "America's First Discipline: American Indian Studies," in Clifford E. Trafzer. ed., *American Indian Identity: Today's Changing Perspective*. Sacramento: Sierra Oaks Publishing Company. 1985.

Cohen, David William. "The Undefining of Oral Tradition," *Ethnohistory*, Vol. 36, No. 1, Winter 1989, 9–18.

Coleman, Michael C. "The Mission Education of Francis La Flesche: An American Indian Response to the Presbyterian Boarding School in the 1860s," *American Studies in Scandinavia [Norway]*, Vol. 18, No. 2, 1986, 67–82.

Costo, Rupert. "Moment of Truth for the American Indian," in J. Henry, ed., *Indian Voices: First Convocation of American Indian Scholars*. San Francisco: Indian Historian Press. 1970.

Crazy Bull, Cheryl. "A Native Conversation About Research and Scholarship," *Tribal College Journal*. Vol. 9, No. 1, Summer 1997, 17–23.

Curtin, Philip D. "Field Techniques for Collecting and Processing Oral Data," *Journal of African History*, Vol. 9, No. 3, 1968, 367–385.

Dale, Edward E., ed., "The Journal of Alexander Lawrence Posey, January 1 to September 4, 1897," *Chronicles of Oklahoma*, Vol. 45, No. 4, Winter 1967–68, 393–432.

Davis, Logan J. "Turtle Mountain Celebrates Another Milestone," *Tribal College: Journal of American Indian Higher Education*, Vol. 9, No. 2, Fall 1997, 48–50.

Dobkins, Rebecca J. "Expect a Different Story: Portraying the Contemporary Plateau." *American Anthropologist*, Vol. 102, No. 2, (June 2000), 330–336.

Dunaway, David King. "The Oral Biography," *Biography*, Vol. 14, 1991, 256–266.

Ellen, Roy F. "What Black Elk Left Unsaid: On the Illusory Images of Green Primitivism," *Anthropology Today*, Vol. 2, No. 6, December 1986, 8–12.

Ellis, Richard. "The Duke Indian Oral History Collection Project," *New Mexico Historical Review*, Vol. 48, No. 1, Summer 1997, 259–263.

Faris, David E. "Narrative Form and Oral History: Some Problems and Possibilities," *International Journal of Oral History*, Vol. 1, 1980, 159–180.

Figlio, Karl. "Oral History and the Unconscious," *History Workshop Journal*, No. 26, 1988, 120–132.

Finnegan, Ruth. "A Note on Oral Tradition and Historical Evidence," *History and Theory*, Vol. 9, 1970, 195–201.

———. "How Oral Is Oral Literature?" *Bulletin of the School and African Studies*, Vol. 37, No. 2, 1974, 52–64.

Fixico, Donald L. "The Muscogee Creeks: A Nativistic People," pp. 30–43 in Arrell M. Gibson, ed., *Between Two Worlds, The Survival of Twentieth Century Indians*. Oklahoma City: Oklahoma Historical Society. 1986.

———. "American Indians (The Minority of Minorities) and Higher Education," pp. 103–124, in Benjamin P. Bowers, Terry Jones, and Gale Auletta Young, eds., *Toward the Multicultural University*. Westport, CT: Praeger. 1995.

————. "Ethics and Resonsibilities in Writing American Indian History," *American Indian Quarterly*, Vol. 20, No. 1, Winter 1996, 29–39.

————. "The Struggle for Our Homes: Indian and White Values and Tribal Lands," pp. 29–46, in Jace Weaver, ed., *Defending Mother Earth: Native American Perspectives on Environmental Justice*. Maryknoll, NY: Orbis Books. 1996.

————. [14 articles on American Indian Studies Programs] *Indigenous Nations Studies Journal*, Vol. 2, No. 1, Spring 2001, 3–111.

Fogelson, Raymond D. "On The Varieties of Indian History: Sequoyah and Traveller Bird," *Journal of Ethnic Studies*, Vol. 2, Spring 1974, 105–112.

Fontana, Bernard L. "American Indian Oral History: An Anthropologist's Note," *History and Theory*, Vol. 8, No. 3, October 1969, 366–370.

Foreman, Grant. "The Story of Sequoyah's Last Days," *Chronicles of Oklahoma*, Vol. 12, No. 1, March 1934, 25–41.

Fitzgerald, J. A. and W. W. Ludeman. "The Intelligence of Indian Children," *Journal of Comparative Psychology*, Vol. 6, No. 4, August 1929, 319–328.

Galla, Amareswar. "Indigenous Peoples, Museums, and Ethics," in Gary Edson, ed., *Museum Ethics*. New York and London: Routledge. 1997.

Gaskin, L. J. P. "Centenary of the Opening of George Catlin's North American Indian Museum and Gallery in the Egyptian Hall, Piccadilly. With a Memoir of Catlin." *Man*, Vol. 40, February 1940, 17–21.

Gilmore, Paul. "The Indian in the Museum: Henry David Thoreau, Okah Tubbee, and Authentic Manhood," *Arizona Quarterly*, Vol. 54, No. 2, 1998, 25–63.

Goodburn, Amy. "Literacy Practices at the Genoa Industrial Indian School." *Great Plains Quarterly*, Vol. 19, No. 1, Winter 1999, 35–52.

Goodpasture, Albert V. "The Paternity of Sequoyah, the Inventor of the Cherokee Alphabet," *Chronicles of Oklahoma*, Vol. 1, No. 2, October 1921, 121–130.

Guardippe, Norman. "Mending the Broken Circle," in E. K. Caldwell, ed., *Dreaming the Dawn: Conversations with Native Artists and Activists*. Lincoln: University of Nebraska Press. 1999.

Guida, Marilyn. "Museums and California Indians: Contemporary Issues," *American Indian Culture and Research Journal*, Vol. 21, No. 3, 1997, 163–181.

Hallowell, A. Irving. "Ojibwa Ontology, Behavior, and World Views," in Stanley Diamond, *Primitive Views*.

Hamley, Jeffrey. "An Introduction to the Federal Indian Boarding School Movement," *North Dakota History*, Vol. 61, No. 2, Spring 1994, 2–9.

Harris, Francis. "Places Important to Navajo People," *American Indian Quarterly*, Vol. 17, No. 2, Spring 1993, 151–170.

Harms, Robert. "Oral Tradition and Ethnicity," *Journal of Interdisciplinary History*, Vol. 10, No. 1, 1979, 61–85.

Hassrick, Peter H. "Yesterday's West Lives on at the Buffalo Bill Historical Center," *American West*, Vol. 14, No. 3, 1997, 16–29.

Heintze, Beatrix. "Oral Tradition: Primary Source Only for the Collector?" *History in Africa*, Vol. 3, 1976, 47–56.

Henige, David P. "Oral Tradition and Chronology," *Journal of Africa History*, Vol. 12, 1971, 371–390.

————. " 'In Possession of the Author': the Problem of Source Monopoly in Oral Historiography," *International Journal of Oral History*, Vol. 1, 1980, 181–194.

Henry, Jeanette. "The American Indian in American History," in Rupert Costo, ed., *Indian Voices: The First Convocation of American Indian Scholars*. San Francisco: The Indian Historian Press. 1970.

Hill, Michael J. "Science Should Serve the Community," *Tribal College Journal*, Vol. 7, No. 4, Spring 1996, 12, 13, 44.

Horse Capture, George P. "From the Reservation to the Smithsonian Via Alcatraz," *American Indian Culture and Research Journal*, Vol. 18, No. 4, 1994, 135–149.

House, Patricia, Schlanger, Sarah, and Lillie Lane. "Here, Now and Always." *El Palacio*, Vol. 103, No. 1, 1998, 32–39.

Howard, James. "The Native American Image in Western Europe." *American Indian Quarterly*, Vol. 4, No. 1, February 1978, 33–56.

Hultgren, Mary Lou and Paulette Fairbanks Molin. "Long Rides Across the Plains: Fort Berthold Students at Hampton Institute," *North Dakota History*, Vol. 61, No. 2, 1994, 10–36.

Hutton, Patrick H. "The Problem of Oral Tradition in Vico's Historical Scholarship," *Journal of the History of Ideas*, Vol. 53, No. 1, 1992, 3–23.

Inglis, George Erskine. "Museum of the North," *Canadian Geographical Journal*, Vol. 75, No. 5, 1967, 174–177.

Jett, Stephen C. "Culture and Tourism in the Navajo Country," *Journal of Cultural Geography*, Vol. 11, No. 1, 1990, 85–107.

Keller, Jean A. "In the Fall of the Year We Were Troubled With Some Sickness: Typhoid Fever Deaths, Sherman Institute, 1904," *American Indian Culture and Research Journal*, Vol. 23, No. 3, 1999, 97–117.

Keller, Robert H. Jr. "American Indian Education: An Historical Context," *Journal of the West*, Vol. 13, No. 2, April 1974, 75–82.

Kelley, Klara and Harris Francis, "Places Important to Navajo People," *American Indian Quarterly*, Vol. 17, No. 2, Spring 1993, 151–170.

Kemnitz, Charles. "The Hand of Memory: Forging Personal Narrative," *Genre*, Vol. 16, 1983, 175–189.

Kenny, Michael G. "A Place for Memory: The Interface Between Individual and Collective History," *Comparative Studies in Society and History*, Vol. 41, No. 3, 1999, 420–437.

La Fromboise, Teresa D. and Barbara S. Plake, "Toward Meeting the Research Needs of American Indians," *Harvard Educational Review*, Vol. 53, No. 1, February 1983, 45–51.

Lang, Mabel L. "Herodotus: Oral History with a Difference," *Proceedings of the American Philosophical Society*, No. 128, 1984, 93–103.

Lazzarino, Chris. "Talk of the Nations," *Kansas Alumni*, May 1996, 20.

Lee, Dorothy Lee. "Notes on the Conception of Self among the Wintu Indians," *Journal of Abnormal and Social Psychology*, Vol. 45, 1950, 538–543.

Lester, Joan. "The American Indian: A Museum's Eye View," *Indian Historian*, Vol. 5, No. 2, 1972, 25–31.

Lewis, Anna. "Miss Anna Lewis, Teacher of Alexander Posey at Bacone University," *Chronicles of Oklahoma*, Vol. 45, No. 3, Autumn 1967, 332–335.

Libertus, Sarah. "The New Mille Lacs Indian Museum," *Minnesota History*, Vol. 55, No. 1, 1996, 32–39.

Littlefield, Daniel F. Jr. "Newspapers, Magazines, and Journals," in Frederick Hoxie, *Encyclopedia of North American Indians: Native American History Culture, and Life From Paleo-Indians to the Present*. Boston and New York: Houghton Mifflin. 1996. 428–431.

Lowry, Laura M. "Differences in Visual Perception and Auditory Discrimination Between American Indian and White Kindergarten Children," *Journal of Learning Disabilities*, Vol. 3, No. 4, July 1970, 359–363.

Lurie, Nancy Oestreich. "American Indians and Museums: A Love-Hate Relationship," *Old Northwest*, Vol. 2, No. 3, 1976, 235–251.

Masco, Joseph. "Competitive Displays: Negotiating Genealogical Rights to the Potlatch at the American Museum of Natural History," *American Anthropologist*, Vol. 98, No. 4, 1996, 837–852.

Maynard, E. "The Growing Negative Image of the Anthropologist Among American Indians," *Human Organization*, Vol. 33, 1974, 402–403.

Medicine, Bea. "Responsibilities of Foundations in Native American Programs," in Rupert Costo, ed., *Indian Voices: The First Convocation of American Indian Scholars*. San Francisco: The Indian Historian Press. 1970. 357–364.

Mercer, P. M. "Oral Tradition in the Pacific: Problems of Interpretation," *Journal of Pacific History*, Vol. 14, 1979, 130–153.

Merrill, William L., Ladd, Edmund J., and T. J. Ferguson. "The Return of the Ahayu da: Lessons for Repatriation from Zuni Pueblo and the Smithsonian Institution," *Current Anthropology*, Vol. 34, No. 5, December 1993, 523–567.

Meserve, John Bartlett. "Cadmus of the Cherokees," *National Republic*, Vol. 22, July 1934, 30.

———. "The Cadmus of the Cherokees," *Oklahoma State Bar Journal*, Vol. 5, October 1934, 130–133.

Meyer, Carter Jones. "Edgar Hewett, Tsianina Redfeather, and Early Twentieth-Century Indian Reform," *New Mexico Historical Review*, Vol. 75, No. 2, April 2000, 195–220.

Momaday, N. Scott. "The Morality of Indian Hating," *Ramparts*, Vol. 3, No. 1, Summer 1964, 29–40.

Moore, John H. "Cheyenne Names and Cosmology," *American Ethnologist*, Vol. 11, No. 2, 1984, 291–312.

Morris, Patrick C. and Michael O'Donnell. "U.S. Indian Higher Education," in Duane Champagne, ed., *The Native North American Almanac: A Reference Work on Native North Americans in the United States and Canada*. Detroit: Gale Research Inc. 1994. 869–878.

Moss, William W. "Oral History: An Appreciation," *American Archivist*, Vol. 40, No. 4, October 1977, 429–439.

Nagel, Joane. "American Indian Ethnic Renewal: Politics and the Resurgence of Identity," *American Sociological Review*, Vol. 60, No. 6, December 1995, 947–965.

Nason, James D. "Tribal Models for Controlling Research," *Tribal College: Journal of American Indian Higher Education*, Vol. 7, No. 2, Fall 1996, 17–20.

O'Danachair, Caoimhim. "Oral Tradition and the Printed Word," *Irish University Review: A Journal of Irish Studies*, Vol. 9, 1979, 31–41.

Oliver, W. H. "Oral and Other History," *New Zealand Journal of History*, Vol. 12, 1978, 99–103.

O'Neil, Floyd. "Commentary" on "Perspectives on The Writing of Indian History from the Indian Point of View," in David L. Beaulieu, ed., *Breaking Barriers, Occasional Paper Series*, No. 1, December 1974, 38.

Omock, Robert E. "The Amerind: A Brief Description," *Western Review*, Vol. 8, No. 1, 1971, 35–46.

Oppler, Morris. "Themes as Dynamic Forces in Culture," *The American Journal of Sociology*, Vol. 51, No. 31, November 1945, 198–199, 202.

Ortiz, Alfonso. "An Indian Anthropologist's Perspective on Anthropology," in *Anthropology and the American Indian: Report of a Symposium*. San Francisco: The Indian Historian Press. 1970.

———. "Ritual Drama and the Pueblo World View," in Alfonso Ortiz, ed., *New Perspectives on the Pueblos*. Albuquerque: University of New Mexico Press. 1972. 135–161.

Otis, Morgan G. Jr. "A Native American Studies Program," *The Indian Historian*, Vol. 9, No. 1, Winter 1976, 14–18.

Perrot, Paul N. "Museum Ethics and Collecting Principles," in Gary Edson, ed., *Museum Ethics*. New York and London. Routledge. 1997.

Posey, Alexander. "The Journal of Alexander Lawrence Posey, January 1 to September 4, 1897," *Chronicles of Oklahoma*, Vol. 45, No. 4, Spring 1968, 2–15.

———. "Journal of Creek Enrollment Field Party 1905 by Alexander Posey," *Chronicles of Oklahoma*, Vol. 46, No. 1, Spring 1968, 2–15.

Reno, Thomas R. "A Demonstration in Navajo Education," *Journal of American Indian Education*, Vol. 6, No. 3, May 1967, 1–5.

Reyhner, John. "The Case for Native American Studies," in Dane Morrison, ed., *American Indian Studies: An Interdisciplinary Approach to Contemporary Issues*. New York: Peter Lang. 1997.

Ridington, Robin. "A Sacred Object as Text: Reclaiming the Sacred Pole of the Omaha Tribe," *American Indian Quarterly*, Vol. 17, No. 1, Winter 1993, 83–99.

Riney, Scott. "Education by Hardship: Native American Boarding Schools in the U.S. and Canada," *Oral History Review*, Vol. 24, No. 2, Winter 1997, 117–123.

Rips, Lance J. and Margaret E. Stubbs, "Genealogy and Memory," *Journal of Verbal Learning and Verbal Behavior*, Vol. 19, 1980, 705–721.

Ritchie, Donald A. "The Oral History/Public History Connection," in Barbara J. Howe and Emory L. Kemp, eds., *Public History: An Introduction*. Malabar, FL: Krieger. 1986. 57–69.

Ruoff, A. Lavonne Brown. "American Indian Oral Literature," *American Quarterly*, Vol. 33, 1981, 309–326.

Sanders, Thomas E. "The Museum of Manitou," *Indian Historian*, Vol. 5, No. 3, 1972, 7–12, 22.

Schusky, Ernest L. "The Evolution of Indian Leadership of the Great Plains, 1750–1950," *American Indian Quarterly*, Vol. 10, No. 1, Winter 1986, 65–82.

Seligman, Haim. "Is Oral History a Valid Research Instrument?" *International Journal of Oral History*, Vol. 10, No. 3, 1989, 175–182.

Southwick, Sally J. "Educating the Mind, Enlightening the Soul: Mission Schools as a Means of Transforming the Navajos, 1898–1928," *Journal of Arizona History*, Vol. 37, No. 1, Spring 1996, 47–66.

Spear, Thomas. "Oral Traditions: Whose History?" *History in Africa*, Vol. 8, 1981, 165–181.

Standing Bear, Luther. "The Future of the Indian," in Charles Hamilton, ed., *Cry of the Thunderbird: The American Indian's Own Story*. Norman: University of Oklahoma Press. 1972.

Stannard, David. "American Historians and the Idea of National Character: Some Problems and Prospects," *American Quarterly*, Vol. 23, No. 2, May 1971. 202–220.

Stefon, Frederick J. "Richard Henry Pratt and His Indians," *Journal of Ethnic Studies*, Vol. 15, No. 2, 1987, 86–112.

Stevens, Philip. "The Uses of Oral Tradition in the Writing of African History," *Tarikh*, Vol. 6, No. 1, 1978, 21–30.

Swisher, Karen. "Why Indian People Should Be The Ones To Write About Indian Education," *American Indian Quarterly*, Vol. 20, No. 1, Winter 1996, 83–90.

Szasz, Margaret Connell. "Federal Boarding Schools and the Indian Child: 1920–1960," *South Dakota History*, Vol. 1, No. 4, Fall 1977, 371–384.

Thurman, M. D. "Plains Indian Winter Counts and the New Ethnohistory," *Plains Anthropologist*, Vol. 27, 1982, 173–175.

Thornton, Russell. "American Indian Studies as an Academic Discipline," *Journal of Ethnic Studies*, Vol. 5, No. 1, Fall 1977, 1–15.

———. "American Indian Studies as an Academic Discipline," *American Indian Culture and Research Journal*, Vol. 2, Nos. 3–4, 1978, 10–19.

Tompkins, Jane. "At the Buffalo Bill Museum—June 1988." *South Atlantic Quarterly*, Vol. 89, No. 3, Summer 1990, 525–545.

Tonkin, Elizabeth. "Implications of Oracy: an Anthropological View," *Oral History*, Vol. 3, Nos. 1–2, 1975, 41–49.

———. "The Boundaries of History in Oral Performance," *History in Africa*, Vol. 9, 1982, 273–284.

Tooker, Elizbeth. "A Note on the Return of Eleven Wampum Belts to the Six Nations Iroquois Confederacy on Grand River, Canada," *Ethnohistory, The Bulletin of the Ohio Valley Historic Indian Conference*, Vol. 45, No. 2, Spring 1998, 219–236.

Trafzer, Clifford. "Native American Studies," in Frederick Hoxie, ed., *Encyclopedia of North American Indians: Native American History, Culture, and Life From Paleo-Indians to the Present.* Boston and New York: Houghton Mifflin. 1996.

Trennert, Robert A. "And the Sword Will Give Way to the Spelling Book: Establishing the Phoenix Indian School," *Journal of Arizona History,* Vol. 23, No. 1, Spring 1982, 35–58.

———. "Corporal Punishment and the Politics of Indian Reform," *History of Education Quarterly,* Vol. 29, No. 4, Winter 1989, 595–617.

Underwood, Mary L. "Bay Mills Focuses on Students," *Tribal College: Journal of American Indian Higher Education,* Vol. 7, No. 4, Spring 1997, 32.

Vansina, Jan. "Oral History in Africa: The Documentary Interview," *African Studies Bulletin,* Vol. 8, No. 2, 1965, 9–14.

Washburn, Wilcomb E. "American Indian Studies: A Status Report," *American Quarterly,* Vol. 27, No. 3, August 1975, 263–274.

West, Francis. "Oral Tradition," *History and Theory,* Vol. 5, 1966, 348–352.

Whorf, Benjamin Lee. "An American Indian Model of the Universe," in Dennis Tedlock and Barbara Tedlock, eds., *Teachings From the American Earth; Indian Religion and Philosophy.* New York: Liveright. 1975. 121–129.

Wiget, Andrew O. "Truth and the Hopi: An Historiographic Study of Documented Oral Tradition Concerning the Coming of the Spanish," *Ethnohistory,* Vol. 29, No. 3, Summer 1982, 181–199.

Wileto, Paul. "Diné College Struggles to Synthesize Navajo and Western Knowledge," *Tribal College: Journal of American Indian Higher Education,* Vol. 9, No. 2, Fall 1997, 11–15.

Willard, William. "Montezuma on the Missouri: A Centennial of Sorts," *Wicazo Sa Review,* Vol. 5, No. 2, 1989, 34–38.

Williams, Samuel C. "Nathaniel Gist, Father of Sequoyah," *East Tennessee Historical Society's Publications,* No. 5, 1933, 39–54.

———. "The Father of Sequoyah: Nathaniel Gist," *Chronicles of Oklahoma,* Vol. 15, No. 1, March, 1937, 3–20.

Wilson, Terry P. "Custer Never Would Have Believed It: Native American Studies or Isolation: An Alternative Model for Native American Studies Programs," in *American Issues in Higher Education.* Los Angeles: American Indian Studies Center, UCLA. 1981.

Wolfe, Tom. "The 'Me' Decade and the Third Great Awakening," *New York,* August 23, 1976, 26–40.

Dissertations and Theses

Breuing, Robert C. "Hopi Perspectives on Formal Education." Ph.D. dissertation. University of Kansas. 1973.

Papers and Keynote Addresses

Fixico, Donald L. "American Indian Minds in Public Schools," Invited Keynote Presentation, California Content Standards and American Indian Civics and Government Symposium, Humboldt State University, Arcata, CA, and D-Q University, Davis, CA, April 5–6, 2001.

———. "Institutionalizing American Indian Intellectualism and Traditional Knowledge," Annual Conference "In Partnership," May 31-June 3, 2001, Saskatchewan Indian Federated College, Saskatoon, Saskatchewan, Canada.

Howe, Craig et al. *25th Anniversary Conference and Celebration Meeting Ground.* Chicago: D'Arcy McNickle Center for the History of the American Indian. 1997.

Lomawaima, Tsianiana. "Changing Paradigms in Ethnography," American Society for Ethnohistory Annual Meeting, Portland, Oregon, November 7, 1996.

Mission Statement for Haskell Indian Nations University, approved by National Board of Regents, Haskell Indian Nations University, Lawrence, Kansas, May 11, 2000.

Mission Statement from Proposal for Indigenous Nations Studies Program, University of Kansas, submitted March 6, 1997 to Provost David Shulenburger by the Indigenous Nations Studies Task Force of the University of Kansas, Lawrence.

"Tribal Colleges: Shaping the Future of Native America," The Carnegie Foundation for the Advancement of Teaching, 1989.

Online Sources

Bay Mills Community College Website, Brimley, Michigan, http://www.bmcc.org/nish/toc/Generalinfo.html, April 16, 2001.

"A Bridge to Our Future: Crownpoint Institute of Technology," May 20, 2002, http://www.cit.cc.nm.us/location_and_history.html

Cankdeska Cikana Community College Website, May 20, 2002, Fort Totten, North Dakota, http://www.littlehoop.cc/

College of Menominee Nation Website, May 20, 2002, Keshena, Wisconsin, http://www.menominee. edu/newcmn/Intro.htm

Dull Knife Memorial College Website, May 20, 2002, Lame Deer, Montana, http://www.montana.edu/~wwwai/DKMC.html

Eiteljorg Museum of American Indians and Western Art Website, May 20, 2002, Indianapolis, Indiana, Http:www.eiteljorg.org/

First National American Indian University," *Educational Update Online,* New York City, October 15, 2001, http://www.educationupdate.com/Oct01/Oct01_articles/col_indian.html

Fond du Lac Tribal and Community College Website, May 20, 2002, Cloquet, Minnesota, http://www.fdl.cc.mn.us/

Fort Berthold Community College Website, April 16, 2002, http://www.fortbelknap.cc. mt.US

Heard Museum Website, May 20, 2002, Phoenx, Arizona, http://www.heard.org

Institute of Indian Arts Website, n.d., http://www.iaiancad.org/institute.htm

Keweenaw Bay Ojibwa Community College Website, www.kbocc.org, March 20, 2002.

Lac Courte Oreilles Ojibwa Community College Website, www.lco-college.edu, March 20, 2002.

Leech Lake Tribal College Website, May 20, 2002, Leech Lake, Minnesota, http://www.lltc. org/

Mashantucket Pequot Museum and Research Center Website, May 20, 2002, Mashantucket Pequot Tribe, Mashantucket Pequot Reservation, Mashantucket, Connecticut, http://www.mashantucket.com

Mission for Fort Belknap College, Website, n.d., http://www.fortbelknap.cc.mt.us/mission.html

Mission Statement for Haskell Indian Nations University, Approved by National Board of Regents, Haskell Indian Nations University, May 11, 2000, http://www.naes.indian.com/catalog/schools.htm

NAES College Information Website, May 20, 2002, Chicago, Illinois, http://www.naes.indian.com/catalog/schools.htm.

Nebraska Indian Community College Website, May 20, 2002, Winnebago, Nebraska, http:www.thenicc.org/

Northwest Indian College Website, May 20, 2002, Bellingham, Washington, http://www.nwic.edu/

Plato's quote, http://www.crystlinks.com/healingcircle.html, May 20, 2002.

Red Crow Community College Website, May 20, 2002, Alberta, Canada, http://www./redcrowcollege.com/mission.htm

Southwestern Indian Polytechnic Institute, website, April 16, 2001, http://www.sipi.bia.edu/history.htm

Sinte Gleska University Website, May 20, 2002, Rosebud Sioux Reservation, South Dakota, http://www.sinte.indian.com/history.html

Sisseton Wahpeton Community College Website, May 20, 2002, Sisseton, South Dakota, http://www.swcc.sd.us

Sitting Bull College Website, May 20, 2002, Fort Yates, North Dakota, http://www.sittingbull.edu/History.htm

Stone Child College Website, May 20, 2002, Rocky Boy Agency, Montana, http://www.montana.edu/wwwscc/index.html

TOCC–History of Tohono O'odham Community College Website, May 20, 2002, Sells, Arizona, http://www.tocc.cc.az.us/history.htm

"Tribe Connections in the Pacific Northwest," Fort Belknap Agency Website, May 20, 2002, http://www.montana.edu/~wwwse/fbc/FBCHIST.HTML

Turtle Mountain Community College Website, May 20, 2002, Bellcourt, North Dakota, http://www.turtle-mountain.cc.nd.us/

United Tribes Technical College Website, May 20, 2002, Bismarck, North Dakota, http://www.unitedtribes.tech.com

Vancouver Museum Website, May 20, 2002, Vancouver, British Columbia, http://www.vanmuseum.bc.ca/inside/history.htm

White Earth Tribal and Community College Website, May 20, 2002, Mahnomen, Minnesota, http://www/.wetcc.org/charter%20bylaws.htm

INDEX